199983

A Da Capo Press Reprint Series

**FRANKLIN D. ROOSEVELT
AND THE ERA OF THE NEW DEAL**

GENERAL EDITOR : FRANK FREIDEL
Harvard University

SEVEN STRANDED
COAL TOWNS

Division of Research
Work Projects Administration

Research Monographs

Works Progress Administration
Division of Social Research
Research Monograph XXIII

Title:- # SEVEN STRANDED COAL TOWNS

A Study of an American Depressed Area

By Malcolm Brown. and John N. Webb

DA CAPO PRESS • NEW YORK • 1971

A Da Capo Press Reprint Edition

This Da Capo Press edition of *Seven Stranded Coal Towns* is an un-
abridged republication of the first edition published in Washington,
D.C., in 1941. It is reprinted by permission from a copy of the original
edition owned by the Harvard College Library.

Library of Congress Catalog Card Number 76-165680
ISBN 0-306-70355-6

Published by Da Capo Press, Inc.
A Subsidiary of Plenum Publishing Corporation
227 West 17th Street, New York, N.Y. 10011
All Rights Reserved

Manufactured in the United States of America

SEVEN STRANDED
COAL TOWNS

Farm Security Administration (Rothstein).

"There's nothing here but just coal."

A Miner's Back Yard in Carrier Mills, Ill.

FEDERAL WORKS AGENCY

John M. Carmody, *Administrator*

WORK PROJECTS ADMINISTRATION

Howard O. Hunter, *Commissioner*

Corrington Gill, *Assistant Commissioner*

DIVISION OF RESEARCH

Howard B. Myers, *Director*

SEVEN STRANDED COAL TOWNS

A Study of an American Depressed Area

By

Malcolm Brown

and

John N. Webb

•

RESEARCH MONOGRAPH XXIII

1941

UNITED STATES GOVERNMENT PRINTING OFFICE, WASHINGTON

Letter of Transmittal

WORK PROJECTS ADMINISTRATION,
Washington, D. C., January 9, 1941.

Sir: The problem of "derelict," economically wrecked areas in the United States has long been of particular concern to the Work Projects Administration. More than any other agency of the Government, the WPA bears responsibility for relieving their extraordinary unemployment burden, and, indeed, for preventing utter collapse in these communities which private industry has abandoned.

This is no light responsibility. Before the initiation of the national defense program, one could identify some fifty-odd separate, chronically depressed areas scattered across the country. Within them were concentrated about one-tenth of the total United States population, about one-sixth of all the unemployed, about one-fifth of all the recipients of public assistance.

Franklin, Saline, and Williamson Counties, Ill., a part of the southern Illinois coal field, constitute one such area. These three counties, and especially seven selected coal towns within the counties, are the subject of the present report.

The southern Illinois problem, as the report shows, is threefold. In the first place, three out of every four jobs which formerly existed in Franklin, Saline, and Williamson coal mines—the area's sole industry—have today disappeared, swept away by either mine abandonment or mechanization. Recent years of Nation-wide recovery have not halted this trend; at the beginning of 1941 the southern Illinois coal mines employed fewer men than at any time during the preceding quarter of a century.

Secondly, no new industries have appeared to fill this gap in the area's economy. For two generations coal-town businessmen have campaigned ardently for "outside industry" to supplant the declining coal industry. By 1941, however, these campaigns had still to win their first industry and to create their first lasting job in Franklin, Saline, and Williamson Counties.

Meanwhile—and this is the third essential of the problem—the size of the area's population has suffered only a slight decline over a period of 20 years.

Thus, intense local unemployment has become almost a normal state of things. Thousands of good workers have had no jobs for many years. Thousands of youth, blocked from entering industry, have reached their most productive years without ever having held a

III

job.   Nearly half the people are dependent on public aid year after year, and intense poverty is common.

The conditions necessary for the dissolution of the depressed areas are of course implicit in the circumstances of their origin.   Either the declining industry must be rejuvenated, or it must be supplanted, or the people must move away—obviously there are no other solutions.

The National defense program will eventually bring temporary relief of one kind or another to many of the depressed areas.   In southern Illinois, for example, the immediate prospect is not totally black, in spite of the continued stagnation of the local coal industry Since this report was written, coal-field unemployment has already been slightly reduced by the emigration of young workers to defense areas.   Two years from now the coal field expects to have 6,000 new defense jobs of its own at the War Department's proposed ordnance plant on Crab Orchard Lake near Herrin.

Such developments do not justify a complacent outlook upon the problems of the depressed areas.   The decline of depressed-area unemployment, waiting as it must upon the solution of Nation-wide unemployment, is likely to be much slower than might be hoped for. And whatever improvement the depressed areas may enjoy will in most cases disappear with the passing of the national emergency. Aggravated crisis within the depressed areas will be among America's foremost postdefense problems.

The present study was made in the Division of Research under the direction of Howard B. Myers, Director of the Division.   The report was prepared by Malcolm Brown and John N. Webb, of the Social Research Section.   Special acknowledgment is made to M. Starr Northrop, who supervised the census of population and unemployment; to Elizabeth J. Greenwood, who supervised the survey of buying patterns among the long unemployed; to William G. Nowell and D. C. Smith, who conducted research into the history and other special aspects of the community; to Rebecca Pfefferman, who supervised the preparation of tabular and graphic materials and assisted in the analysis; to Albert Westefeld, who assisted in the analysis of chapter VII; to Frances McDonald, who prepared the manuscript for publication; and to Roy E. Stryker, of the Historical Section, Division of Information, Farm Security Administration, for the photographs used.   Warm thanks are extended also to the scores of residents of southern Illinois—particularly to union officials, working miners, and the unemployed—who patiently assisted the research workers in their inquiries.

Respectfully submitted.

CORRINGTON GILL,
Assistant Commissioner.

HON. HOWARD O. HUNTER,
Commissioner of Work Projects.

Contents

ILLUSTRATIONS

Figures

Photographs

Seven Stranded Coal Towns

XIII

INTRODUCTION

CERTAIN AMERICAN communities have borne far more than their share of unemployment and relief since 1929. Some were already reporting typical middepression unemployment rates at the time of the 1930 Census, 6 months after the stock-market crash. During the operation of the Federal Emergency Relief Administration (1933–1935) some were accustomed to carrying as much as half or more of their entire population on the relief rolls. The 1936 recovery passed them by. And in the trough of the 1937 recession they reported 3 times, 10 times, some even 50 times higher unemployment rates than their more fortunate neighbors at the other end of the scale. These communities, comparable to the industrially decadent "black districts" of Great Britain, are America's depressed areas.

The problem of depressed areas is considerably more serious than is generally realized. Late in the decade of the 1930's (before the national defense program was initiated) one could identify some fifty-odd distinct depressed areas in the United States.[1] These areas contained an aggregate population of 13 million, about one-tenth of the total population of the United States. In January 1935 more

[1] The use of counties as the geographical unit for identifying depressed areas conditions the results obtained. County data conceal pockets of unemployment which more detailed data would reveal. New York City, for example, doubtless contains a number of "depressed areas," but they cannot be isolated by the use of existing data.

The areas were identified on the basis of their relief load in January 1935 and the percent of gainful workers reporting unemployment in November 1937. The lower limits of the identifying measures were arbitrarily set to include specified areas which had been shown by case studies to be, beyond reasonable doubt, chronically depressed areas.

Several well-known "problem areas" were not "depressed areas" according to the measures used. In particular, the greater part of the Cotton Belt was excluded, since it reported relatively low relief and unemployment throughout the 1930's. No attempt was made to include plane of living as a criterion.

These figures will, of course, bear substantial revision when the data on earnings and duration of unemployment in the 1940 Census are available.

than 3½ million persons in these areas received general relief, and they accounted for nearly one-fifth of the total relief population of the United States. In November 1937 the depressed areas contained more than 1½ million totally unemployed workers, and their *excess* of unemployment over their average share was equal to the *total* unemployment of Chicago, Detroit, Los Angeles, and Cleveland combined.

THE ORIGIN OF DEPRESSED AREAS

Depressed areas come forcefully to public attention only during a period of general unemployment. Superficially, they then appear as merely another manifestation of the depression itself, as the depression's special victims, where unemployment has struck hardest and persisted most stubbornly. It would be a mistake to suppose that the distinction between the depressed areas and their neighbors ends with this observation. Beyond the general problems of the depression, depressed areas are a special problem in themselves.

In one sense a depressed area is nothing new on the American scene. Essentially it is a modern instance of a community whose basic function has been rendered unprofitable by noncyclical trends in the pattern of economic interrelations. During the past 100 years there have been scores of such communities. In the past, however, two opposing forces have usually come into play, preventing the full development of a depressed area.

In the first place, the workers not needed in a given community might move away and find work elsewhere. Thus, with the depletion of the western gold fields in the 1880's the population simply decamped, sometimes to the last man. Even as late as the 1920's half the population of numerous central Georgia counties were still able to pick up and move out after the boll-weevil invasion. More often, however, wholesale emigration was unnecessary; ordinarily the community itself could rebuild its wrecked economic base by shifting to an expanding industry. New Bedford, for example, shifted from whaling to textiles; South Bend turned its wagon industry to manufacturing automobiles; Key West became a shipping center when its cigar industry collapsed. Baltimore, Louisville, St. Louis, and numerous other American cities have passed through such metamorphoses since the Civil War.

After 1929 both of these self-healing remedies failed. The general disappearance of job opportunities not only checked the exodus of surplus workers from the declining communities but often turned the stream backward. As a result, "redundant" workers found themselves for the first time stranded in large numbers within areas where opportunity had disappeared. The possibility of developing substitute industries to absorb the unemployed locally also vanished;

investors who shunned the depressed areas in prosperous times found even less reason for favoring them afterwards. On top of all, the general depression intensified the decline within these communities, and hastened the economic degeneration already latent. Overnight the long-developing difficulties reached maturity. Unemployed workers piled up by the thousands, the relief load soared, and poverty became the lot of a great part of the people. At this point the problems of the depressed areas achieved sudden recognition.

The Vulnerable Communities

Not all areas are equally vulnerable to this type of disintegration; in the aggregate, depressed areas have their own peculiar characteristics. Although several diversified areas have been identified as depressed, highly specialized areas—whether engaged in extractive or manufacturing industries—are predominant. The vulnerability of such communities is clearly related to the narrowness of their economic base.[2] Depletion, as in the stranded oil fields and lumbering districts; or the loss of markets, as in depressed cotton-growing areas and bituminous coal fields; or technological obsolescence, as in several steel-processing centers; or the emigration of industry, as in stranded cigar and textile centers—these forces paralyze the sole foundation of economic life in the specialized communities. Without buffer industries, whole areas are disrupted.

Isolation of one sort or another is a second characteristic of the depressed areas identified. Several areas, especially those devoted to extractive industries, are set off at a great distance from the nearest labor market, so that the emigration of workers is extremely difficult. Specialized skills tend to immobilize stranded workers in some of the depressed areas, particularly in the coal fields and steel centers where technological changes have played special havoc. In other areas, the problem is complicated still further by ethnic isolation, involving not only Negroes, but also important Spanish-language groups in Florida and Texas. Finally, such depressed areas as the Appalachian and Ozark Highlands are isolated by a singular culture pattern. In each instance, the dispersion of "redundant population," difficult enough in any case, is made even more difficult.

The Effects

Internally, the pathology of a depressed area also follows its own special logic. The extraordinary impact of unemployment, often

[2] It does not follow that all specialized communities are vulnerable; indeed, quite the contrary is true. Many of the least depressed communities are also specialized—the Iowa food-industry cities, the Piedmont textile districts, and the Connecticut metalworks cities, for example.

involving half or more of an entire labor force, leads to qualitative differences of the utmost gravity. The youth problem, for example, takes on a new aspect, for a large proportion of the younger workers grow into their most productive years without ever knowing the experience of a job in private industry. The long unemployed—those experienced workers who have not worked in private industry for a year, 2 years, even 5 years—form a substantial part of the entire labor force, and thousands of workers in middle age give up all hope of ever working again.

Some of the workers, particularly the youth, leave the community to seek work elsewhere, and a few get jobs. But the great majority, pauperized by bank failures, foreclosures, and years of unemployment, lack the resources as well as the contacts necessary for migration, and they never get away. Many who leave eventually come home again. Spontaneous migration does not proceed rapidly enough to diminish appreciably the size of the population. Such migration as does occur drains away the ablest workers, leaving a people heavily weighted with the aged, and laying the basis for even more serious problems in years to come.

The people of the depressed area are helpless in the face of the disaster. Enthusiastic campaigns to rebuild the economic base—"to land outside industry"—fritter away without producing substantial results. The attempt to save the tottering industrial structure by a return to more primitive techniques creates as many problems as it solves. Subsistence farming for the unemployed finds many willing recruits, but in practice it has usually been ineffectual. The bankrupt local governments are powerless to carry on their normal activities, let alone to give relief to the unemployed. Large-scale grants from the Federal and State Governments are required to save the community from utter collapse.

THE SOUTHERN ILLINOIS COAL FIELD

Franklin, Saline, and Williamson Counties, in southern Illinois, are such an area. These three counties have long been of special interest to the Work Projects Administration because they have required, year after year, WPA employment quotas three or four times greater than average American communities of the same size. In order to get full information on the characteristics and problems of this depressed area—and in turn, to throw light on the problems of depressed areas generally—the WPA Division of Research conducted a detailed survey of the community in 1939. The results of this survey are the subject of the present report.

The principal Illinois coal field consists of 13 counties extending nearly 200 miles southward from the center of the State in the shape of the letter "C." The top of the field is at Springfield, the center at East St. Louis, the bottom at Harrisburg, Ill., 50 miles north of Paducah, Ky. In the northern part of this area coal mining is only one of several diverse activities (except in two specialized coal counties); and in several counties it holds a distinctly minor position in the total economy. South of East St. Louis, however, the size and frequency of the mines encountered gradually increases, while the farms become poorer and other industries gradually disappear. At the very bottom of the field are Franklin, Saline, and Williamson Counties, almost entirely dependent upon a group of gigantic coal mines.

The Three Counties

Of the three counties Franklin is by far the most important coal producer, mining nearly 9 million tons in 1939. In spite of its reverses during recent years, Franklin is still one of the half-dozen leading coal-mining counties in the United States and the top producer west of the Appalachians. Franklin County coal is all "deep-vein," lying 300 to 600 feet below the surface of the prairie. It can thus be recovered only by shaft mining.[3] Ample sources of capital, together with several peculiar advantages in the seam,[4] have led to large-scale operation; one of the Franklin County mines is the largest on earth, and three others have a daily output of more than 5,000 tons. Franklin County operators have also been able to take advantage of most of the recent revolutionary advances in coal-recovery techniques, so that in 1941 the Franklin County mines were among the most modern and efficient shaft mines in the United States.

Saline County, with a 1939 output of over 3½ million tons, ranks fourth among the Illinois coal-producing counties. In the northern part of the county the coal is recovered by deep-vein shaft mines similar to those in Franklin County, though somewhat smaller. Towards the south, however, the seam rises gradually to the surface of the prairie, so that shaft mining is no longer necessary. Along the southern edge of the seam a considerable area of coal lies under an overburden of only about 100 feet. In this area several highly efficient slope mines [5] have recently been developed. Further south

[3] A shaft mine is one in which loaded pit cars are hoisted from the underground workings to the surface by means of a system of tandem elevators, or "cages," operating in a vertical shaft.

[4] The No. 6 seam in Franklin County lies almost level, and is relatively free from faults. The underground transportation system can accordingly radiate great distances off the central shaft without encountering difficulties.

[5] In slope mines coal is brought to the surface either by means of an inclined track on which the pit cars run, or on an inclined belt conveyor. In either case, the elaborate system of cages and hoists used in shaft mines is eliminated.

still there is an area with an overburden of 60 feet or less. Here the coal is recovered by strip mining,[6] the most efficient of all mining methods.

Williamson County, once the leading coal county in Illinois, ranked only eighth in 1939 with an output of 2½ million tons. Like Saline, Williamson County mines both deep-vein and shallow-vein coal; hence it uses the three recovery techniques—shaft mining, slope mining, and stripping. In addition, there are in Williamson some one-hundred-and-fifty-odd small, makeshift workings called "gopher holes,"[7] where farmers and displaced workers from the great mines near by dig shallow-vein coal for the local trade. These mines, which work the leavings of the coal lands under the most primitive technical conditions, represent a return to handicraft methods of production under the stress of the depression.

The one other primary industry is agriculture. There are scattered, small communities of prosperous farmers within the three counties, particularly in Saline County, which has, indeed, been partially stabilized by its farm economy. By and large, however, the land within the area is poor; erosion has taken a heavy toll in some sections; and many of the farms are too small for profitable operation. For generations farmers throughout "Egypt"[8] have counted themselves lucky when they raised half the corn crop regularly grown on the richer lands 100 miles to the north. As a matter of fact, several of the purely agricultural southern Illinois counties adjoining the coal field are more depressed than the coal counties themselves.

There are 140,000 people living within the area of the 3 counties, more than half of them living in some twenty-odd coal towns ranging in size from 500 to 13,000 population. The majority of these people are descended from settlers who came into Illinois between 1870 and 1910 from the West Kentucky hills; thus, in speech and numerous folkways, the area is at bottom culturally homogeneous with the western Appalachians and distinctly unlike the Illinois Corn Belt communities. In addition to the Kentuckians, several large foreign-born groups—principally Italians, Hungarians, Croatians, and Ukrainians—settled in southern Illinois between 1900 and 1920 for work in the mines. Finally, Williamson County contains a separate Negro settlement of about 3,000 persons.

---

[6] In strip mines huge power shovels first remove the overburden from the seam, then simply load out the coal in the open air.

[7] "Gopher holes" are officially known as "local" mines, because they produce coal for the trucking trade and are distinguished from the "shipping" mines, which produce for railway shipment. Most of them employ from 5 to 10 workers for a short season at substandard wages.

[8] "Egypt" is the local name for the southernmost one-fourth of Illinois, lying south of a line drawn between Vincennes, Ind., and St. Louis, Mo. The three coal counties are in the heart of this district.

The Study of the Depressed Area

The present study is based mainly upon three primary sources of information. The first source is a census of unemployment and population, conducted between December 1938 and March 1939 in seven coal towns selected to present a fair cross section of the non-agricultural population. The towns chosen were:

County and town	Population (1939)
Franklin County:	
West Frankfort	12, 733
Zeigler	3, 017
Saline County:	
Carrier Mills	2, 234
Eldorado	4, 620
Williamson County:	
Bush	643
Herrin	9, 608
Johnston City	5, 353

This list includes the larger towns as well as the small mine villages, towns where mine mechanization was complete as well as the towns dependent (at the time) on hand loading, and it includes the most prosperous towns remaining in the area as well as the most utterly depressed. This survey was supplemented with a detailed study of the buying patterns of long-unemployed families in four of the seven towns.

The second step in the research was a thorough examination of all pertinent local records on the development of the community. Special emphasis was given to courthouse records dealing with coal-land ownership, real-estate transfers, real-estate values, the distribution of the tax load, and tax delinquency. The minutes kept by the county commissioners and county supervisors were traced for information on the history of poor relief, and for the record of all county and township expenditures. Local newspaper files covering 40 years in the life of the coal field were read in detail to reconstruct the history of the community.

Finally, field research workers informally discussed the problems of the coal field with hundreds of local residents. All sections of the community were covered in this work, and each of the dozens of conflicting points of view expressed was carefully considered. Ministers, merchants, editors, coal operators, bankers, public officials, relief case workers, and teachers were interviewed, together with scores of workers of all types—miners at the face, union officials, shopkeepers, clerks, farmers, and the unemployed.

The organization of the report may be briefly outlined. Chapter 1 traces the economic history of the three counties through two decades of the great southern Illinois coal boom. The condition of the coal field in 1939 is described in chapters II and III, with special reference to the peculiarities of a depressed labor market. The decline of the Franklin, Saline, and Williamson coal industry is discussed in chapter IV, and the parallel collapse of local enterprise is traced in chapter V. Chapter VI deals with the various local attempts, all more or less futile, to solve the communities' problems. Chapter VII discusses the emigration of workers from southern Illinois since the dark days first set in. The extraordinary record of relief in the three counties is presented in chapter VIII. Finally, chapter IX discusses the general problem of depressed areas, with an analysis of the possible solutions that might be attempted.

SUMMARY

FEW COMMUNITIES in America are more specialized than Franklin, Saline, and Williamson Counties, three contiguous counties in the southern Illinois coal field. Outside of agriculture, which has never prospered on the relatively sterile lands of southern Illinois, the three counties have only one industry—coal.

Between 1900 and the middle of the 1920's coal mines served the community well. For a quarter of a century the southern Illinois coal industry enjoyed a dramatic growth, employing an ever-increasing number of miners to produce coal for an ever-expanding market. More than 100 mines hoisted coal each day in the 3 counties. Sesser had 3 mines, Benton had 4, Johnston City had 8, Pittsburg had 3, and 16 mines operated in and around Herrin.

About 15 years ago, however, the southern Illinois field began to lose markets rapidly to rival coal fields and to competing fuels. Prosperity suddenly ended. The few mines which survived were saved only by the continual introduction of new laborsaving techniques, with the result that increased efficiency displaced thousands of workers. Sixty of the hundred mines were abandoned and more thousands of miners were thrown out of work. At last there were no mines left in Sesser, in Benton, in Johnston City, in Pittsburg; and of Herrin's 16 mines, only 1—equipped with the most modern and efficient machinery—remained.

In the wake of mounting unemployment came great waves of bankruptcies and foreclosures. A total of 34 coal-town banks collapsed within 2 years, and 7 million dollars in savings were swept away. The building and loan associations, to whom a large part of the population was debtor, found themselves unable to collect high interest on property that had suddenly become almost worthless. There followed score upon score of repossessions, and hundreds of building-and-loan houses were razed for secondhand lumber. Little businessmen by the dozens closed their doors. The tax structure collapsed.

UNEMPLOYMENT

The disintegration of the local coal industry has left the three counties economically prostrate. At no time during the past 4 years has less than one-third of the population been dependent on public assistance and the proportion rose to half for short periods during both 1938 and 1939. In the seven towns surveyed, more than two-fifths of all available workers were unemployed at the *peak* of the 1939 mining season; in Johnston City 60 percent were unemployed; in the little mine village of Bush unemployment claimed four out of every five workers. The distress of the coal towns had apparently become still more grave by the early autumn of 1940, when 4 of the larger mines operating at the time of the 1939 survey had been abandoned and their 1,200 employees dismissed.

The great majority of the unemployed in the coal towns fall into two groups. The largest of these consists of the long unemployed. As the local labor market tightened year after year, there came a time when a man who lost his job was not likely to find another. His qualifications, his experience, his union, even his friends, could do him little service, for job opportunities had all but vanished. Unemployed workers thus became in the course of time long-unemployed workers. By 1939 half the coal-town unemployed consisted of experienced workers who had held no private job for at least 1 year.

Among the long-unemployed workers coal miners are of course most numerous. The displaced miners, as a group, reported continuous unemployment for an average of more than 5 years at the time of the study. The group was, moreover, heavily weighted with older workers whose industrial experience had been confined principally to loading coal by hand, an occupation now largely obsolete in southern Illinois. The rest of the long unemployed had been discharged from a score of industries devoted either to servicing the community or to servicing the coal industry itself. Since the coal field contains virtually no manufacturing industries, very few operatives were included among the unemployed.

The second major unemployed group was composed of youth who had reached working age and who had found no job after months and even years in the labor market. By 1939 one unemployed worker in every three was a new worker who had *never* held a job in private industry. Four-fifths of all the unemployed were thus either long-unemployed or inexperienced workers.

PROSPECTS FOR NEW EMPLOYMENT
At the Mines

It is obviously impossible to predict the extent of the market for southern Illinois coal during the next few years. The University of Illinois is now developing a technique for briquetting southern Illinois coals and making them smokeless; if perfected, the technique would, of course, increase the demand for southern Illinois coal. On the other hand, the field suffers increasing competition from a great oil and gas pool recently brought into production at Salem and Centralia, Ill., only 75 miles from Herrin.

The effects of the national defense program on the southern Illinois coal industry cannot be clearly foreseen. If one supposed that the community could again market as much coal as it produced in 1917—a somewhat dubious assumption—the prospects for reemployment at the mines would still be extremely meager. The efficiency of the average southern Illinois miner has exactly doubled since 1917. The tonnage mined in 1917 required 25,000 miners; the same tonnage could be mined in 1941 with only 12,500 miners, fewer than were *actually* employed at the bottom of the depression in 1933.

New Industries

For 30 years the coal towns have campaigned ardently to secure new industries to supplant the declining coal industry. They have offered subsidies to outside manufacturers; they have donated land and buildings; they have offered guarantees against unionization; for many years they have advertised the industrial advantages of the community. But the few investors who have accepted such offers have long since failed; and three decades of attempting to broaden the area's economic base must be accounted an utter failure.

EMIGRATION

There has been a slight population decrease in southern Illinois since the decline of the coal industry first began. In 1920 the 3 counties contained 157,000 persons; in 1930, population had fallen to 150,000 persons; and by 1940 it had declined to 140,000 persons. Over a period of two decades, the area thus lost 10 percent of its population. Population decrease, however, has lagged far behind the decline in economic opportunity. During the period when population was declining 10 percent, the number of men employed at the coal mines fell from 29,000 to 10,000, a drop of 66 percent.

The migrants who have left southern Illinois during the past decade have consisted principally of youth of both sexes. In the older age groups emigration has been insignificant; among the very old, indeed, there has recently been a net *increase* from migration. These tendencies have resulted in a rapid "aging" of the general population, thus storing up more serious problems for the future of the community. Emigration of coal-town youth in response to defense activity will doubtless be accelerated in the immediate future. Among the older workers, however, emigration will still be hindered by the fact that years of unemployment and relief have left large sections of the population without the resources necessary for migration in search of work.

Chapter 1

THE ORIGINS OF A VULNERABLE COMMUNITY

LESS THAN two decades ago the southern Illinois coal field was riding the crest of a prolonged and spectacular boom. At that time the coal industry of Franklin, Saline, and Williamson Counties had behind it a record of more than 20 years of uninterrupted advance, and it was still expanding. The territory between the towns of West Frankfort and Benton was being surveyed for the site of the New Orient, the largest coal mine ever developed. Workers were in demand. Nearly every school boy was going into the mines as soon as he finished the eighth grade. Herrin residents remember those years as the time when "you could stand on the roof of the city hall and see smoke from 16 mines every day." Coal-town service enterprises—the banks, the stores, the real-estate agencies, the building and loan associations—reflected the activity at the mines and flourished more dramatically than the coal industry itself.

The prosperity of the area appeared in those times to be as solid as one could hope for. The three counties were built on coal, and coal was basic to the American economy. The southern Illinois coal reserves, then as now, were never spoken of except in terms of being "almost inexhaustible." Above all, the great natural advantages of the coal field—the level-lying coal deposit, the 8-foot seam in the No. 6 coal, the high B. t. u. and low sulphur content, the flat top land, and the short run to Chicago ("largest coal market in the world")—seemed to assure the favorable competitive position of southern Illinois coal for years to come. Two decades ago a person would have supposed that the three counties were to have a vastly different future from the one which actually lay in store.

Today the southern Illinois coal field presents a picture, almost unrelieved, of utter economic devastation. The years since 1923 have

1

seen the community lose three out of every four of its mines. They have seen a half-dozen once lively coal centers gradually sink to ghost towns. They have seen the building-and-loan bubble burst in every coal town and every bank throughout the greater part of the coal field driven into bankruptcy. They have seen employment shrink until two out of every five workers were "surplus" at the busiest season of the year, while the public-assistance load climbed until it included more than half the entire population of the three counties. They have seen the coal boom subside and give way to hopeless poverty.[1]

How did so radical and unexpected a decline in the fortunes of Franklin, Saline, and Williamson Counties come about? One may hear many pat answers to this question. The "Jacksonville Scale," which set up a higher wage for Illinois miners than was paid in competing nonunion fields, is usually isolated as the one villain in the piece. But one may justifiably wonder what connection the Jacksonville Scale, abandoned in 1928, could have had with the failure of coal-field banks in 1932, with the foreclosure of miners' homes in 1935, or with tax delinquency in 1940.

Another common explanation is that the miners "couldn't stand prosperity" when they earned high daily wages during the middle 1920's,[2] that they "squandered their money on silk shirts" and automobiles, that they failed to save for a less prosperous time, and that their current plight is somehow a just recompense for earlier folly. But careful examination shows that the legend of the "silk-shirt era," as retold today, is built as much on fancy as on fact. In any case, the accumulation of savings in banks that were eventually to crash could hardly have altered the history of the coal field. One will also be told that the present condition of the three counties was brought on by loading machines, or by the Herrin riots in 1922, or by the movement off the farms between 1900 and 1930.

Actually, the story of distress in the southern Illinois coal field cannot be reduced to a simple, single cause. The complex forces at work upon the fortunes of the three counties can, however, be separated into two main threads. One of these is the coal industry itself, whose rise and fall of course played a dominant, though not a lone, role in the history of the coal field. The other thread, less often

---

[1] This was written late in 1939, before the national defense program got under way. In September 1940 a field research worker revisited the community and found its condition in no way improved. Three mines which were operating when this study was conducted had been abandoned by September 1940, displacing 1,250 men.

[2] Such, for example, is the judgment of a writer who discussed another declining American coal field in *Harpers Magazine*, March 1940, p. 412 (Rice, Millard Milburn, "Footnote on Arthurdale"). This general attitude is also popular among coal-town businessmen.

recognized, lies in the structure of local finance and enterprise which was created in response to the activity of the mines, but which often ran a strange independent course of its own. To understand each of these threads in the history of the coal field, it will be profitable to begin with their origins 40 years ago, when southern Illinois first became one of America's important coal fields.

THE COAL BOOM

Discovery and Consolidation

At the turn of the twentieth century the great coal deposits of Franklin, Saline, and Williamson Counties were for the most part still undiscovered. Here and there a few small mines had started commercial operation, some as early as the 1880's, but for many years development proceeded slowly. According to the legend, prospectors had believed that the district's coal occurred only in pockets, so that if drillers found coal in one place their discovery was taken as proof that coal could not be found elsewhere in the neighborhood. Several decades of hit-and-miss exploration had turned up only a few isolated "pockets," one at Carterville, one at Johnston City, and one at Marion—all in Williamson County—and one at Ledford in Saline County.

Not long before 1900 came the first realization that southern Illinois might have a coal deposit of Nation-wide importance. A group of small landowners near the present town of Herrin had become skeptical of the accepted notions about coal occurrence in southern Illinois and had started drilling on a plot of poor farmland midway between the Carterville and Johnston City mines. At 150 feet below the surface they struck a rich 9-foot seam of high quality coal. Soon afterward new drill holes were put down and coal was found to run all the way across Herrin's Prairie from Carterville to Johnston City.

The new Herrin field, some thirty-odd square miles of coal, was the small investor's opportunity. Only three large blocks of coal were consolidated, two of them coming under the control of directors of the Missouri Pacific Railroad. The rest of the new field was parceled out to numerous small promoters, each taking up blocks varying from 200 to 1,000 acres. Williamson County coal all lay so close to the surface that exploitation usually required only a small accumulation of capital, and the new operators set to the work of development immediately. By 1900 three new mines in western Williamson County were already hoisting coal, and more than a score of others were being planned.

There were certain investors who took very careful note of the Herrin discovery. Among these were the more powerful Chicago mineowners and retail coaldealers, who observed that the northern

Illinois fields were rapidly playing out and that a newly discovered high-grade coal, mined close at hand, might soon command the mid-western fuel market. By 1903 this group was fortified with earnings made during the Chicago coal famines (which followed the great anthracite strikes) and were ready to move on to larger enterprises. Several wildcat coal promoters, fresh from the job of opening new coal properties at New River, or the Hocking Valley, or Kansas, or Indiana, were looking for newer fields to exploit. Steel manufacturers were anxious to find a coking coal somewhere near their Chicago mills. Most interested of all were the railroads, not only because of their operating needs, but also because they were deep in a plan to organize the soft-coal industry as a subsidiary of the carriers, just as Pennsylvania anthracite had already been organized.

The Herrin discovery had brought into question all the old notions about coal occurrence in southern Illinois and suggested the existence of large undiscovered deposits. The four groups of investors responded quickly to the suggestion. Throughout 1900 drill crews prospected quietly across eastern Williamson County. Land dealers followed, buying up the land. Within a short time about 15 sections of coal land east of Johnston City had been consolidated and purchased by the Illinois Central, and another block of 4,000 acres was taken up by the Illinois Steel Company. North of Herrin, a wildcatter financed by John W. (Bet-a-million) Gates took title to another large block of Williamson coal. A leading Chicago coaldealer bought two operating mines at Marion and drove a railroad from Williamson into the heart of Saline County, buying up the mineral rights along the way.

The most startling discovery was still to come. About 1900 a wealthy young Chicago promoter named Joseph Leiter bought out the patent rights on a special coking process, and started a search for a coking coal. Eventually he experimented with Carterville coal and thought it satisfactory (mistakenly, as it later developed). After an unsuccessful attempt to buy the Carterville mine, Leiter hired a geologist to discover whether similar coal might be found near by. The geologist concluded that the Carterville seam ran northward into Franklin County; and when test drill holes were sunk, the cores showed that there existed beneath 400 feet of overburden a new field more extensive and valuable than any yet discovered in southern Illinois. In 1903 Leiter bought a solid square block of 7,000 acres, started sinking a shaft, and built the company town of Zeigler.

By 1904 the findings of Leiter's geologist had brought America's largest corporations scrambling for land in southern Illinois, and especially in Franklin County. The Chicago, Burlington, & Quincy Railroad bought some 10,000 acres of coal land at Valier, and started extension of its tracks to the coal field. The United States Steel

Corporation took up the greater part of two townships east of Benton. The Missouri Pacific consolidated an extensive block of coal at Bush; the Illinois Central took over twenty-thousand-odd acres north of Carterville, together with an operating mine; and the Frisco Lines got control of a block between Benton and West Frankfort. A wildcatter and a northern Illinois operator bought a couple of townships of mineral rights in Franklin and Williamson. In Saline a coal operator controlled by the New York Central Railroad bought up thousands of acres from Eldorado to Carrier Mills.

The pattern of coal ownership which has since dominated the southern Illinois field was firmly established by 1907, when the last stray mineral rights were brought under control. In the gaps between the great coal blocks of Franklin and Saline Counties a few small investors—some local, some absentee—had gained a foothold; and in western Williamson County, where the boom first started, the small holders were numerous. But the great majority of the coal had come into the hands of about a dozen companies, holding from 10 to 50 sections each. Four of these holdings were "captive" to the railroads, that is, held with a view to supplying the railroads' own coal needs.[3] Two others were captive to steel manufacturers. The other half-dozen great blocks were held by companies connected more or less directly with Chicago and St. Louis coaldealers. The fortunes of the southern Illinois coal field were dependent from the start upon these few absentee operators and their successors, and the decisions of these Chicago, New York, and Boston investors were in the course of time to make their share of history in the three counties.

Labor

The Illinois miners' union and the southern Illinois coal field were born at the same time and grew up together. In 1898, just at the opening of the first mine on Herrin's Prairie, the United Mine Workers of America (Illinois District) won their first considerable victory in the State and successfully negotiated contracts with most of the Illinois operators. Nearly all of the few small mines that had already started operation in Williamson and Saline Counties signed contracts in 1898, and the transition to collective bargaining at each new mine developed after 1898 came for the most part without great strain or friction.

There were, however, two significant exceptions, which had a profound influence on the history of the southern Illinois union. In 1899 a Carterville operator had decided to import Negro miners to

---

[3] The original railroad plan for controlling all the output of the field was wrecked by the Hepburn Act of 1906, which prevented railroads from engaging in the coal business except to supply their own operating needs.

break a strike at his tipple. Inevitably, violence followed and numerous persons were killed. This tactic isolated the operator and led most of the community to support the strike. The operator was eventually driven to bankruptcy, and finally, after 7 years of nonunion operation, he gave way to an operator who immediately signed a contract with the union. A similar incident occurred in Franklin County, where another isolated operator tactlessly housed his strikebreakers in a stockade protected with Gatling guns. Again there was violence, again the community supported the strikers, again the union won after years of bitterness. In 1910, when this last nonunion mine started operating under union contract, collective bargaining had become a part of the natural order of things in the southern Illinois coal field.

The Product of the New Field

Even before the great landholdings were consolidated, the rush to develop the field had begun. From 1900 through 1904 Williamson and Saline Counties saw 29 new mines opened and during the next 3 years another 21 mines started hoisting coal. In Franklin County the Zeigler shaft was rushed to completion and began hoisting late in 1904. The next year two other Franklin County mines opened, followed in 1907 by five more (appendix table 1). By 1907 southern Illinois coal had become a competitor to be reckoned with in every midwestern coal market from Bismarck to Chicago.

The new coal had many substantial advantages. In competition with the dwindling supply of coal from northern Illinois, southern Illinois coal had to meet a somewhat higher freight rate, but mining costs were so favorable that they offset the freight differential. In competition with Indiana coal, southern Illinois also had a slight disadvantage in freight rates to Chicago (though not to St. Louis), but most Indiana coals were of poorer quality. The chief fuel on the Chicago market of better quality than southern Illinois coal was a soft coal from the Hocking Valley of Ohio and Pennsylvania anthracite, both of which had to bear a far higher freight rate than southern Illinois coal.

The investors who opened the field provided a different kind of advantage. Joseph Leiter was able to spend a considerable sum of money advertising Zeigler, and thereby helped to build a reputation for all the Franklin County coal. The new Williamson mines cashed in similarly on the advertising of a Carterville operator who had made "Carterville prepared lump" well known on the Chicago market before the boom started. Several of the mines had enough capital to provide washers and other cleaning equipment, a new departure for the time. The railroad mines were helped along with ready-made contracts and sometimes special rates, while freight rebates came to the aid of several favored independent operators. Finally, many of the new mines were closely tied to the larger Chicago coaldealers, who naturally pushed the sale of coal from their own tipples. Thus, throughout the early period the West Virginia and Kentucky coal jobbers, who were later to affect so decisively the fortunes of southern Illinois, were still begging orders from office to office in Chicago, and offering their coal on consignment to overcome the reluctance of midwestern buyers.

Prosperity

Under all these favorable influences, the new field pushed rapidly into the midwestern coal market. Year after year the sale of southern Illinois coal increased. Coal output and mine capacity expanded with an amazing regularity. Each year saw more men digging coal in the three counties than the year before. At times the growth was rapid, as in the early discovery years and the World War boom. At other times—in the depression of 1907 and the prewar slump—the growth was slower. But every single year for a quarter of a century, from the discovery of coal on Herrin's Prairie in 1896 until the postwar depression in 1921, there was always some advance and never a backward step (figs. 1 and 2).

The magnitude of growth during the long period of steady advance was particularly impressive: the average net increase in employment each year between 1900 and 1923 was 1,400 men. The average growth of coal output during the same period was 1 million tons, roughly equal to the total output of the field during the year 1900. From 1900 to 1923 an average of two mines was abandoned per year, but an average of six new mines started hoisting coal (see appendix table 1). At the beginning of the coal boom southern Illinois coal supplied only an insignificant part of the demand on the Chicago and St. Louis markets; at the end, the three counties were by far the greatest coal-producing region west of the Appalachians and one of the two or three leading coal regions in the United States.

There was only one catch to this remarkable record of advance: the growth of production was constantly being outrun by the growth of mine capacity. For, while output was advancing at the rate of a 1-million-ton increase annually, the field's capacity to produce coal was being increased at the average rate of 2 million tons annually. Throughout the long coal boom, this tendency had caused periodic difficulties. The field was only a few years old when the cry of "cutthroat" competition was first heard, and the complaint that rivals sold their coal "below the cost of production" was reiterated year after year. As early as 1905 attempts were made to form combines in southern Illinois which would control supply, and despite repeated failure, the attempts were repeated every few years until as late as 1926.

Fig.1—MEN EMPLOYED AT SHIPPING COAL MINES IN FRANKLIN,
SALINE, AND WILLIAMSON COUNTIES, 1900–1921

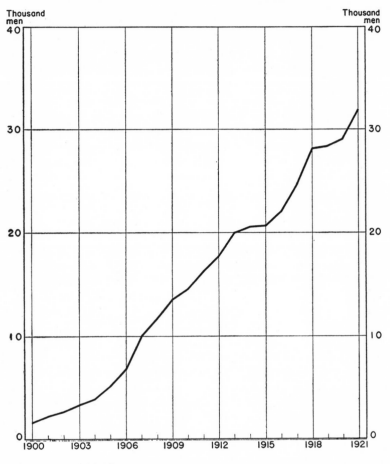

Source: Appendix table 2.   WPA 3635

The symptom of overexpanded mine capacity was a tendency for the work year to contract as time passed. In the discovery period a work year of 220 days was not uncommon (appendix table 3). Such a work year indicated a brisk demand for coal. Capital responded readily to the demand and flowed into the field faster than was needed. Capacity thus increased rapidly and soon far outran production (fig. 2). By 1911 the work year had fallen to only 165 days. At this point new investment slackened, production began to catch up again with capacity and the work year lengthened.

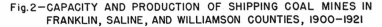

Fig.2—CAPACITY AND PRODUCTION OF SHIPPING COAL MINES IN
FRANKLIN, SALINE, AND WILLIAMSON COUNTIES, 1900–1921

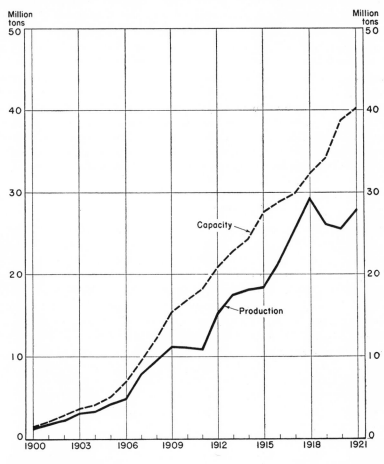

Source: Appendix table 3.   WPA 3636

The extraordinary wartime demand for coal started a new cycle.
In 1918 production soared, the work year lengthened to 254 days,
capacity in excess of output nearly disappeared. But again, and
on a bigger scale than ever before, capital flowed into the field, and
capacity soared again as huge new mines, developed to meet the
wartime demand, started hoisting coal. In 1919 peace and the
postwar coal strike halted the expansion of output. By 1920 the
work year had fallen back to 183 days. The time had come for
further growth of the market for southern Illinois coal. Unless

it continued to expand—as it had for a quarter of a century—calamity was certain.

At the peak of the boom in the early 1920's coal had become not only the leading industry in Franklin, Saline, and Williamson Counties but virtually the only industry. Coal had made the once poor farming community rich and prosperous, and had made it an important cog in American industry. But coal had also made the three counties vulnerable. Their welfare had come to depend solely upon the great impersonal coal market and upon the accidents which determined their position in competing for the market. An increase in the demand for steel, a mild winter in the Dakotas, a change in the price of crude oil, the installation of domestic stokers in Minneapolis, a wage cut in the Harlan County coal mines, a new freight rate from West Virginia to Lake Erie—all such remote occurrences had come to mean the difference between prosperity and poverty in southern Illinois.

THE STRUCTURE OF LOCAL ENTERPRISE

Local bankers and businessmen in the southern Illinois coal field have had very little direct connection with coal mining itself. When the rapid development of the southern Illinois coal field began in 1900, the three counties were a poor and isolated farming community. Local capital, which existed mainly in the form of poor farm land and deposits in small rural banks, was altogether inadequate for the opportunity at hand.[4] Only a few local entrepreneurs were able to gather enough capital for speculating in coal-land options, let alone for extensive development of producing mines. From the first the absentee investors controlled the greater part of the output of the southern Illinois mines, and not many years passed before they had almost complete ownership. No combination of local capital was ever strong enough to gain a lasting or important foothold in the mining industry.

The coal operators, on the other hand, were not able to set up any extensive system of company-town paternalism in southern Illinois. Unlike the mountain districts of West Virginia and Kentucky, the Illinois prairies provided the coal companies with no monopoly on townsites. Moreover, the Illinois miners, many of whom were drawn from farms and rural villages near the mine tipples, were organized early enough to prevent the operators from requiring residence on company property as a condition for a job. While several company towns and company stores were built early in the development of the southern Illinois field, they were soon forced to compete with inde-

---

[4] In 1900 bank deposits in the three counties totaled $523,403, scarcely enough to develop a single good-sized coal property.

"Orient Number One Blows Work."

One of the Big Franklin County Mines.

pendent towns near by. Under such circumstances, company towns had no particular purpose.[5] By 1910 the job of housing and servicing the rapidly growing population of the coal field had passed in large part to local entrepreneurs in real estate and banking.

Real Estate

With local entrepreneurs excluded from direct participation in the coal industry, real-estate values came to be the foundation of the financial structure of the coal towns and the basic form of wealth available to the community itself. The banks, the building and loan associations, and the local governments themselves were in large part built upon the security represented in real-estate values. An important key to an understanding of the development of the southern Illinois coal communities thus lies in the history of its real-estate activity.

The sudden transformation of Franklin, Saline, and Williamson Counties from a poor farming area into one of America's leading coal fields naturally created a boom in town real estate. The sudden influx of new workers soon led to a housing shortage, and new building became a very real need. Actual need, in turn, soon brought less tangible factors into play. Undue optimism was inevitable. An enthusiastic local newspaper computed (somewhat incorrectly) that southern Illinois coal would not be exhausted until A. D. 9279. The flow of capital into the field during the discovery years appeared to make the outlook still brighter; if the great financiers of America "had faith in southern Illinois," its future was indubitably assured.

Moreover, the early stages of the real-estate boom brought the rise of the real-estate promoters, local businessmen who were in most instances connected with the banks, the building-supply houses, the larger stores, or the building and loan associations. These entrepreneurs busied themselves with buying up farm land on the periphery of the growing towns, subdividing it into town lots, and offering it to the public at the end of an intensive advertising campaign. Making a frank appeal to speculators and promising that investment in real estate would "return a handsome profit," the promoters carried on a thriving business. Their activity is reflected in figure 3–A, which shows the number of deeds for town lots recorded in the three counties from 1900 to 1921.

---

[5] The town of Zeigler, for example, continued to be a company town through a period of nonunion operation at the Zeigler mine from 1904 to 1910. In 1910 the Zeigler mine signed a contract with the miners' union. The lands around the tipple were then opened up for real-estate promotion.

Fig. 3 - INDICES OF LOCAL BUSINESS ACTIVITY IN FRANKLIN,
SALINE, AND WILLIAMSON COUNTIES, 1900-1921

A. NUMBER AND AVERAGE VALUE
OF DEEDS FOR TOWN LOTS

B. ASSETS AND NEW LOANS OF BUILDING
AND LOAN ASSOCIATIONS

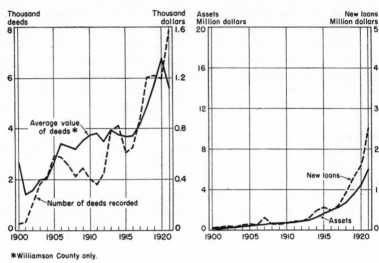

*Williamson County only.

C. BANK DEPOSITS

D. TAXES EXTENDED AND COLLECTED

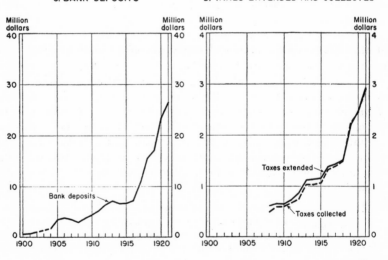

Source: Appendix tables 21, 22, 23, and 24.

WPA 3637

Real-Estate Speculation

Although the development of the southern Illinois coal industry was constant year after year for two decades, the real-estate boom did not progress evenly. Periodically the turnover in town lots showed strong speculative tendencies, and for a short time the activity of the real-estate promoters would run far ahead of the activity justified by the actual condition of the industry. The periods of inflation would then pass into periods of relative depression. The local entrepreneurs, seeing the foundation of their local financial structure weakened, immediately would become apprehensive and start to plan ways and means "to halt the decline of property values." But as long as the coal industry continued to expand, these fears would soon be allayed. Before many years had passed, the activity of the mines would catch up once more; increased real-estate activity would again increase and another period of land-value inflation would set in.

The real-estate boom thus rose in waves of alternating inflation and depression. The first of the waves began with the discovery of coal in Franklin County in 1902. Within a short time drilling crews were set up in all parts of the field, and month by month the full significance of the discovery became clearer. The most important deposit of coal west of the Appalachians had been found, and everyone thought he had a chance to get in on the ground floor in the community,[6] if not in the industry. The real-estate promoters went to work (fig. 4). By 1906 such typical advertisements as this were appearing weekly:

> Just 18 months ago the first car of coal was shipped from the _____ field, since which time _____ has doubled her population and is now the home of 4,000 people . . . the most conservative predict that within 3 to 5 years, _____ will be a city of 15,000 people. . . .
>
> We believe these lots will be worth at least 50 percent more by this time next year. As an investment, whether for holding or disposing of quickly, or for improvement and occupation . . . an investor cannot lose but on the contrary is bound to make a handsome profit. . . . An increase in value of 50 percent in a year is quite conservative.

[6] The accounts of the early activity in the coal field read like descriptions of an oil boom. In 1904 a coal-field visitor wrote: "We had heard much about the magic city of _____, to which people were flocking from everywhere. . . . We found it was one of the busiest and most thriving towns we had ever seen. . . . On almost every street new homes were going up. The song of the saw and hammer was everywhere in the air. People walked fast. They were all busy and they were happy." Another visitor reported in 1903, "Villages have sprung up where but yesterday the land was yielding a bounteous wheat crop. Cities have greatly enlarged their area and population and the whole section is alive to the possibilities of the future."

Fig. 4 - AN APPEAL TO REAL-ESTATE SPECULATORS FROM
THE FRANKLIN COUNTY INDEPENDENT
October 1906

This advertisement, one of the scores that
appeared, ran as a half-page spread

After a few years of such hysteria, the first boom in real estate had
gone far beyond all reasonable bounds. The promised increment of
50 percent a year failed to materialize, and sales of real estate slackened sharply. Soon afterward came the depression of 1907, which
for several years slowed the rate of growth of the local coal industry.
The real-estate business became progressively more sluggish, and
property values wavered. As this slump continued it caused considerable anxiety among local businessmen and real-estate dealers,
who were fearful above all of their wavering property values; this was
the first local intimation of the vulnerability of the one-industry
community. It led to the first schemes for bringing in outside
industry, which—significantly—were coupled with real-estate promotion drives.[7]

---

[7] See pp. 97, 98. One of the main arguments advanced to raise local money for
factories in 1912 was that new factories "would make a veritable boom in real-
estate values." One town naively computed that for every 100 new factory jobs
created, an increment of $420,000 would be added automatically to the total
value of the town's real estate.

By 1912 the inflated land prices resulting from the first wave of speculation had been absorbed in large part by the constant increase in the number of employees working in the mines. During the same year the real-estate dealers launched their second sales campaign, based on the prospect of establishing factories in the coal field.[8] Once more the invitations to get sudden profits from real-estate speculation was freely extended:

> Lots in the addition, as soon as the stove factory and foundry are built, should be worth more than is now asked.
> Lots in Factory Heights will change hands at an increase in value. The dust had not settled on the roads before Mr.———was offered an advance of $25 upon his lot purchase. Likewise Mr.———was offered $12.50, as well as many others.

Once more the turnover in town lots began to climb (fig. 3–A), and a second real-estate boom got under way. "The past sale of lots," said one newspaper, "is only the beginning of a greater sale of lots."

The second real-estate boom lasted 3 years. Those who had invested their money in the various "Factory Heights" additions to the coal towns in 1913 and 1914 were to be sadly disappointed soon afterward when the factories that had been promised failed to arrive. At the same time the rate of growth of employment in southern Illinois coal mines was again slowed down by the short depression which accompanied the first years of the World War. As soon as the factory promotion schemes were clearly discredited in 1914, there followed a second slump in real-estate activity. This slump was short-lived, however. Before 2 years had passed, the activity of the mines had again caught up with real-estate expansion and a third wave of inflation had started.

The World War and the years immediately following brought the real-estate boom to its final climax. The unprecedented demand for southern Illinois coal, beginning in 1916, attracted thousands of new workers to the coal field and created a critical housing shortage. Dozens of jerry-built "shotgun houses," assembled in 24 hours, were erected in every town. Rents and real-estate values soared. As figure 3–A shows, the activity of the real-estate promoters once more

---

[8] The schemes advanced in 1912–1915 proposed to raise funds for subsidizing new industries out of the profit from the sale of lots near the projected factory site. See pp. 97–98.

The economics of these schemes was explained as follows: "The amount necessary to secure [these] factories will be less than $100,000, and if this money be raised by the sale of lots, the increase in [real-estate] values will make the lots an exceptional investment, especially when we consider the certain [added] population of 5,000 to 6,000 people who will be compelled to use these same lots for residences."

began to increase, reaching a new record in 1917 and continuing to climb rapidly through the period of the war.[9]

The strike of 1919 and the postwar depression failed to deflate the real-estate boom. The housing shortage persisted, and even the coal companies which had long since abandoned the company-town system were forced to build houses in order to hold their workers. The productive capacity of the field continued to increase as new mines, started during the war, began actual operation. The financiers of New York, Boston, and Chicago also continued to demonstrate their optimism about the future of the field by their policy of absorbing the smaller producers throughout the three counties. In 1920 the miners started a relatively long period of steady work at wages well above the wartime scale. With this last period of prosperity, the wave of real-estate speculation reached its third and final peak, far above the highest wartime levels.

The Building and Loan Associations

During the period of the development of the southern Illinois coal field local entrepreneurs had organized—in very leisurely fashion—a number of mutual building and loan associations in the larger coal towns. Some of these associations were headed by the building-supply dealers, who had discovered that the home-loan system encouraged building and at the same time provided ample returns on the money invested. Also included among the directors of the associations were most of the real-estate promoters whose activities were traced in the preceding section, the leading bankers and professional people, and occasionally one or two of the more important coal-town merchants.

By 1918 there were 20 such associations operating in the 3 counties. Their activities, however, had played no important part as yet in the life of the communities, even though the communities were already nearly full-grown. The total assets of the associations in 1918 were only about 2¾ million dollars, and the number of new loans issued had not yet passed the 1-million-dollar mark (fig. 3–B). By this time the towns in the 3 counties had already been built from sleepy rural villages containing, all told, less than 15,000 persons at the turn of the century to active towns with a total population of more than 80,000. The coal towns had grown to maturity quite without the assistance of building-and-loan financing.

---

[9] The boom was apparently not altogether spontaneous. The usual fanfare in connection with the sale of lots in a new subdivision continued during the war boom, with free transportation, free picnic lunch, and brass bands provided for the customers. One promoter gave each purchaser of a lot a chance on a two-story house, which was later deeded to the person holding the lucky number after the lots were sold.

In the midst of the 1920 housing famine many families who were unable to find places to rent were forced to buy lots and build their own houses. In order to build in the emergency, however, a considerable sum of money was needed quickly; and for the first time in the history of the coal field, the miners began to turn to the building and loan associations for loans. Within the space of 4 years the amount of new loans issued by the associations quadrupled. By 1921, when new loans passed the 2½-million-dollar mark for the first time, the associations were doing 10 times the business they had enjoyed when the war began. The beginning of intense activity among the home-loan associations thus coincided with the period in which the real-estate activity in the coal towns reached the final and record peak discussed in the preceding section (fig. 3–B).

The sudden spurt in the home-loan business during the housing boom in 1920 and 1921 had built up a sizable backlog of capital for the associations. The interest rate was high—interest and "premiums" netted more than half a million dollars in 1921 on total loans of over 5½ million dollars—hence, local capital flowed freely into the growing loan enterprises (appendix table 23). Installment payments on association stock sold in connection with the original loans provided other capital; by 1921 the associations had accumulated 2½ million dollars for loans from this source alone. On this basis the associations prepared themselves for a long and profitable business.

Banking

Southern Illinois banking has always been the private domain of local businessmen rather than of absentee coal operators. The banks in the coal field have accordingly not dealt directly in any large degree with the coal-mining industry, and the job of providing banking facilities and credits to the mines has fallen to Chicago and St. Louis banks. Local banks have perforce confined their activities to servicing the miners, farmers, and merchants within the community—to receiving the savings of the miners, carrying the deposits of local merchants, and providing credit for the community itself.

Until the time of the World War these functions did not assume great importance. Mine wages were not high, and the community's share from the coal industry went principally into physical expansion of housing and inventories, rather than into cash surplus. Another difficulty faced by local bankers before the war was that the foreign born, who comprised a large part of the working population, were traditionally suspicious of "the banking institutions of this country." Instead of depositing their money in the local banks, they preferred to send it to Europe for deposit in government-controlled savings banks.[10]

[10] For this reason the local businessmen welcomed the Postal Savings System. See p. 83.

Bank deposits thus accumulated slowly during the period which saw the greatest development of the coal field. During the first real-estate boom (1900–1906) they increased from ½ million dollars to nearly 4 million dollars. Some of this increase, however, was subsequently lost during the depression of 1907. The period of the second real-estate boom (1911–1913) brought deposits to more than 7 million dollars; but again a recession which accompanied the first years of the war wiped out a part of the gains. Not until the beginning of wartime activity in the coal field did the local banking business come into its own. (See appendix table 24.)

The World War simultaneously increased the pay roll in the coal field—through a lengthened work year, higher wages, and the creation of thousands of new jobs—and cut off the flow of savings to Europe. Under these circumstances, bank deposits shot upward at an amazing rate. While it required 16 years for the three counties to accumulate their first 7 million dollars in bank deposits, the second 7 million dollars was deposited in less than 2 years during 1917 and 1918. After the war a further rise in wages and employment continued to increase deposits; from 15½ million dollars in 1918, deposits climbed to almost 26½ million dollars in 1921. For each dollar deposited in coal-field banks in 1916 there were nearly $4 on deposit in 1921 (fig. 3–C).

The sudden skyrocketing of bank deposits was interpreted in the coal field to be a reflection not only of the prosperity of the community—which no one could deny—but of its "soundness" as well. A local newspaper boasted:

> All the banks are in a most healthy and prosperous condition and reflect our prosperity in a most emphatic manner. We are enjoying the greatest measure of sound, substantial prosperity and growth in our history.

Even the foreign born cast off their suspicions and began to deposit their money in the local banks.

THE TAX STRUCTURE

The Changing Tax Base

Before the rapid development of southern Illinois coal reserves got under way in 1900, the lands, improvements, and personalty of farms represented the chief form of wealth in Franklin, Saline, and Williamson Counties; and what little tax income was required to keep up the limited tasks of local government was paid almost altogether by farmers. As the coal mines were developed, three other forms of taxable wealth were created: coal in the ground, assessed sometimes with top land and sometimes separately as mineral rights; coal-land improvements in the form of tipples, hoisting, and screening equipment, etc.; and residence and business property in the growing coal towns. The tax base was accordingly shifted from farm property to the community's new property. The manner of the shift, determined as it was by the informal and empirical approach of local tax assessors, was to have far-reaching effects upon the later life of the coal field.

The contribution of farm property to the total assessed valuation of the three counties continued to be important in spite of the growth of the coal industry. The State of Illinois had long followed a tradition of "encouraging" the coal industry through favorable taxation. At one time coal mines were even declared to be exempt from State (but not local) levies; and although the courts later decided otherwise, the forces which made for the original exemption continued to operate through other channels. Since their earliest contacts with the great absentee coal operators, local tax assessors in the three counties appear to have been lenient in appraising mine property. And when the assessors did not take this approach the operators' lawyers were not slow to appear before the local equalization boards demanding adjustments.

In any case, it appears that the burden of taxes outside the coal towns was not shared equitably between farmers and coal operators. By 1913 the gross value of products from the mining industry was roughly four times that of products from the farms in the three counties.[11] Yet the assessed valuation of all real property connected with the coal industry was only half that of farm property. During the war period this disproportion was heightened, as wartime prices for coal pushed the value of mining products up to about eight times the value of farm products. After the war there was a general adjustment of rural assessments; but the coal industry, which was still producing about four times as much gross value as the farms, even then carried no more assessed valuation than the aggregate farm land of the community (appendix table 20). The attitude of the local assessors toward the coal industry may be illustrated by the valuation of a typical mine property: In 1924 the company's real property was assessed on the basis of half its full-and-true value at 2 million dollars, and was accordingly judged to have a full value of 4 million dollars.

---

[11] For value of farm products in the three counties during the period 1910–1925 see Bureau of the Census, *Thirteenth Census of the United States: 1910*, Agriculture Vol. VI, 1913, pp. 442–445; *Fourteenth Census of the United States: 1920*, Agriculture Vol. VI, Part 1, 1922, pp. 365–409; and *United States Census of Agriculture: 1925*, Part 1, 1927, pp. 520–547, U. S. Department of Commerce, Washington, D. C.

For the value of mine products during the same period see *Mineral Resources of the United States*, issued annually by the U. S. Geological Survey, Washington, D. C., for the years 1910 through 1923 and by the Bureau of Mines, U. S. Department of the Interior, Washington, D. C., for the years 1924 ff.

During the same year an impartial and reputable mining engineer appraised the value of the same property at 27 million dollars.

While the coal operators tended to benefit at the expense of the farmers in the apportionment of rural taxes, they also benefited at the expense of the townspeople in the division of the total tax load of the three counties. County-wide expenditures—for maintaining the county offices, county roads, poor farms, etc.—were from the start borne more heavily by town property than by coal property.[12] No matter how fast coal-property valuations might increase during the coal boom, they were always accompanied by greater increases in the valuation of town lots (appendix table 20).

In terms of actual tax collections, the disproportionate division of the tax burden between coal towns and coal operators was far greater. It naturally fell to the towns to maintain their own strictly local services, such as the police force and the fire department. But the burden of providing revenues for the schools also fell principally upon the towns. The mines, located in almost every instance beyond the city limits of the towns, paid taxes in rural school districts where few people lived, while thousands of the miners' children went to school in the towns, where the mine operators contributed nothing. Even the high schools, whose district boundaries frequently included an entire township, were often financed largely by the coal towns because the miners' homes were not located in the same townships as the mines. The most important source of tax revenue in the three counties thus came to be coal-town real property. The local governments rested on the same foundation as the banks and the building and loan associations.

The Rise of Tax Income

Until the time of the World War taxation in Franklin, Saline, and Williamson Counties presented no special problems. The services of the local government were restricted to paying the county judges, juries, and sheriffs, patching up the roads now and then, and maintaining a somewhat primitive school system. The coal industry had grown up in the midst of a backward agricultural community, and as far as the function of local government was concerned, the rural shell was not cracked until the industry reached maturity. Not until the beginning of wartime activity in the coal industry did the community undertake to do the work it had long neglected.

One pressing job was to build roads. As late as 1917 a drayman starting from Herrin in the early morning to deliver a load of

---

[12] Railroad property valuation also increased progressively, but it played a small part in the total property valuation, and is therefore not included above. Personal property is also omitted from this discussion because its assessment appears to have been distributed much like real property.

merchandise in Marion, 10 miles away, would not return home until dark. The scope of the independent towns was particularly restricted by inadequate roads. Miners depended on railroad transportation to get to their work in out-of-the-way mines, and where railroad connections were poor, the independent towns lost population and trade. From Benton, for example, it was possible to ride 7 miles by train to work in the Buckner mine; but there was no transportation to Rend City, which was only 6 miles away. Rend City, accordingly, became a company town, with consequent inconvenience to the miners and losses to the businessmen of Benton.

The school system was also clearly inadequate for the needs of the community. In 1912, when the total population of the 3 counties was about 110,000 persons, the expenditure for public high schools was only $64,000, scarcely enough to maintain even a semblance of a high-school system. Elementary schools were similarly hampered by an amazing expenditure per student of $10 per year.[13] Many of the school buildings were so old and unsanitary that they had been condemned wholesale by the State. For many years the schools had not kept pace with the growth and added wealth of the community, and one of the first jobs needed at the time of the World War was to expand and overhaul the education system.

In 1919 the State of Illinois changed the assessment rate of all taxable property from one-third to one-half of full-and-true value. The three counties took advantage of the broadened base, and not only readjusted valuations according to the new State regulation, but reconsidered assessments generally and raised them still further. In this way the tax base was increased in 1 year from about 22 million dollars to over 40 million dollars. At the same time the total levy of the three counties jumped from 1½ million dollars to almost 2¼ million (fig. 3–D). The long-awaited local improvements could get under way at last.

In the early 1920's the community thus began to assume some of the more important responsibilities it had neglected. The coal towns set about to provide themselves with sidewalks, gravel streets, sewage disposal, and city water. The school system was expanded. The problem of caring for widows and for the blind began to enter— however dimly—into the consciousness of the county officials. The local government officials recognized that increased population had brought new needs, and they made provision for new expenditures for policing, fire protection, and all the regular services of the towns and counties—including the cloud no bigger than a man's hand, pauper relief.

---

[13] The cost per pupil in schools throughout the country during the same period was $36. *Report of the Commissioner of Education for the Year Ended June 30, 1913.* Vol. II, U. S. Bureau of Education, Washington, D. C., 1914, p. 34.

Chapter II

A DEPRESSED AREA

JOBS IN THE southern Illinois coal industry were still plentiful in 1926. Franklin, Saline, and Williamson coal production for the year set a new postwar mark and, indeed, almost equaled the wartime record itself. Southern Illinois coal went upon the world market for the first time in 1926, when European buyers ordered several trainloads of Franklin County coal for export through New Orleans. The world's record for coal tonnage hoisted in an 8-hour shift at a single mine—held for years by one or another southern Illinois operator—was broken many times during the year as the New Orient in Franklin County proceeded every month or so to surpass its own previous record. The working miners enjoyed a satisfying degree of economic independence. If a miner disliked his boss, or if he objected to lax safety practices, or if he found his earnings falling because of poor coal, he could always quit his job, knowing that in a week or so he could find another one. Youth, too, had an agreeable choice to make in 1926: They could, if they wished, take advantage of the excellent new high schools recently built throughout the coal field; or they could go to work at the mines as soon as they were grown.[1]

The Franklin, Saline, and Williamson mine pay roll in 1926 amounted to about 40 million dollars, enough to provide a comfortable livelihood for the entire working population and enough to initiate a boom in the trade and service industries. Miners were averaging between $50 and $60 for each 2-weeks' work in 1926, and sometimes "a pay" would run as high as $100. The automobile dealers, the

[1] "As quickly as boys became of any size, their fathers took them to the mine. Boys could not see the necessity for going to school when the almighty dollar could be earned so easily." Carstens, Arthur and White, Ina, *A Semi-Stranded Area*, unpublished ms., Federal Emergency Relief Administration, Washington, D. C., 1935, p. 18.

grocers, the clothing merchants, the furniture and music stores all flourished, and the newspapers carried advertisements for grand pianos, Earl Carroll's Vanities, and men's $10 shoes as well as for necessities. When someone discovered a destitute family living on a garbage dump near Sesser, the entire community was shocked. Bank deposits in the three counties increased 3 million dollars in 1926, bringing the aggregate to 32 million dollars and breaking still another prosperity record. "The thing for our people to do," said a local newspaper that year, "is to settle down to a life of enjoyment and contentment."

But there was little time left for either enjoyment or contentment, for the collapse came quickly. Within less than a decade the whole structure of prosperity lay in utter ruin. Where great noisy tipples had stood, one found a few years later only weed-covered railroad sidings, crumbling mine buildings, and scrub oaks growing in the silent mine yards. Sesser once had three mines and Benton had four; all were abandoned. Johnston City had eight mines, and they were all abandoned too. Out of the 16 mines which could once be seen from the Herrin city hall, 15 were gone forever. Throughout the 3 counties, 109 mines were abandoned from 1923 through 1938, leaving the countryside dotted with industrial tombstones—burnt-out slack piles, rotting tipples, here and there a smokestack standing alone in the middle of a pasture—to mark the graveyard of almost 20,000 jobs. (See appendix table 1.)

Of course not all the mines had been abandoned; most of the largest mines, indeed, were still operating. But they too had undergone great changes. The old atomistic system of coal recovery, based upon pairs of independent, versatile hand loaders, had almost disappeared from Franklin, Saline, and Williamson Counties. The center of underground activity was now the great, new, automatic coal loaders, which could put as much coal into pit cars within a minute as hand loaders could load in an hour. Men were now organized into gangs; their jobs were simplified and specialized; the tempo of their work was heightened. At Herrin and Carrier Mills, operators had reorganized the haulage system too; the standard system of hoisting coal in cages running in a vertical shaft was replaced by a simple endless belt, fed underground by rubber-tired trucks. All in all, mine efficiency had nearly doubled.

The coal towns had been transformed. Whole crowded sections of the larger coal towns had fallen into decay. The paint had worn off the houses, windows long broken were patched with cardboard and adhesive tape, foundations had rotted away, leaving the roofs sagging and the walls askew. Other sections of town, where the miners' homes had been repossessed and razed for secondhand lumber, had vanished altogether. Block after block of vacant store space lined the business streets, testifying to the ruin of scores of businessmen. In some of the towns one found families living in tents, in shanties built on the garbage dumps, in chicken houses. A half dozen once active mine villages had degenerated into dilapidated, crowded, poverty-ridden rural slums.

In a few short years the coal towns had seen many strange things happen. Out of every four coal diggers who had once worked in the mines, only one—who counted himself exceedingly lucky—still held his job; and even so his yearly income had shrunk from $1,350 to $700. Sometimes singly, sometimes in batches, a total of 34 coal-town banks had collapsed, and some 7 million dollars in savings had been swept away. The high schools had suddenly filled to overflowing; but the teachers went unpaid, and members of the graduating classes regularly took their places in the ranks of the unemployed. The coal towns had seen families reduced to living on a dole as low as 78 cents a week, had seen outside charities set up soup kitchens for their undernourished children, and had seen thousands of their people at hunger's door.

What had happened? To begin with, the community had lost half its coal market, three-fourths of its coal-mine jobs, and four-fifths of its mine pay rolls, the community's basic income. No new industries whatever appeared to fill these gaps in the coal towns' economy. And meanwhile, the size of the population in the three counties suffered only an insignificant decline. In brief, the community no longer offered support for a large section of its population.

UNEMPLOYMENT AND UNDEREMPLOYMENT

Just how serious the economic plight of the southern Illinois coal field had become may be judged, first of all, on the basis of the extent of unemployment among its workers and families. Statistics on unemployment are provided in a special survey of unemployment conducted in seven southern Illinois coal towns between December 1938 and March 1939.[2]

The Labor Force

At the time of the special census roughly two-fifths of the entire population of the coal towns were workers: that is, they came within

[2] The census determined the employment status of workers as of a "census week" just prior to enumeration. The census week was changed from town to town as the enumeration progressed, but was never changed within a town. Enumeration began in Bush on December 19, 1938, with reference to the census week December 11–17, 1938. The latest census week used was March 12–18, 1939, applied in Herrin.

Throughout chapters II and III, all mention of employment, unemployment, and labor-market status refers to the workers' activities during the census week.

one of three categories—employed persons, unemployed persons actively seeking work, or persons normally employed but temporarily neither working nor seeking work (appendix table 10). Compared with the labor force in four American cities,[3] this proportion appears to have been somewhat small. Among males the difference was not great, though the seven coal towns did have a smaller proportion of males in the labor force. The difference was principally the result of a much smaller proportion of female workers in southern Illinois, where only 18 percent of all females were workers, as compared with 24 to 36 percent in the four cities. The fact that coal mining offers no job opportunities for women obviously accounts for this difference. The important point is that numerous persons who might have sought work under other circumstances were not seeking work in southern Illinois. Such persons are not, of course, counted among the community's workers, and hence are likewise excluded in the count of the unemployed.

The Unemployed

The census of unemployment in the seven coal towns was timed to coincide with the peak of the year's mining activity,[4] and it accordingly shows employment in the best possible light. The census caught Eldorado, for example, just after one mine had resumed work after a period of bankruptcy and reorganization, and just before a second mine shut down for the springtime slump. At Herrin the enumeration found another mine crew briefly enjoying the only stretch of employment it had had since 1937. Many other workers reporting private employment during the census period had only

[3] The same survey of unemployment was also conducted in Birmingham, Ala.; New Bedford, Mass.; Toledo, Ohio; and San Francisco, Calif., at about the same time as the southern Illinois census. In the seven coal towns 41 percent of the population were workers; in Birmingham, 47 percent; in New Bedford, 51 percent; in Toledo, 45 percent; in San Francisco, 52 percent. For data on Birmingham, Toledo, and San Francisco see Webb, John N. and Bevis, Joseph C., *Facts About Unemployment*, WPA Social Problem Series Number 4, Division of Research, Work Projects Administration, Federal Works Agency, Washington, D. C., 1940. The data on New Bedford are derived from *The Decline of a Cotton Textile City: A Study of New Bedford*, a manuscript in preparation by Seymour L. Wolfbein, Division of Research, Work Projects Administration.

[4] An index of seasonal variation in coal tonnage in Franklin, Saline, and Williamson Counties for the period 1922–1937 shows that the peak of activity occurs between October and March, and the low point between April and August. Peak activity is regularly more than double the activity at the slack period. This remarkably wide seasonal fluctuation results in part from the timing of union stoppages, which ordinarily begin on April first of an "agreement year," i. e., a year in which a new union contract must be negotiated. But in other years, the seasonal fluctuation is still very wide. Southern Illinois, unlike the Appalachian fields, gets little business from the summertime Great Lakes coal traffic.

recently resumed work or were soon to be laid off to face months of summertime unemployment. The mine work week was also longer than average during the census period, so that underemployment was at its minimum, too, for the year.

But even under peak-season activity, the community's workers suffered a staggering loss through unemployment (fig. 5).

Fig 5 - UNEMPLOYMENT AND UNDEREMPLOYMENT IN 7 SOUTHERN ILLINOIS COAL TOWNS AND IN BIRMINGHAM, NEW BEDFORD, TOLEDO, AND SAN FRANCISCO

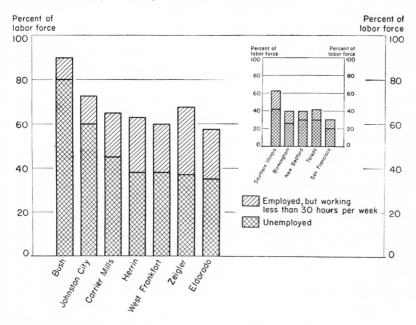

Source: Appendix table 10.   WPA 3639

A good, simple rule of thumb for evaluating the gravity of unemployment might be about as follows: When 10 percent of a community's labor force is unable to find a job, the community has begun to suffer appreciably. When unemployment climbs to 20 percent, a depression of serious consequences exists. And when unemployment reaches 30 percent—a figure rarely reached by most American communities and still more rarely maintained over any period of time—the community must be judged to be in extremely desperate circumstances.

According to this scale, the predicament of southern Illinois will be clear; throughout the seven towns 41 percent of all available workers had no jobs at the time of the census. In Johnston City, the hardest hit of the larger coal towns, unemployment had climbed to 60 percent; and in the little mine village of Bush, unemployment claimed four out of every five workers. In Zeigler and West Frankfort, two of the most active coal towns in Illinois, more than one-third of the workers were without jobs. Eldorado, which had (at the time) suffered far less than most of its neighbors from either mine mechanization or abandonment, was the most favored of the seven towns. Yet even there, more than one-third of all the available workers were found to be unemployed.[5] (See appendix table 14.)

Underemployment

Tradition provides that southern Illinois mines shall work with the entire mine crew or else not work at all. If there are orders for coal, every man works; but if there are none, nobody works. Slack business at the operating mines accordingly means fewer days worked rather than fewer men working, underemployment rather than unemployment. During the past few years 1 or 2 workdays a week have been the standard summertime schedule in southern Illinois, and even in the winter most of the mines run only 3 or 4 days unless the weather is severely cold. A second scheme for spreading work also reduces the length of the work week. According to agreement between the operators and the union, men displaced by machinery at a given mine have the right to "divided time" at the remaining jobs, and the reduced work is rotated so that all the men on divided time will work less in order that no one may lose his job altogether.

The practice of spreading work in the seven towns has doubtless helped to prevent unemployment from becoming even greater than it is. Yet underemployment can be nearly as disastrous to a worker's welfare as complete lack of work. A worker who is allowed only 1 or 2 days of employment a week cannot meet his normal living expenses, and he is sometimes considered ineligible for public assistance [6] as long as he holds a job bringing in any income at all. The extent of underemployment is another important index to the plight of the southern Illinois coal towns (fig. 5).

---

[5] By comparison, the survey of Birmingham showed 26 percent unemployed; New Bedford, 30 percent; Toledo, 30 percent; and San Francisco, 20 percent. The actual difference between southern Illinois and the four cities was probably even greater, for the wintertime survey would have found the four cities at their worst and the coal field at its best.

[6] Shortly after the survey was completed, Illinois workers became eligible to receive compensation for either total or part-time unemployment. Coal miners are now permitted to draw compensation for underemployment, but only for a part of each year. Miners underemployed at the peak season would get little help from the compensation system, since most of their benefits would be used up in the summertime slump.

In Bush and Johnston City, where few were working at all during the special census, obviously there could be little underemployment either; and the full effect of division of work is best seen in the more active towns—Eldorado, West Frankfort, and Zeigler—where underemployment had become little less widespread than unemployment itself. Throughout the seven towns a shortened work week added substantially to the general distress of the workers. Not only were two available workers out of every five without jobs altogether, but one out of five was working less than 30 hours per week.[7]

DISADVANTAGED WORKERS

The shadow of the general industrial decline in southern Illinois falls in one way or another upon most of the workers in the coal towns. No age group and no class of worker has escaped considerable damage from the disrupted labor market. Some sections of the working population, however, have borne more than the average burden of unemployment, and have been disadvantaged in relation to other sections of the depressed community.

Throughout American industry young and old workers bear the heaviest brunt of unemployment, and the same general tendency governs the depressed labor market in the southern Illinois coal field. The tendency operates, however, with several qualifications and exceptions which grow out of the special rules for employment at the coal mines. Instead of being left to "natural forces," the labor market for miners is controlled within limits by the terms of the union contract.

Employment Policy in the Mines

Although the union contract reserves to the coal operator "the right to hire and fire," the right is substantially abridged in actual practice. An operator may after due warning discharge a miner for violation of safety rules, for unwarranted absence from work, for gross inefficiency and irresponsibility, for "vile and abusive language," or for physical incapacity to perform his duties. Short of these reasons, the union

---

[7] In Birmingham 10 percent of the available workers were employed less than 30 hours a week; in New Bedford, 7 percent; in Toledo, 8 percent; and in San Francisco, 11 percent.

Incidentally, the prevalence of underemployment in southern Illinois does not mean that excessively long working hours were eliminated. Where trade and service workers were organized, it is true, the work week tended to be short. But in the unorganized industries, a 70-hour work week was by no means uncommon. One family was discovered in which the father, a coal miner, had been working 7 hours a week in the mines, while his son worked 72 hours a week in a gasoline station.

In the 7 coal towns, 11 percent of all employed workers worked 60 hours or more, as against 9 percent in New Bedford, 7 percent in San Francisco, 10 percent in Toledo, and 14 percent in Birmingham.

protects the miner in his job.   The practice of replacing older workers with more active youngsters is not permitted, for example.   Nor can the operator indulge in periodic bolt-from-the-blue dismissals "to keep up morale," nor discharge surplus workers after the installation of coal-loading machines, nor pare down the mine crew for a period of slack operation.   These restrictions on firing of course restrict hiring as well, and virtually eliminate labor turnover at the operating mines.

A second important tradition fixes the miners' job rights to a particular shaft, whose fortunes become their own.   As long as a shaft continues to hoist coal, the entire mine crew is reasonably certain of some kind of a job (though by no means certain of a living wage the year round, particularly when divided time is widespread).   When a shaft reopens after a period of suspension, all available members of the original mine crew must be rehired, for suspension does not cancel a miner's job rights.   But if a shaft is abandoned, the job rights of its entire crew automatically disappear; and its miners are cast adrift to take their own chances of finding other jobs.   The selection of those who shall be thrown out of work is thus governed more by the fate of each individual mine than by the characteristics of the miners themselves.[8]

From time to time a few new jobs for coal miners are created, either by the opening of new mines or the extension of the underground workings at operating mines.   The operators may fill these jobs with whomever they please, and as a result hirings—unlike dismissals—are highly selective.[9]   Neither older displaced miners nor inexperienced youth have much chance at the new jobs.   Most of them go to a special group of workers, usually young and active, and usually chosen from the abandoned mines of the company which is hiring.   New jobs

[8] There has been one significant departure from this tradition.   In 1932 the local unions at most of the larger Franklin County mines split.   Several thousand miners withdrew from the United Mine Workers of America, established a new union, the Progressive Miners of America, and struck against a new agreement. The strike failed and the miners lost their jobs.   It happened that at the time most of the struck mines were already mechanized, and their crews were heavily weighted with displaced hand loaders getting on in years and working on divided time.   The dismissal of the strikers enabled the operators both to abolish the surplus jobs and to remove the older hand loaders from the mine rolls.   It also enabled them to rebuild the mine crews according to such standards as they chose. The new employees at the struck mines automatically acquired the same job rights that govern every union mine, and the labor market was frozen again.

[9] Job rights are not company-wide.   If an operator abandons one mine and opens another at the same time, he may choose whom he pleases from the crew at the abandoned mine, and reject whom he pleases, in building a crew for the new mine.   In this process the older workers are eliminated.

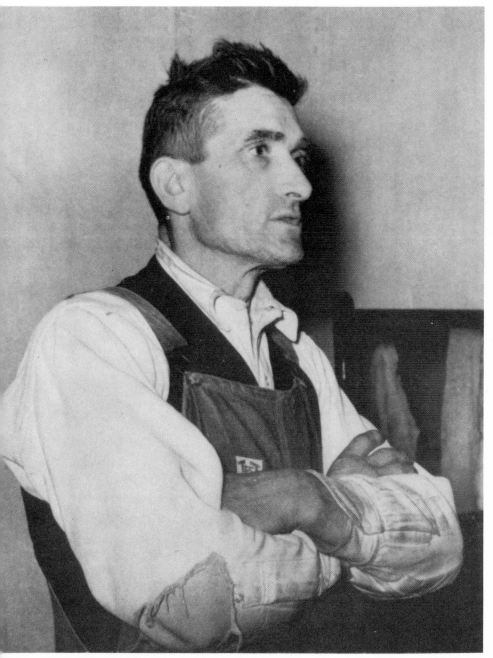

"When I think about the future I get the blues so bad I can't stand it."

Unemployed Southern Illinois Miner.

have been so rare in recent years, however, that even the preferred workers have benefited from them but little.

All these policies add up essentially to this: Youth coming of working age are virtually barred from the mines, for all the available jobs are taken. Able-bodied older workers who have put in a lifetime of service to the mines are reasonably certain of work unless their mines are abandoned; but if they ever do lose their jobs, they stand practically no chance to work underground again. The middle group of active experienced miners is likewise protected except against mine abandonment; and when they lose their jobs, they hold the best odds—such as they are—to return to work if new jobs are created.

Hiring policies in the coal towns' retail and service industries offset these tendencies in part. A few of the older workers displaced from the mines have been able to pick up unskilled jobs here and there, and a few others have opened up little stores, beer parlors, hamburger stands, and the like in the coal towns. Jobs in the coal-town stores, garages, filling stations, utilities, and offices are open to anyone who can qualify for them; youth are not only acceptable but usually favored as applicants. But the service industries are little less depressed than the mining industry itself; job turnover is small, and few jobs are available. Whatever job opportunities they offer do not neutralize the basic employment patterns determined by policy at the mines.

Unemployment Among Coal Miners

The shrinkage in the number of coal miners employed in southern Illinois has been brought about in two different ways. First of all, there have of course been thousands of dismissals, resulting either from the abandonment of mines or from the unsuccessful Progressive Miners of America strike in 1932. But other miners have left the industry for a variety of reasons not connected with dismissals. Death and permanent disability resulting from mine accidents alone retire about 1 percent of the total mine crew in Franklin, Saline, and Williamson Counties each year; and the expected mortality from natural causes runs to another 1 or 2 percent. In the course of a year a number of additional miners leave the labor market because of illness, age, and removal to another job or another community. The sum of all these causes reduced the total labor force at the mines by perhaps as much as one-fourth between 1929 and the time of the special survey of the seven towns.

With the normal flow of inexperienced new workers into the coal industry checked, the loss of workers through death and withdrawal from the labor market produced a substantial net decrease in the size of the labor force attached to coal mining,[10] and further, a decrease in the *incidence* of unemployment among miners who continued to be available for work. In 1939, paradoxically, unemployment among coal miners—that is, among those who reported coal mining as their usual occupation—was less severe than among the coal-town working population as a whole (appendix table 11). Unemployment claimed every third coal miner, but two-fifths of the transportation workers, two-fifths of the manufacturing and mechanical workers, and four-fifths of those without a usual occupation. Only the trade and professional workers fared better than the miners.

Outsiders sometimes think of the unemployment problem in the coal towns as being almost exclusively one involving coal miners. Actually, as figure 6 shows, coal miners constituted only about one-fourth of the unemployed. Considerably more numerous among the

Fig. 6 - INDUSTRY OF USUAL OCCUPATION OF UNEMPLOYED
WORKERS, BY SEX, 7 SOUTHERN ILLINOIS
COAL TOWNS

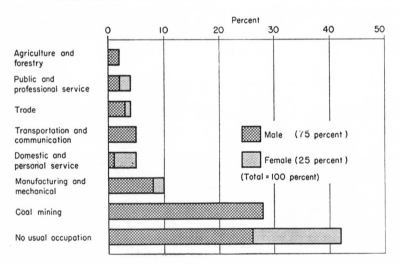

Source: Appendix table 12.   WPA 3640

[10] The decrease in the size of the labor force when neither replacements nor dismissals are made to any extent is apparent in the process by which divided time "works itself out" and disappears over a period of a few years. Zeigler mine No. 2, for example, installed new machines in 1936 and cut the number of available jobs from 900 to 650. The "surplus" workers, numbering 250, then began to share work with the "necessary" workers. In 1936 the surplus shrank to 200 miners, in 1937 to 100 miners, in 1938 to 70 miners, and in 1939 the surplus— together with divided time—disappeared altogether.

unemployed were the workers without a usual occupation, a group composed mainly of youth who had been blocked from normal entry into the labor market.[11] Experienced workers from all industries other than coal mining also formed a larger proportion of the unemployed than the displaced coal miners.

Age and Unemployment

Like most American communities, the coal towns showed least unemployment in the middle age groups, a higher incidence among the older workers, and the highest incidence of all among youth (fig. 7).[12] But because of the peculiar labor-market tendencies in southern Illinois, the variation among the three age groups was not exactly what might be expected in the operation of a more "normal" labor market. While older workers were disadvantaged by comparison with the middle group, their relative disadvantage was not as great as

Fig. 7 - PERCENT OF LABOR FORCE UNEMPLOYED IN 7 SOUTHERN ILLINOIS COAL TOWNS AND IN BIRMINGHAM, NEW BEDFORD, TOLEDO, AND SAN FRANCISCO, BY AGE GROUP

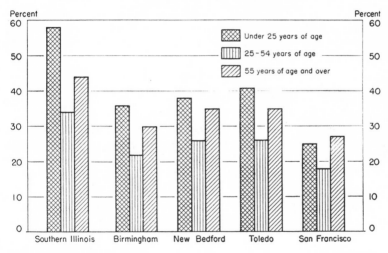

Source: Appendix table 14.   WPA 3641

[11] See p. 41.

[12] The percents of workers unemployed in each age group in four American cities at about the time of the southern Illinois survey were as follows:

City	Under 25 years	25–54 years	55 years and over
Birmingham, Ala.	36	22	30
New Bedford, Mass.	38	26	35
San Francisco, Calif.	25	18	27
Toledo, Ohio	41	26	35

commonly prevails. On the other hand, the relative disadvantage of youth was intensified beyond normal expectation.[13]

Youth in the Depressed Area

Even beyond the general unemployment problem in southern Illinois, coal-field youth are a special problem in themselves, a disadvantaged group within a depressed area. Since they have little opportunity to enter the coal mines, they make up an insignificant part of the mine force. Out of 3,789 coal miners at work in the 7 coal towns, only 227 were under 25 years of age (appendix table 13). Cut off in such fashion from the basic employment of the community, coal-field youth suffer an exceedingly high proportion of unemployment.

Among all the workers under 25 years of age in the 7 towns, nearly three-fifths (58 percent) were unemployed at the time of the census (appendix table 14 and fig. 7). In the most active of the 7 towns, nearly half the youth were jobless; in the most severely depressed town the proportion rose to almost 9 out of every 10. In contrast, the incidence of unemployment among youth in four American cities ranged from a low of 25 percent in one city to a high of 48 percent in another. Coal-field youth clearly bear an extra burden of unemployment, both by comparison with the other workers within the depressed area itself and also by comparison with the youth in other areas.

FAMILY UNEMPLOYMENT

Unemployment among a community's workers does not tell exactly the predicamênt of a community's families. The loss of a job in a family with more than one worker employed is not quite as serious as the loss of a job in a family with a single breadwinner. An unemployed worker does not necessarily mean a family out of work. On the other hand, some families in every community have no workers

---

[13] The varying disadvantage of young and old workers, computed as the ratio of the percent of unemployment among the young and old workers in each city to the percent of unemployment among the middle age group in each city, appears as follows:

City	Under 25 years	25–54 years	55 years and over
7 southern Illinois coal towns_____	170	100	126
Birmingham, Ala_____	164	100	136
New Bedford, Mass_____	146	100	135
San Francisco, Calif_____	139	100	150
Toledo, Ohio_____	158	100	135

The incidence of unemployment among the older coal-field workers was only 26 percent higher than among the middle group, but in four American cities it ran from 35 percent to as high as 50 percent above the incidence in the middle group.

The incidence of unemployment among coal-field youth was 70 percent above that of the coal-town middle group; in three American cities, however, the differential against youth was 39 percent to 64 percent.

at all, and would be without means of support even though all the community's gainful workers were employed. The family is an economic as well as a social unit. Its economic resources, as far as employment is concerned, depend upon the number of workers it contains. The more workers a family has, the better its chances of having at least one member employed. In the seven coal towns the distribution of families by the number of available workers per family was not out of the ordinary. About one-tenth of the families had no workers at all, more than two-thirds had only one worker, and one-fourth had two workers or more; apparently, these proportions are about what would be expected in most nonagricultural American communities.[14] With no more than a normal distribution of workers in coal-town families, the heavy incidence of worker unemployment naturally took a heavy toll in family unemployment (fig. 8).[15]

Fig. 8 – UNEMPLOYMENT AMONG FAMILIES IN 7 SOUTHERN ILLINOIS COAL TOWNS AND IN BIRMINGHAM, NEW BEDFORD, TOLEDO, AND SAN FRANCISCO

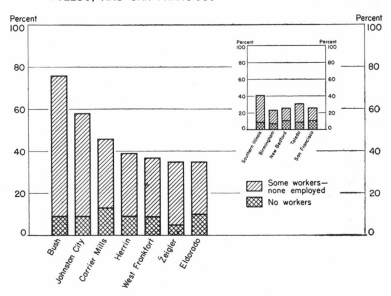

Source: Appendix table 15.　　　　　　　　　WPA 3642

[14] Approximately the same proportions were found in Toledo and San Francisco. In Birmingham and New Bedford, however, the number of families with two workers or more was considerably higher, because of the employment of females in the textile and domestic-service industries.

[15] Families in the seven coal towns, like those elsewhere in the country, suffered less from unemployment when they contained more than one worker. Among families with one available worker, 40 percent had no employment. But among families with two available workers or more, 25 percent had no member employed.

Throughout the seven towns two families out of every five held no job in private industry, either because they contained no worker or because their worker members were unable to find jobs. Even in the most active coal towns, every third family still held no job in private industry. In Johnston City the families with no member employed made up nearly two out of every three families, and in the village of Bush they made up nearly four out of every five. (See appendix table 15.) In contrast, four American cities reported only about one-fourth of their families without jobs.[16]

Some of these, the families without workers, were not necessarily a depression problem, of course. Families in which the head is a woman with dependent children, or in which the head is incapacitated by injury or disease, or is aged and too feeble to work would presumably exist in about the same proportion in good times as well as bad, though their problem naturally becomes more acute when the depression cuts off whatever support they may have had in better times from relatives. But the great majority of the families without jobs were not of this type; more than three-fourths of them contained one or more available workers, none of whom was able to find a job. Moreover, the families which did hold private jobs were not necessarily as fortunate as this classification implies. Some of them had earnings so low that they still required public assistance (appendix table 15). Others contained jobless workers who doubtless felt the distress of unemployment no less acutely than if the entire family had been out of work.

Whether the state of the southern Illinois labor market is measured in terms of families or workers, the conclusion is the same. Between one-third and two-thirds of the people—depending on the circumstances of the individual towns—were "surplus" at the busiest season of 1939; and a considerable part of the remainder were none too secure, as the figures on underemployment reveal. The seven coal towns have undergone a depression so severe that today they take their place, not, as before, among the most prosperous American communities, but among the most prostrate. In the 1920's superlatives were applicable to the prosperity of the coal field. Today, superlatives are again applicable, but they are the old ones reversed.

---

[16] In Birmingham 7 percent of the families had no workers and an additional 16 percent had workers without jobs; in New Bedford and San Francisco the proportions were, respectively, 11 percent and 15 percent; and in Toledo, 9 percent and 22 percent. Note that the proportion of families without workers in the four cities was roughly the same as in the seven coal towns.

Chapter III

LONG UNEMPLOYMENT IN THE DEPRESSED AREA

THE WORKERS employed in most "normal" American industrial communities are constantly shifting and changing. A part of the labor force will always be losing its jobs; another part will be returning to work; a third part will be entering industry for the first time. The constant labor turnover means that at any given time a considerable part of the unemployed will have been out of work only a short time, and will have a reasonable chance of shortly returning to work. This situation reflects itself in a relatively short duration of unemployment among a cross section of all the jobless workers.

In the southern Illinois coal field there was also once a time when an unemployed worker could find another job without much trouble. But as more and more mines shut down, as more and more stores, garages, banks, and other local businesses disappeared, jobs became increasingly difficult to find. Men at work held to their jobs tenaciously; mobility from job to job was stopped; the labor market was frozen. At last there came a time when a man who had lost his job was very unlikely to find another. His qualifications, his experience, his union, even his friends might do him little service, for job opportunities had all but vanished. Such was the prevailing condition of the coal-town labor market at the time of the special unemployment survey in 1939.

The constantly narrowing chance for reemployment in the coal field reflects itself in the long period of unemployment reported by the coal-town jobless workers. Long unemployment, in turn, implies a whole train of consequences for a people who were prosperous only a short time ago. It means drastically reduced income and dependence upon public aid. It means the sacrifice of the normal accumulations against want and old age, and the destruction of former living standards. It also means immeasurable anxiety, hopelessness, and despair.

37

DURATION OF UNEMPLOYMENT

The average duration of unemployment among all the unemployed workers in the seven coal towns is shown in appendix table 16 and figure 9.

Fig. 9 — AVERAGE*DURATION OF UNEMPLOYMENT SINCE LAST FULL-TIME JOB OF WORKERS IN 7 SOUTHERN ILLINOIS COAL TOWNS AND IN BIRMINGHAM, NEW BEDFORD, TOLEDO, AND SAN FRANCISCO

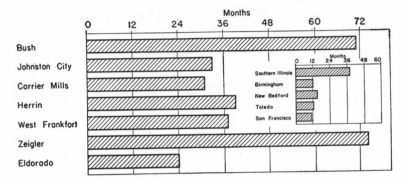

*Median.
Source: Appendix table 16.

WPA 3643

These figures, it must be remembered, do not indicate the time lost through unemployment during the past few years, but only the time elapsed since the last 2-weeks' job of at least 30 hours' work each week. Workers who had picked up occasional odd jobs would shorten the average duration and put the best face on the matter. Even so, the figures are almost incredible. The record of experienced [1] and able-bodied workers out of a job for an average of from 2 to 6 years is an extraordinary showing for a cross section of all the unemployed in an area. What unemployment of such duration means as a measure of the general economic collapse of the coal towns will be clear by comparison with four American cities, where the average duration of unemployment during the same period was roughly 1 year. Coal-town workers in southern Illinois had not only suffered half again as much unemployment as might have been expected in an "average" community during 1939, but their unemployment had lasted three times as long.

---

[1] Duration of unemployment could not, of course, be computed for the numerous new workers in the seven towns who had never had a full-time job in private industry. This group is discussed later; see pp. 40-43.

Displaced Miners

Although coal miners enjoy a measure of security as long as the mine employing them continues to work, those who have lost their jobs face a particularly difficult problem. Once a miner is out of the mines, his chances of returning are small, especially if he happens to be an older worker. Unemployed coal miners accordingly reported the highest average duration of unemployment of all the major industrial groups within the coal towns. Half of all the unemployed coal miners had been out of work for 68 months or more—over 5½ years. (See appendix table 17.)

Unemployed coal miners' time out of work increased with their age. Among those over 55 years, for example, the average duration of unemployment was 6½ years. Unemployed miners under 45 years, on the other hand, had been out of work about half as long. This difference reflects a somewhat more favorable labor market for the younger displaced miners. Avenues closed to older displaced miners are not altogether closed to the younger men. Some of them have been rehired in other mines, some have moved away, a few—probably very few—have shifted to other industries. In spite of these advantages, however, even the most favored among the unemployed miners had still been out of work for an average of more than 3½ years.

The displaced coal miners in southern Illinois are obviously a disadvantaged group of workers. Out of work for more than 5 years on the average, skilled workers in a declining industry, replaced by machines, lacking the resources and the qualifications to seek work in another labor market, likely in many cases, indeed, to spend the rest of their days outside of private industry, these workers suffer long unemployment at its worst.

The Rest of the Long Unemployed

If we arbitrarily set up 1 year of unemployment as a convenient dividing line between "short-term" and "long-term" unemployment, we may identify that part of the labor force which has suffered most through loss of work. In the 7 coal towns there were 3,117 such long-unemployed workers (appendix table 17). They constituted nearly one-fourth of all the experienced [2] workers in the coal towns and almost three-fourths of all the experienced unemployed workers. We may make a further distinction and identify the workers unemployed more than 3 years as the "very long" unemployed. There were 2,223 such workers in the coal towns. They made up about one-seventh of all workers and roughly half of all the unemployed. Who were these workers?

---

[2] The term "experienced" applies to workers who have had a full-time private job.

Coal miners made up by far the largest single group of these long and very long unemployed. The remainder were distributed among scores of other industries, with no significant concentration in any one industry. When combined, however, these other industries contributed one long-unemployed worker for each one contributed by the coal mines. The burden of unemployment in a one-industry community falls not alone on workers in the main industry.

Fig. 10 - INDUSTRY OF LAST FULL-TIME JOB OF WORKERS UNEMPLOYED MORE THAN I YEAR AND MORE THAN 3 YEARS IN 7 SOUTHERN ILLINOIS COAL TOWNS

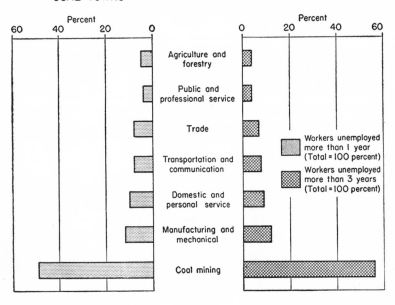

Source: Appendix table 17.   WPA 3644

Inexperienced Workers

Inexperienced jobless workers—if they exist in unduly large numbers—have the same significance as long-unemployed workers. The problem of the long unemployed is their difficulty in recovering a place they once held in industry. The gravity of their problem is implied in the lapse of time since they last worked. The problem of the inexperienced workers is their difficulty in finding their first jobs in industry. Since lapse of time is difficult to measure in this situation, the unemployment problem among new workers may be shown in terms of the number of inexperienced workers in the labor market.

Farm Security Administration (Rothstein).

"Times are sure bad for everybody. But the young ones—they got it worse."

A Young Southern Illinois Worker.

Youth

As we have seen, coal-town youth suffer an extremely high incidence of unemployment; nearly three workers out of every five under 25 years of age were jobless at the time of the special survey. This figure tells only a part of their predicament. Ordinarily, the economic problems of youth consist more in the kinds of jobs they get—the wages they receive, the hours they work, the insecurity of their jobs—than in their failure to get jobs of any sort. A recent study of urban youth in the labor market has shown that however many problems young workers faced, most of them have at least held a job at one time or another.[3] In the southern Illinois coal field, however, quite another situation prevails. A substantial part of the coal-town youth are not only unemployed, but have still to find their first job.

Nearly two-fifths of the new generation of workers in the coal towns have come to their best productive years without ever having held a full-time job in private industry. In the more severely stricken towns the proportion rose to half of all young workers; and even in the most active of the towns surveyed more than one-fourth of the youth had never been employed. Among all the coal-town youth who were jobless at the time of the special survey, nearly two-thirds had never held a full-time job at any time in the past. (See appendix table 18.)

In most American industrial communities the case for youth—bad as it is—has one relieving feature: unemployed youth are at least future workers. At any given time, it is true, a section of youth are in the position of awaiting their turn in industry. But in the course of time most of them will presumably be drawn into private jobs. Youth generally do not fall into the category of the long unemployed. In the southern Illinois coal field, however, even such qualified optimism is not possible. Looking at the problem of coal-town youth as one of waiting for work, one will conclude that for many the wait must be very long indeed. The general predicament of youth in the depressed area suggests an analogy with sections of youth in postwar England and Germany, the "lost generation" which has grown to middle age without every knowing the experience of a private job.

The Rest of the Inexperienced

Although most of the inexperienced coal-town workers were youth, a few were older workers. Among the workers under 25 years nearly two-fifths were inexperienced; among the workers over 25 years, only about 1 in each 20 was inexperienced (appendix table 18).

---

[3] Payne, Stanley L., *Disadvantaged Youth on the Labor Market*, Series I, No. 25, Division of Research, Work Projects Administration, Federal Works Agency, Washington, D. C., 1940.

Fig. II— WORKERS UNDER 25 YEARS OF AGE WHO NEVER HELD A
FULL-TIME JOB, 7 SOUTHERN ILLINOIS COAL TOWNS,
BIRMINGHAM, NEW BEDFORD, TOLEDO,
AND SAN FRANCISCO

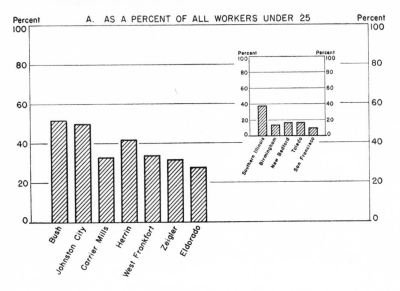

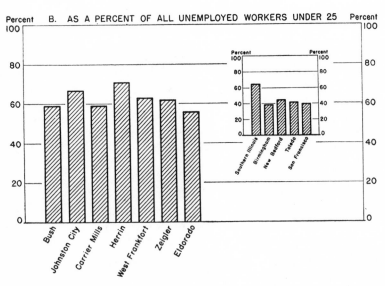

Source: Appendix table 18.

WPA 3645

Many of these, naturally enough, were in the age group 25–29 years, and represent persons who have been unsuccessfully seeking work over a period of some years. Others, of course, represent new entrants to the labor market, and in particular, inexperienced women forced by circumstances to seek work for the first time at near middle age or beyond. It may be noted, however, that these older inexperienced workers formed a smaller part of the total coal-town labor force than would be expected in most communities.

Work-Program Employment

Obviously, a workingman cannot maintain himself and his family for 1 or 2 years—let alone 5 years—without work. The first shock of long unemployment may perhaps be taken up by accumulated reserves, by savings accounts, life-insurance policies, and home ownership. In southern Illinois, however, the early years of the depression wiped out a great part of the community's reserves through bank failure, lapsed payments, and the collapse of real-estate values. Once these resources had vanished, and once the debts with landlord, grocer, and butcher had reached the limits allowed, some form of public assistance became essential.

At the time of the special survey employment on the work programs [4] was the principal form of assistance available to the able-bodied unemployed; and the proportion of the unemployed holding work-program jobs was, again, unusually high (fig. 12).

Ordinarily, the proportion of unemployed workers on the work programs remains low. For the country as a whole an estimated 20 to 25 percent of the unemployed had work-program jobs at about the time of the coal-town survey. Depressed areas are an exception to this general rule. The rate of labor turnover is low, the long unemployed form an unduly large group of workers, and the normal activity of seeking a job has little chance of success. In southern Illinois the work programs have necessarily become indispensable props to the economic life of the community.

The work programs for youth were of special importance to the coal towns. Nearly half the unemployed coal-town youth, and well over one-quarter of all the youth in the labor market, held jobs on either the NYA, the CCC, or the WPA. In contrast, four American cities reported an average of about 20 percent of the unemployed youth, and 7 percent of the youth in the labor market, holding work-

---

[4] As used here this term includes the Works Progress Administration, the National Youth Administration, the Civilian Conservation Corps, and other emergency work programs of the Federal Government. Of these, the WPA is by far the largest.

program jobs.[5]   On the basis of a given number of unemployed youth, the coal towns thus had more than double the work-program employment of a cross section of urban youth.   And on the basis of a given number of youth in the labor market, the extent of work-program employment in the seven coal towns was four times greater.

Fig. 12 - PERCENT OF UNEMPLOYED WORKERS ON WORK PROGRAMS *
        IN 7 SOUTHERN ILLINOIS COAL TOWNS AND IN BIRMINGHAM,
        NEW BEDFORD, TOLEDO, AND SAN FRANCISCO

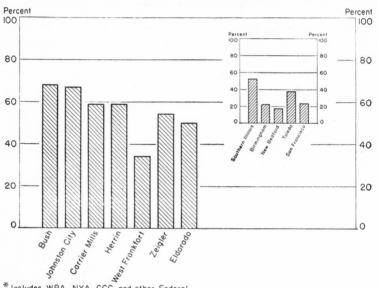

* Includes WPA, NYA, CCC, and other Federal
emergency programs.

Source: Appendix table 10.   WPA 3646

Long-Unemployed Families

Long unemployment is a family disaster.   A substantial number of coal-town families, it will be recalled, had none of their workers employed in private industry at the time of the southern Illinois unemployment survey.[6]   These families had frequently been without private employment for a period of some years.   Long-unemployed

---

[5] In the seven coal towns, 48 percent of the unemployed youth and 28 percent of all youthful workers were on the work programs.   In Birmingham the proportions were, respectively, 30 percent and 7 percent; in New Bedford, 20 percent and 6 percent; in Toledo, 18 percent and 10 percent; in San Francisco, 17 percent and 5 percent.   The ratio of WPA to NYA to CCC among youth varies considerably.   In the seven coal towns it was 2–2–1.   In Birmingham the ratio was 5–5–1; in New Bedford, 1–1–2; in San Francisco, 1–3–1; in Toledo, 5–3–1.

[6] See pp. 34–36.

families were common not only among the coal-town families with only a single worker, but among the multiworker families as well.

Among coal-town families whose worker members were unemployed, one group had had no job in private industry for more than a year at the time of the survey. Two-thirds of all the unemployed families fell within this group.[7] Another group of families contained only workers who had never held a full-time job in private industry. A great many of these families were of course young couples who had married before the head could find a job. Others were mature families in which the breadwinner's responsibility had fallen to a youth or to an older inexperienced female head. Every ninth unemployed family in the coal towns surveyed was such a family. All told, nearly four-fifths of the unemployed families contained only inexperienced or long-unemployed workers. (See appendix table 19.)

These are the families who have borne the heaviest burden of the coal field's decline. A few years ago they were as necessary in the community as any other coal-town families; today they are "surplus" population, and a great gap separates them from the normal economic life of the coal towns. Their common experience is less income, greater dependence on relief, and more of all the stark compulsion of poverty than prevail among their neighbors in the depressed area.

THE LIVING STANDARDS OF THE LONG UNEMPLOYED

The various indexes of economic disturbance, marshaled in this and the preceding chapter, show the southern Illinois coal field to be a critically depressed community. In human terms, what does this fact mean? What does it mean to say, for example, that two-fifths of the coal-town labor force is jobless, or that four out of every five unemployed families in the coal towns have had no work for a year or longer? As an approach to these questions, the principal findings of a special survey of buying patterns among 149 long-unemployed coal-town families conducted in the spring and summer of 1939 are presented.[8]

Income

The income of the long unemployed is derived almost entirely from various forms of public assistance. WPA employment alone accounted for 81 percent of all the families' income during an average month; direct relief, old-age assistance, CCC, and NYA together provided another 12 percent of all income. The small remainder—

---

[7] We leave out of account here the families which contained no workers at all.

[8] The survey included only families which contained one worker or more. Dependency growing out of the absence of workers in the family unit is not represented in the 149 families surveyed.

7 percent of all income—came from earnings on odd jobs picked up here and there in the coal towns, from gifts, and from the sale of various possessions.[9] The average income of the families from all these sources was $39.30 per month—$471.60 per year. The average size of family dependent upon this income was 3.5 persons.

Expenditure Patterns

An average monthly income of about $40—plus some supplementation by surplus commodities for large families—must thus provide all of a long-unemployed family's needs. The resulting problem in household finance is difficult indeed. Each family must try to stretch this income to satisfy the butcher, the baker, the grocer, the landlord, the dry-goods merchant, the moving-picture manager, the pastor, the utility company, and the doctor. When the money does not go around the alternatives are clear. The family may possibly run into debt, although the chances of finding a creditor are not good. Otherwise the family must simply do without and not only put up with discomfort but even get along without necessities.

The resulting predicament of the families is shown in the level of buying choices they must make. Early in the winter, for example, one housewife was faced with the urgent need for both a new heater and a winter coat, but she had money enough for only one. After long thought she decided that a heater was more needed, and she bought one on the installment plan. Three months later, however, she wished she had bought the coat because "it would have cost less and we wouldn't have to owe for it." In another family an unemployed miner's wife was ill, but had no doctor. "We doctor ourselves," she said; "every time you get the doctor it takes that much off what you have to eat." Another couple had 30 cents saved to celebrate their wedding anniversary. The problem then was how to spend it, whether to buy a dish or go to the movies. They decided at last to go to the movies and do without the dish. Another family chose to have the kitchen stove repaired in preference to replacing worn-out shoes, another traded food for pillow slips, and so on.

The sum of all these choices between competing needs creates a pattern imposed by the "must" items in subsistence living Each family spends its money in its own way, but as the following table indicates, there is less choice involved than one might think.

---

[9] Barter is not included as a part of income. Nevertheless, some of the barter transactions among the long unemployed take on considerable importance, not to say complexity. One family, for example, set out to buy a house which had been ruined by the Ohio River floods. This deal, involving $30, was achieved through these steps: (1) trading a hog to pay for part of the house, (2) mortgaging a cow to pay the rest, and (3) selling the cow to pay for new shingles and the electric light deposit.

Percent Distribution of Expenditures of Long-Unemployed Families in 3 Southern Illinois Coal Towns

Item	Total	Carrier Mills	Zeigler	West Frankfort
Total	100	100	100	100
Food	51	50	49	51
Clothing	9	7	16	8
Personal care	1	1	1	1
Housing	11	11	9	12
Household operation	6	5	7	6
Furniture, furnishings, and household equipment	5	6	4	4
Medical care	3	3	5	3
Transportation	6	5	4	6
Recreation	1	2	1	1
All other	7	10	4	8

Food

When incomes fall, the relative importance of food increases, not only because food is the most urgent of a family's needs, but also because habits of diet are powerful and tend to be maintained after other living habits have disintegrated. Ordinarily, even in families living on short income, the cost of food occupies no more than one-third of a family's total budget; and as income increases, the cost of food falls considerably below a third. Among the long-unemployed families in the coal towns, however, food purchases accounted for exactly half of all cash expenditures. Out of the $40 which the average family was able to spend each month, $20 went for food.

In spite of the important position of food expenditures in the budgets of the coal-town long unemployed, a generally satisfactory diet was by no means provided. According to the accepted standards for measuring adequacy of diets, 10 cents per person is considered to be the minimum cost per meal in a budget to be used over any long period of time; and between 7.5 and 8 cents is the absolute bottom for an "emergency" budget designed to tide a family over a short period of poor luck. But the average sum available to the long-unemployed families in southern Illinois was 6.3 cents a meal. Moreover, this allowance was not a temporary expedient, but had become more or less permanently established over a period lasting for many families as long as 7 or 8 years.

In the process of stretching their cost per meal further than it should have to go, the families have become accustomed to several serious deficiencies in their diets. Flour, corn meal, beans, potatoes, and bacon are necessarily the basic foods consumed. Fresh milk is almost excluded from the average menu, even when there are small children in the family, and canned milk is substituted. Oleomargarine takes the place of butter. Fresh vegetables are likewise absent throughout the winter and spring, and in the summertime as well unless a family has a garden of its own. Unsalted meat is usually foregone except for the biweekly pay-day celebration, the husband's lunch on WPA workdays, and an occasional supper of hamburger, wieners, shank bone, or some other cheap meat. Families wanting more fresh meat—the central European immigrants in particular—must trim their budgets elsewhere to make up the difference.

As the number of mouths to be fed increases, the burden of providing enough food of the right kind naturally becomes more difficult. In the very large families, however, the difficulty is partly relieved by surplus commodities. "If it weren't for surplus commodities," said one housewife, "we couldn't navigate at all."

Many families also raise a part of their own food. Though by no means universal, gardens, chickens, and even pigs and cows were common, and they doubtless helped to improve the quality of many a long-unemployed family's diet. They did not, however, solve the families' food problems—as outsiders so often suppose. Nor were they always a net financial gain; feed for cows and chickens, canning supplies, seeds, and the like were items of considerable importance in the family budgets.

Clothing

Very little of the long-unemployed families' income goes for clothing. Out of the average income of $40 a month, 9 percent, or about $3.60, was spent on clothes. Over the course of a full year, clothes would cost the average long-unemployed family about $43, which would be less than one-third the amount provided in synthetic "maintenance" budgets, and less than half the amount provided in minimum-standard "emergency" budgets.

As the wife of a long-unemployed miner commented, "You can promise your back, but you can't promise your stomach." The job of keeping a family clothed is accomplished through a variety of ingenious makeshifts in order that money which would otherwise be spent on clothing may be diverted to apply on more pressing needs. Flour sacks, sugar sacks, and feed sacks are made over for a wide variety of needs, ranging from underwear and sheeting to washrags and curtains. The life of every garment is stretched to the limit; clothes are always made over, patched, and handed down from person to person until "when they're finished, they're about gone." For necessary replacements many families depend on secondhand clothing, or on castoff clothes donated by more prosperous relatives. Surplus commodity clothing—much of it made in the WPA sewing rooms—helps the larger families. Often replacement is not possible from any source. Some families had no shoes for winter weather and some had none at all; some were forced to send their children to school in rotation; on washday it was not unusual for family members to be confined to the house until their clothes were dry.

"Ten years ago you wouldn't of knowed it was the same house."

The Home of an Unemployed Miner in Franklin County, Ill.

The families' clothes are usually 3 or 4 years old. Few have good dresses or suits; and a clean housedress or overalls—sarcastically called "blue serge"—serve for special occasions as well as everyday use. Inadequate clothing often results in changed social habits. Many families have not attended church since they wore out their last Sunday clothes, and visiting beyond the neighborhood is similarly handicapped. An unemployed miner complained, "See my pants, a patch here, a patch there, and I have to go to town like this. I have to buy for the kids first, they go to school. But I have to go among people too, once in a while."

Housing

Housing, like clothing, was subject to considerable skimping. The cash cost of housing in the budgets of the coal-town long unemployed absorbed 11 percent of the total cash outlay, and averaged about $50 per family over the period of a year. About half the families still held title to their houses and paid somewhat less than the average, while the families who rented paid somewhat more. In both situations, however, unpaid housing obligations tended to accumulate, either as delinquent taxes among owners or as past-due rent among the tenants.

Both owned and rented houses had often passed into the advanced stages of disrepair. Roofs leaked ("like all outdoors"); windowpanes were cracked and sometimes missing altogether; floors sagged and doors were pulled askew from the rotting of underpinning; the paint on most of the houses had long since worn away. "But if you'd come to my house 10 years ago," said a miner's wife, "you wouldn't of knowed it was the same house." In spite of all these hardships the houses were almost invariably kept clean and neat, and decorated with the best that had come to hand—with crocheted work, bright lithographed calendars, and religious mottoes.

City water, and often electricity as well, had been sacrificed. Out of all the long-unemployed families interviewed, 80 percent had no running water and 95 percent used outside toilets. Bathtubs had become an equally rare luxury. Every third family had had the electricity turned off and had reverted to kerosene lamps. Gas for cooking was available to most of the communities, but only 3 percent of the long-unemployed families could afford to use it. In spite of the intense summertime heat in southern Illinois, half the long-unemployed families used no ice.

Medical Care

Southern Illinois long-unemployed families bear their full share of illness. Deficient diets extended over any period of time will leave their mark; and the insecurity and worry of long unemployment can contribute to a variety of disorders. Moreover, when illness does come to the families of long-unemployed workers it is likely not to be properly treated. Many of their small disorders grow into chronic undiagnosed ailments simply because the families cannot afford proper medical care. All these difficulties produced a rather unusual record of disability among the long unemployed in the coal towns. During the year ending June 30, 1939, the members of the families interviewed were disabled for an average of 25 days each.[10]

The cash outlay for medical care absorbed about 5 percent of total cash expenditures of the long-unemployed families, and in a full year it cost an average of about $23 per family. This outlay, however, took care of only a small part of the total charges made against the families for medical care. Accumulated debts for past medical care amounted to an average of $34 per family at the end of the period covered. In most cases the families accepted this debt as a real obligation against their future income.

But there is a limit to credit for even such necessaries as medical care. Many of the services that the families needed they did without. Hospitalization, for example, was quite out of the question for long-unemployed families. One unemployed worker "nearly went crazy with the toothache all summer," but could not afford to get treatment. A schoolboy had to drop out of school for a whole year because the family could not buy glasses for him. In one family a diabetic had neither proper diet nor insulin. Many persons had not been able to buy false teeth after their own were extracted. And there were instances in almost every family of home treatment for illness which would ordinarily call for medical care.

Other Needs

Several other types of wants have a necessary claim on the long-unemployed families' income. Transportation, which in most families involves nothing more than rides from home to the WPA project and back, is a substantial and inescapable item. The cost of household operation is somewhat reduced by the cheap fuel available in all the coal towns—where "gopher-hole" coal sells for as little as $1.50 a ton; but even so, the cost of fuel and lights still absorbed 6 percent of the family income. The families had also cut their expendi-

---

[10] It should be borne in mind that the families studied were not "unemployable," but that each contained one available worker or more.

The National Health Survey discovered that during 1935 and 1936 the average annual disability per person in the population at large was 9.8 days, and that among relief recipients generally the average was 16.3 days. See Division of Public Health Methods, *The National Health Survey: 1935–1936*, Preliminary Reports, Bulletin No. 2, Sickness and Medical Care Series, National Institute of Health, U. S. Public Health Service, Washington, D. C., 1938, p. 4.

tures for furniture and household equipment to the absolute minimum, but they could not eliminate this cost. Replacement of worn-out equipment, particularly worn-out stoves, took up 5 percent of all the expenditures of the long-unemployed families, and the biweekly installment payment to the furniture store was one of their more common obligations. All of these supposedly minor and supposedly nonessential items, together with a meager expenditure for recreation (1 percent) and for "other" expenses, took one-fourth of all the cash outlay of the long-unemployed families.

Hand-to-Mouth Living

The long-unemployed families do not make allowance for all the miscellaneous needs that must in the course of time absorb a considerable part of their incomes. Certain needs are constant—food, for example, and electric lights, rent, transportation, and recreation. These items are, in practical terms, the families' necessities, and they absorb most of every pay check. But there are occasional needs that can no more be avoided than the grocery bill itself. The doctor's bill is one of these items, and prescriptions, clothing, replacement of household equipment, and repairs to roofs, floors, windows, and the like are others. With most of the monthly income already spoken for, these unexpected needs will in most cases throw the families into debt. And no sooner is one debt paid than others must be assumed, so that the families live perpetually in the midst of a struggle to pay off their small obligations.

There is another difficulty. Expenditures among the long unemployed are naturally gauged to their full monthly income. But sometimes there are misfortunes. A WPA worker may lose time through bad weather, or illness, or failure to be transferred to a new project, or he may be laid off altogether. From time to time every long-unemployed family must draw less than the expected full pay. In this situation, the budget is invariably thrown out of gear. Again the family must go into debt, and frequently nothing but the corner grocer's credit will stand between it and hunger.

Any approach to the broader questions of the southern Illinois depressed area must take into account the current economic predicament of the long unemployed. The families are without reserves of any sort. Nearly all are in debt for their current needs,[11] and they live

---

[11] There are two types of debts among the long unemployed. There are the "old debts," running to as high as $1,000 in a single family, accumulated in most cases during the years when there was no relief for the unemployed. The extent of old debts is amazing; a small corner grocery in one coal town, for example, had bad debts amounting to $40,000. There is no chance whatever that the old debts can be repaid. The other type, the "current debt," which is kept distinct from the old debt, is far smaller, and is recognized as a real obligation.

from day-to-day. Self-initiated remedies for the predicament of the long unemployed have thus long since become impossible. The back-to-the-farm movement, for example, would require capital which the families do not have and could not get. Spontaneous migration of family units must likewise be ruled out as a possible solution, for migration also requires reserves which the families simply do not possess.

Chapter IV

THE DECLINE OF THE SOUTHERN
ILLINOIS COAL INDUSTRY

When UNEMPLOYED southern Illinois coal miners explain the causes of the predicament in which they now find themselves, they invariably begin with the statement: "There is nothing here but just coal." The statement is almost literally true. There is, of course, some agriculture. Farm land in the three counties is generally poor, however; average farm income is exceedingly low; and a considerable part of the coal field has never been put under cultivation. Compared with coal, agriculture is a minor contributor to the economic life of the community. There are also a few primary manufacturing establishments—a flour mill, a packing house, a brick plant—but their total pay roll has scarcely exceeded 200 workers at any time within the past 15 years. The rest of the working population is dependent upon either the mines, the industries which are subsidiary to mining, or the area's trade and local service industries. The fortunes of the coal industry and the fortunes of Franklin, Saline, and Williamson Counties are inseparable.[1]

THE NATION-WIDE COAL DEPRESSION

Overexpansion of Mine Capacity

The underlying causes of the long depression in southern Illinois are the difficulties which beset the bituminous coal industry throughout

---

[1] The recent discovery of oil near Benton, in Franklin County, does not alter this fact. Ironically enough, the first effects of the discovery were more detrimental than helpful. Few of the local unemployed found work on the drilling crews which suddenly went to work all over the coal field, for these crews were manned almost altogether with skilled workers originally brought from Texas and Oklahoma. The influx of these migrants intensified the already critical shortage of housing in the coal towns. The community will apparently not even benefit greatly from royalties, since the great bulk of the mineral rights are of course owned by the absentee coal operators.

53

the United States. Since the turn of the century bituminous coal mining has been "unstabilized." During the period of a rapidly expanding coal market (1900–1918) the productive capacity of the coal industry was developed faster than coal consumption. Anticipating future profits through occasional coal famines and through a constantly expanding market, optimistic investors not only continued to pour unneeded capital into the industry but also failed to abandon inefficient operations. Overexpansion of capacity led in turn to bitter and prolonged price wars. In order to keep the mines working and thus protect their investment against heavy shutdown losses, operators were forced in slack times to dump coal on the market for whatever it would bring. The many prewar attempts to control competition among the operators, whether by merger or trade agreement, were unsuccessful; and the industry was already in serious difficulty as it entered the wartime boom.

High coal prices during the World War intensified the top-heavy condition of the soft-coal industry. When the wartime peak of 579 million tons in production was reached in 1918, America's coal-mine capacity (i. e., the output possible under 280 days operation) had risen to 650 million tons. After the war was over and output began to decline, capacity continued to grow. The postwar shift in production from the union fields to the nonunion fields in Kentucky and West Virginia resulted in the development of hundreds of new mines not justified by the demand for coal. By 1923 mine capacity had risen to 885 million tons, while production stood at 565 million tons.[2]

Loss of Markets

Just when overexpansion reached its height in the years after the war, the coal industry suddenly began to lose markets. Petroleum, natural gas, and hydroelectric power became serious competitors with coal for both the industrial and the domestic fuel trade. In 1918 these three sources of power had supplied only 18 percent of the total energy consumed in the United States. But by 1922 they supplied 32 percent, and in 1927 their share further increased to 36 percent. Bituminous coal fought a losing battle; between 1918 and 1927 its share in the total energy consumed dropped from 70 percent to 55 percent.[3]

Simultaneously, American industry began to make substantial improvements in fuel-burning efficiency. Railroads, which consume more bituminous coal than any other industry, had burned 174 pounds of coal per 1,000 ton-miles in 1920. By 1927 the consumption

---

[2] Bureau of Mines, *Minerals Yearbook*, U. S. Department of the Interior, Washington, D. C., 1936, p. 562.
[3] *Ibid.*, 1937, p. 810.

of coal for the same amount of hauling was only 131 pounds, a decrease of one-fourth. Central electric power stations, another large consumer of coal, burned 3.04 pounds of coal per kilowatt-hour in 1920, but burned only 1.84 pounds in 1927, a decrease of 39 percent. Increased efficiency in fuel burning was also recorded for the manufacture of cement and pig iron.[4]

Liquidation of Surplus Capacity

In the face of this situation liquidation of surplus coal capacity was inevitable. The postwar record for coal production in the United States was set in 1926, when total output reached 573 million tons. Three years before this record was made, however, the industry began a rapid deflation in terms of both mines and men. Between 1923 and 1926, 138 million tons of mine capacity were abandoned, and 100,000 miners were displaced from their jobs. During the last 3 years of "prosperity" in the 1920's nearly 100,000 more miners were displaced. Further widespread abandonment of coal mines brought capacity in 1929 down to a point only 27 percent above actual output, and for a short time the industry was more nearly stabilized than at any other time since before the World War.[5]

The depression intensified all the basic difficulties of the bituminous coal industry. Between 1929 and 1932 a third group of 100,000 miners lost their jobs, cutting the total number of miners employed to the lowest point since 1902. Actual tonnage fell to 310 million, the lowest since 1904. Total productive capacity, however, declined only slightly during this period, so that by 1932 capacity was again almost double actual output.[6] The result was rampant cutthroat competition, and in turn a rapid lowering of wages and working standards.

Recovery—but the Problems Remain

With the adoption of the coal code under the National Industrial Recovery Act, the coal industry began a period of steady recovery, though at a slower pace than the recovery of industry in general because of competition with rival fuels. In 1936, when the volume of all industrial production had recovered to 1927 levels, America's output of bituminous coal had risen only to the level first reached in 1912. The 7-hour workday established by the National Recovery

[4] Yaworski, Nicholas; Spencer, Vivian; Saeger, Geoffrey A.; and Kiessling, O. E., *Fuel Efficiency in Cement Manufacture, 1909–1935*, Report No. E–5, National Research Project, Works Progress Administration, Philadelphia, Pa., April 1938, pp. 1–15.

[5] Bureau of Mines, *op. cit.*, 1936, pp. 562–563.

[6] *Ibid.*, pp. 562–563.

Administration coal code raised the total number of workers employed from 406,000 in 1933 to 458,000 a year later. In 1936 total men employed stood at 477,000, and in 1937 at 492,000, an increase of 86,000 over the bottom year of the depression.[7] But these increases reabsorbed less than half of the workers displaced between 1926 and 1932.

The year 1938 wiped out the greater part of these gains. Total soft-coal output dropped to 349 million tons for the year, the level of production prevailing in 1908. The number of men employed was cut from 492,000 to 441,000, and the greater part of the employment gains made after 1932 was canceled. In 1939 soft-coal output showed a substantial recovery, increasing 13 percent over 1938. Yet preliminary estimates put the total number of workers employed at 437,000, or 4,000 less than had been employed in 1938.[8]

THE POSTWAR POSITION OF SOUTHERN ILLINOIS COAL

The general postwar decline in the American coal industry found the once favored competitive position of southern Illinois coals vastly changed. Of course, the favorable freight haul to Chicago and St. Louis remained. A ton of mine-run coal from Herrin continued to enter the Chicago market with an initial freight-rate advantage; in 1939 this differential amounted to 35 cents over western Kentucky, $1.14 over northern West Virginia and western Pennsylvania, and $1.34 over southern West Virginia. Indiana and central Illinois coals, however, were still favored by lower rates than southern Illinois, which bore 30 cents more than Sullivan, Ind., and 40 cents more than Taylorville, Ill.

Competition

The quality of southern Illinois coal still compared favorably with any other coal mined west of the Appalachians [9] Hocking Valley, Ohio, coals—originally the chief high-grade soft-coal competitor of southern Illinois—had virtually disappeared from the midwestern market.

---

[7] *Ibid.*, 1937, p. 799; 1938, p. 694.

[8] *Ibid.*, 1940, pp. 779, 780.

[9] Southern Illinois No. 6 seam coal is superior in B. t. u. to all other midwestern coal except that mined from No. 6 and No. 11 seams in Hopkins County, Ky. In ash content it averages better than all leading coals from the midwestern fields with the exception of those from No. 4 seam Vigo County, Ind., and No. 6 seam in Sullivan County, Ind., and Hopkins County, Ky. In volatile matter, southern Illinois coal averages superior to all leading midwestern coals except coals mined in No. 5 seam Sullivan County, Ind., and No. 6 seam of Vermillion County, Ill. In sulphur content its low-sulphur coals are superior to leading midwestern coals with the exception of No. 4 seam coal from Vigo County, Ind.

Shortly before the World War, however, a new high-grade Appalachian coal appeared on the Chicago market, and as time passed its inroads into the southern Illinois trade became increasingly severe. This was Pocahontas (low-volatile) coal, which outranked southern Illinois in all the standard quality criteria. Pocahontas coal had an additional advantage in that it burned with less smoke than any other soft coal. As the agitation for control of the urban smoke nuisance grew, the competitive position of Pocahontas coal was greatly strengthened. In spite of a high freight rate, smokeless coal became increasingly popular in St. Louis and Chicago.

The southern Illinois coal field also lost heavily in competition with petroleum and natural gas. Midwestern cities, particularly Chicago and St. Louis, were logical terminals for the pipe lines from the new southwestern oil fields, so that natural gas and petroleum could be delivered at particularly low prices throughout the territory covered by southern Illinois coals. After the war oil and gas became serious competitors for the coal industry generally, but especially for Franklin, Saline, and Williamson Counties.

Wage Scales

An equally important reason for the decline of the southern Illinois field lay in the lower wages paid by competing fields. The most intensive period of mine development in southern Illinois occurred immediately after the World War, when total capacity was increased by one-half within the space of 6 years. This expansion was motivated, first, by the belief that the general demand for coal would continue to increase geometrically, just as it had been increasing since the 1870's. And there was a second fateful assumption that the early postwar pattern of union wages, and hence mining costs, in the competing coal fields would not be disrupted.

Immediately after the war the United Mine Workers of America began to lose agreements in one Appalachian coal field after another. At one time or another in the early 1920's, western Kentucky (the nearest competitor to Illinois), eastern Kentucky, Tennessee, Maryland, and nearly all fields in West Virginia began operating on a nonunion basis; after 1926 operators in Ohio and Pennsylvania followed suit. There came a time at last when Illinois was the only leading coal-producing State with a strong miner's organization left intact. In 10 years membership in the U.M.W. of A. had dropped from 386,000 to 80,000, of whom half were in Illinois.

As union influence outside of Illinois waned, the 1919 wage structure in the industry fell to pieces. By 1924 average hourly earnings for hand loaders in Illinois had risen 12 percent above 1919 levels, while wages in West Virginia and Kentucky had decreased between 2 percent and 6 percent (appendix table 4). On this new basis, which remained substantially constant through a period of generally falling wages until 1929, West Virginia and Kentucky were able to double their tonnage output within 8 years. In the depression a second gap appeared. Between 1929 and 1931 the Illinois wage rate stood practically unchanged, while the West Virginia rate fell by one-fifth and the Kentucky rate by about one-tenth. Comparable cuts took effect in Ohio and Pennsylvania. In the next 2 years the Illinois scale was cut 30 percent, but in competing fields the cut was even greater. Before the NRA was established in 1933, Kentucky, West Virginia, Ohio, and Pennsylvania were paying only slightly more than half the Illinois scale. (See appendix table 4.)

These unequal wage rates thoroughly demoralized the coal market. Between 1926 and 1933 the quoted price of mine-run coal from southern Illinois never fell below $1.95 a ton. But mine-run coal from western Kentucky averaged about $1.20 a ton through the whole period, and in 1933 it sold for as little as 70 cents. During the same period West Virginia coal dropped to a low of $1.25, and for a short time smokeless coal was delivered on the Chicago market at a price only 65 cents higher than the delivered price from southern Illinois.

This state of affairs was ended in 1934 when the United Mine Workers once more organized all the principal coal fields. On the basis of union agreements covering almost the entire bituminous coal industry, wage differentials among the competing fields were again brought back to approximately the 1919 pattern. This new stabilization, which was generally welcomed by operators and miners alike, solved one of the most grave and persistent problems of the southern Illinois coal industry. But meanwhile, 10 years of unstabilized mine wages left their mark upon Franklin, Saline, and Williamson Counties.

The Reduced Share of Southern Illinois in the Coal Market

The southern Illinois coal industry lost its tonnage after 1923 even more rapidly than the coal industry as a whole. Immediately after the World War Franklin, Saline, and Williamson Counties mined 5.6 percent of the total United States soft-coal output, and about the same share was maintained through 1926. After the 1927 strike this share began to diminish rapidly. In 1928 the three counties mined 4.6 percent of the Nation's output; in 1930 they mined 4.2 percent; in 1933 their share had fallen to 3.3 percent. Once lost, the share was not easily recovered. In 1938 the three counties still mined only 3.7 percent of the United States total. (See appendix tables 3 and 5.)

The falling price of coal in the 1920's and during the depression required each coal field to make its own particular adjustment, depending

ırm Security Administration (Rothstein).

Abandoned . . . Bush Mine, Franklin County, Ill.

upon its position in competition with rival fields. The nonunion fields of Kentucky and West Virginia were able to keep both tonnage and mine investment intact, but only by cutting wages drastically, eventually to less than half the 1924 level. In Pennsylvania, which bore the heaviest brunt of the general decline, deflation meant widespread abandonment of mines, and, after 1927, the degradation of wages and working conditions as well.

In Franklin, Saline, and Williamson Counties two adjustments in the basic structure of the industry were made: (1) The field abandoned roughly half of its mine capacity, somewhat more than its average share in the Nation-wide deflation. (2) The surviving operators cut their costs by installing coal-loading machinery, which nearly doubled the efficiency of operations and eliminated thousands of workers from the mines.

ABANDONMENT OF MINES

The first effect of the developing coal depression in southern Illinois was a rapid liquidation of mine capacity. The collapse began with the 1922 strike, the longest and most bitterly fought in the history of the field. The strike had several important results. It led to the bloody clash between strikers and strikebreakers which has come to be known as the "Herrin Massacre," and in turn to a boycott against Williamson County coal in northern Illinois. It raised mine wages to a basic scale of $7.50 a day, the rate which became the "Jacksonville Scale" when it was renewed at a Jacksonville, Fla., conference in 1924. Most important of all, the failure of the 1922 strike in west Kentucky and in several Appalachian fields gave one section of the soft-coal industry an opportunity to cut the miners' wages and to destroy the 1919 wage structure.

As soon as the strike was over and the new agreement was signed, mine abandonment started suddenly and in earnest.[10] Thirteen shipping mines were abandoned in 1923, displacing 2,500 miners. Next year 17 more mines were abandoned and 3,800 more miners were displaced. Deflation continued in 1925 with 11 mines closed and 3,000 more miners displaced. (See appendix table 1.)

During these years the growing trend went almost unnoticed. The miners drew high wages under the new contract, and the "silk-shirt era" had begun. Jobs were still plentiful, and most of the displaced

---

[10] Williamson County took the first and the heaviest blows of the deflation. Its position was somewhat injured by the boycott on Williamson coal and by the lurid publicity given to the so-called "Herrin Massacre." It suffered even more, however, from the fact that its principal mines were the first southern Illinois mines to be developed. Williamson mines by 1922 tended to be both small and old, and either had been worked out during the war or had become too inefficient to survive the new competition. See p. 3.

miners were soon rehired. Older coal miners, in particular, were fortunate; for as long as coal was loaded by hand, the operators considered the older workers to be their steadiest and best hands. The New Orient mine at West Frankfort, "largest mine in the world" and the last big mine developed in southern Illinois, was opened in this period and made new jobs for 1,900 coal miners. Among the 9,300 miners who lost their jobs between 1923 and 1925, about 3,000 found their way back into the mines. Most of the rest either went back to school, moved away, or retired to live on their savings or their children's earnings. Only a small number of unemployed had begun to pile up in the three counties.

Southern Illinois miners look back on 1927 as the year that ushered in the hard times. Before the 1927 strike, a miner could still move about from mine to mine with little difficulty. After 1927 all such mobility stopped. Miners were suddenly frozen in whatever jobs they held, or if their mine had shut down, they looked forward to an indefinite period of seeking work. The loading machines had already been installed in several mines, and had begun to take over the hand loaders' work. Older miners were no longer preferred, for alert young workers were wanted to run the new machines. On top of all, a second wave of mine abandonment followed the 1927 strike (appendix table 1). In the period 1927–1929 a total of 29 mines closed permanently in the 3 counties, and 5,000 miners, nearly one-fourth of the total mine crew, were thrown out of work. By the time of the 1930 Census (only 6 months after the stock-market crash) southern Illinois was already deep in the trough of the depression; Franklin County had a higher unemployment rate than any other county in the United States, and the three counties together had nearly four times the average incidence for the country as a whole.[11]

During the first years of the depression mine abandonment continued, though at a slower rate. In the years 1930–1932, 10 mines were abandoned and 2,100 more miners joined the unemployed, who now constituted a sizable part of the entire working population. By 1931 poverty and distress had become commonplace throughout the coal field, and local pauper funds were no longer adequate to provide even food for the unemployed.[12] Jobs in mines which had survived became more and more difficult to find; and although several thousand displaced miners, members of the U.M.W. of A., found jobs in Franklin County after the strike of the Progressive Miners of America in 1932, one . Progressive miner was dismissed for each unemployed miner reemployed.

---

[11] Bureau of the Census, *Fifteenth Census of the United States: 1930*, Unemployment, Vol. I, U. S. Department of Commerce, Washington, D. C., 1931, pp. 317, 318. In Franklin County, 27 percent of all gainful workers were unemployed, in the three counties, 21 percent.

[12] See pp. 128–129.

With the beginning of general recovery in 1933, the market for southern Illinois coal broadened and the tonnage produced in the field increased rapidly. With the increasing efficiency at the larger mines, however, abandonment of smaller mines continued as before. From 1933 through 1938, 28 more mines were permanently abandoned and their combined mine crews, consisting of 3,200 workers were dismissed. In 1939 and 1940 the process continued; during these 2 years five more mines were abandoned and several hundred more men were thrown out of work.

Reasons for Abandonment

While the particular reasons for abandonment varied from mine to mine, the most important cause of the general liquidation was direct economic pressure. The Old Ben Coal Co., the Consolidated Coal Co., the Sahara Coal Co., the Peabody Coal Co., and the C. W. and F. Coal Co. each closed from two to four good mines because they could not operate them profitably. Another group of mines was closed because underground conditions would not permit the installation of loading machines or because the operators could not afford to buy machines. Economic pressure in still another form closed most of the captive mines in the three counties. The United States Steel Corporation mine at Benton was abandoned when changing wage differentials made a shift in operation to the Appalachian field more profitable. A number of captive railroad mines were dismantled and abandoned in order to appease independent operators who were unwilling to ship coal over railroads that bought no coal.

Meanwhile, a number of mines were being closed for other reasons; in many the coal territories had been mined out, and in others the underground workings had been flooded. The coal depression, of course, had little to do with the abandonment of these mines, although operators might have reopened at least one of the flooded mines if the demand for coal had warranted. The important fact is not so much that these mines were abandoned as that they were usually not replaced. Operators who were being forced to abandon good producing mines each year were not eager to develop new mines, and any excess capacity which could be canceled by abandoning worked-out and flooded mines was simply considered so much to the good.

New Mines

In spite of the trend toward restricted operation, a few new mines were opened after 1923. The new mines, however, were far more efficient than the older mines, and they did not provide a great deal of employment. The general tendency of new investment was away from shaft mining; only one of the more important new mines opened since 1923 (the New Orient) is a shaft mine. Slope mining has

expanded considerably since 1923, partly because it requires less investment than shaft mining, and hence is a more flexible operation; and
partly because it permits the added efficiency of semiautomatic conveyor haulage, instead of the elaborate system of pit cars, locomotives,
and cages required in shaft mines. Between 1923 and 1938 some 17
slope mines were developed in Williamson and Saline Counties.[13]
Four of these still survived in 1940, giving employment to about 400
men. A fifth supermechanized slope was opened early in 1940.

In terms of recent new tonnage, the strip mines have contributed
most to the field. After 1923 a total of 14 strip mines began operation
in Saline and Williamson Counties. Five of these mines were still
working in 1940, adding 2 million tons to the total annual capacity of
the two counties. These mines are so extremely efficient, however,
that their employment has been almost negligible. The maximum
employment of all 5 mines is about 400 men, while an equivalent
output in a shaft mine would require approximately 3 times that
number.

Total Effect of Mine Abandonment

Of the two great changes in the southern Illinois coal industry since
the early 1920's, mine abandonment has been far more disastrous to
employment than mechanization. In 1923 the 3 counties had 103
shipping mines with an aggregate yearly capacity to produce 47 million
tons of coal. Thereafter productive capacity decreased almost
uninterruptedly until 1935. In 1939 there were 35 mines left, and
capacity had fallen to 27 million tons, a little more than half of the
peak. (See appendix tables 1 and 3.)

At the peak southern Illinois' 103 shipping mines provided jobs for
36,200 miners. After 1923, 85 of these mines fell by the wayside,
and with their disappearance a total of 21,100 jobs also disappeared.
Meanwhile, mines opened after 1923 (which had survived until 1938)
had added 2,100 new jobs. Liquidation of productive mine capacity
in Franklin, Saline, and Williamson Counties would have eliminated
about 19,000 jobs, nearly half of all those existing in 1923.[14]

---

[13] Slope mining is not possible in Franklin County because of the depth of the
coal below the surface. Slope mines operate in "shallow-vein" coal lying 50 to
150 feet deep.

[14] Mine abandonment has not been uniform throughout the field. Franklin
County, the least seriously affected, lost about one-quarter of its 1923 capacity,
and, as a result, about 9,600 of its peak of 16,200 jobs. Saline County lost
somewhat less than one-third of its 1924 capacity, but nearly half of its jobs.
Williamson was by far the worst hit of the three counties. Since 1923 it has lost
78 percent of its capacity, even with the recent development of three strip mines
and one slope mine. Abandonment of Williamson mines displaced about 11,200
of its 12,900 miners employed in 1923.

Fig. 13—SHIPPING MINES OPERATING AT THE CLOSE OF 1925 AND
1939 IN FRANKLIN, SALINE, AND WILLIAMSON COUNTIES

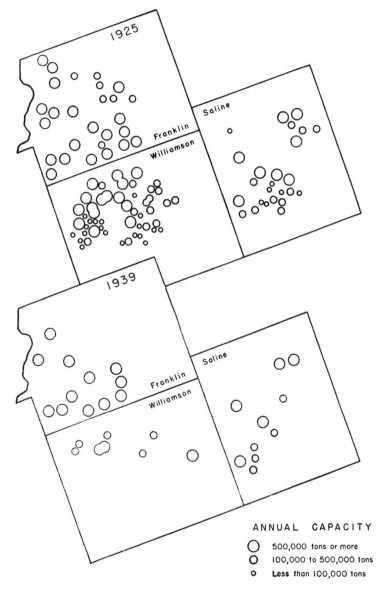

ANNUAL CAPACITY

O   500,000 tons or more
O   100,000 to 500,000 tons
o   Less than 100,000 tons

WPA 3647

MECHANIZATION OF LOADING

The decision to abandon an unprofitable mine is the last resort of coal operators. Each of the larger mines in southern Illinois represents an investment of from 1 million dollars to 7 million dollars in equipment, development cost, and coal lands. As long as the mines continue to run, even at a loss, this original investment continues to have some value based upon the possibility of future profit. But if the mines are dismantled, the operators can salvage only a very small fraction of the capital invested. They must write off as a total loss the cost of sinking the shaft and driving the haulage entries. Much of the equipment, which cannot be used in any other industry, can at best be sold for scrap iron at a few cents on the dollar, or must be left to rust at the mine site. The value of the coal property itself is also frequently lost; the coal territories once opened are usually not recoverable after abandonment, even though the coal itself has not been worked out.

Rather than liquidate their investment on any such basis, or continue trying to protect the investment with mounting deficits, operators will naturally explore even the most difficult possibilities of reducing mining cost. In Kentucky, Ohio, Pennsylvania, and West Virginia a partial "solution" to this problem was found in wage cuts. This solution, which frequently had to be enforced by resort to the yellow-dog contract, espionage, the maintenance of a private industrial police system, and like tactics, was difficult in any case. In Illinois, where the influence of the union continued to be powerful, a parallel reduction of wage costs was not possible. Southern Illinois operators turned instead to laborsaving techniques as a solution to the problem of cutting the cost of mining coal.[15]

This tendency has involved, first, the increasing emphasis on strip and slope mining. Because of the prevailing depth of the coal seam, however, both slope hoisting and stripping are impossible except for a small district near the outcrop in Saline and Williamson Counties, and neither technique can be used in Franklin County. The introduction of stripping and conveyor-haulage slope mines not only failed to benefit the majority of the shaft-mine operators established in the field but actually gave them new competition from within their own districts. The one way to lower costs for shaft-mine operators was through mechanization of underground loading.[16]

---

[15] Southern Illinois operators also met this situation by buying up coal property in Kentucky and West Virginia.

[16] For an exhaustive account of coal-mine mechanization, see Hotchkiss, Willard E. and Others, *Mechanization, Employment, and Output Per Man in Bituminous-Coal Mining*, Report No. E-9, National Research Project, Work Projects Administration, in cooperation with the U. S. Department of Interior, Bureau of Mines, Philadelphia, Pa., August 1939.

Machine Loading

The installation of underground coal-loading machines can be undertaken only where a peculiar combination of circumstances exists. Because of poor underground working conditions, unsteady markets, insufficient coal reserves, or lack of capital to purchase additional expensive equipment, the great majority of the shaft mines in southern Illinois were not able to mechanize. By January 1941 all such mines in Franklin, Saline, and Williamson Counties had been abandoned, and every single mine which survived the period of liquidation was mechanized. From the operator's point of view, this solution has been adequate.

In 1924 the average output of coal per man-day throughout the United States was 4.6 tons. Southern Illinois underground mines, which had not yet begun to install loading machines, were somewhat more efficient, producing 5.3 tons per man-day during the same year. Within the next 5 years, a total of 32 southern Illinois mines installed loaders of one kind or another under the pressure of competition from strip mines and the nonunion coal fields. By 1929 more than one-third of all underground-mine tonnage was loaded mechanically (appendix table 6). During these first years of machine loading, the man-day output in the three counties rose steadily. By 1929 it had increased to 6.0 tons per man-day, while the average efficiency throughout the United States had risen to 4.9 tons (appendix table 8).

The first loading machines installed in southern Illinois were principally pit-car loaders, simple conveyors which hoist coal from the floor of the miner's room and dump it into a pit car, but which still require manual workers to shovel coal into the bottom of the conveyor. These machines speed up loading somewhat, but do not dispense with a large number of workers. In 1929 most of the coal loaded mechanically in the three counties was loaded by these machines (appendix table 6).

The depression forced Illinois operators to hasten their program of mechanization. Between 1929 and 1932 the proportion of coal loaded mechanically underground nearly doubled. During the same period, however, only a few pit-car loaders were installed; instead, operators turned to the more efficient mobile loading machines, which dispense with all manual loading of coal at the face. Efficiency rose quickly under these conditions. In 1932 southern Illinois underground mines were producing 7.3 tons per man-day, as compared with 5.2 tons throughout the United States.

After 1932 shaft-mine efficiency increased still further. New installations of mobile loaders continued. Many of the mines which had originally installed pit-car loaders eventually replaced them with mobile loaders. The proportion of total tonnage loaded by hand dropped steadily from 31 percent in 1932 to 5 percent in 1939. At the beginning of 1941, every ton of coal mined in Franklin County was loaded mechanically, and in Williamson and Saline Counties shaft mines were nearly 100 percent mechanized. Meanwhile, the average output per man-day in southern Illinois underground mines had increased from 7.3 tons in 1932 to 8.9 tons in 1939. In Franklin County, where all hand loading has been eliminated, the 1939 man-day output was 9.4 tons, almost double the output in the county 15 years earlier.

Total Effect of Mechanization

The effect of mechanization may be traced in the record of the 21 southern Illinois shaft mines which had by 1938 installed machines for loading all or part of their coal output. All of these mines were in existence before loading machines were introduced. In 1926, under maximum employment on a hand-loading basis, the annual capacity of the 21 mines was 22 million tons. In 1938 capacity on a machine-loading basis was practically unchanged. In 1926 the mines employed 15,300 men to maintain that year's capacity. In 1938, however, they employed only 9,700 men, of whom about 400 were on divided time and were not necessary for maintaining the capacity (appendix table 7). Without appreciably changing capacity the machines have thus eliminated at least 6,000 miners from the industry in southern Illinois and abolished the jobs of every sixth miner employed in 1926.[17]

A DEPRESSED AREA

The significance of the changes undergone by the southern Illinois coal industry since the early 1920's is shown in figures 14 and 15. Since the deflation of southern Illinois mining first began, nearly three out of every four miners (actually 72 percent) have been squeezed out of the industry. In part, however, employment has declined with tonnage; and it might be supposed—indeed, it is actually believed in many quarters—that a restoration of former tonnage levels would increase mine employment and solve the coal field's unemployment problem.

There is grave doubt that tonnage can be appreciably increased. A great new oil field recently developed only 75 miles from the center of the coal field has brought petroleum competition closer home than

---

[17] Because of division of work, the first direct effect of the machines is to cause underemployment, rather than to throw men out of work. See p. 28. The decrease of 6,000 men employed at the 21 mines came about in several ways: (1) dismissal of men on divided time after the Progressive Miners' strike in 1932; (2) deaths, accidents, etc.; (3) the restriction on new hiring, except at the end of the 1932 strike.

Fig. 14—MEN EMPLOYED AT SHIPPING COAL MINES IN FRANKLIN,
SALINE, AND WILLIAMSON COUNTIES, 1921-1940 *

* 1940 figure is preliminary.
Source: Appendix table 2.

WPA 3648

ever before; and recently invigorated antismoke campaigns in the
Midwest seem likely to intensify still further the competition with
West Virginia smokeless coals. On the other hand, it is true, progress
is reported in developing a new technique for briquetting southern
Illinois slack coals and making them smokeless. But all in all, the
outlook is not promising, even as the national defense program gains
momentum.

We may estimate with somewhat more assurance the amount of
tonnage increase which would be required to restore full employment
in the coal community. Parallel with the shrinkage of the southern

Fig. 15- CAPACITY AND PRODUCTION OF SHIPPING COAL MINES IN
FRANKLIN, SALINE, AND WILLIAMSON COUNTIES,
1921-1940

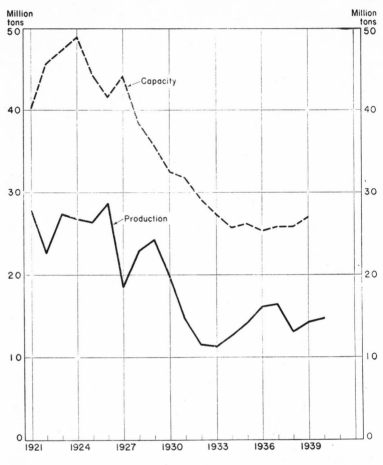

Source: Appendix table 3.

WPA 3649

Illinois coal market has run a highly significant trend in the man-day output of coal. The extension of strip mining and the introduction of mobile loaders in underground mines have increased the efficiency of mining in the three counties by 80 percent since the early 1920's. As a result, the tonnage output of the field can be increased to the highest level ever reached with the restoration of only a small proportion of the jobs that have been eliminated in the decline. The postwar record tonnage for the three counties, established in 1926, was about 29 million tons of coal. At present efficiency, about 3¼ million man-days of labor would be needed to recover this tonnage, or a total mine crew of 16,300 men working 200 days a year. Peak tonnage would thus require the creation of 6,000 more jobs than existed in 1939. Between 1926 and 1939, however, a total of 20,000 jobs disappeared, thus a return to 1926 production levels would require 14,000 fewer workers than were needed in that year. If one assumed a work year of 150 days,[18] there would still be 8,000 fewer jobs. (See appendix tables 2 and 3.)

The predicament of the coal field may be illustrated in another way. The average southern Illinois miner in 1940 loaded 9.4 tons per day, or nearly 1,900 tons per year (200 days). In order for 1926 employment levels to be restored at such efficiency, the three counties would have to market 58 million tons of coal, twice their all-time production record and more than four times the output marketed in 1939. Or, if the 1926 crew were working at present efficiency for only 150 days a year, the output would still be 42 million tons, far more than the highest tonnage ever reached and three times the 1939 output.

---

[18] The 200-day-work-year estimate is actually more realistic than the 150-day estimate, even though the average time worked in the past 15 years has seldom run over 150 days. When demand increases, the work year tends to increase too. Any such extraordinary demand as is implied in these estimates would doubtless increase the work year first and the size of the mine crew later.

Chapter V

COMMUNITY BANKRUPTCY

LOCAL COAL-TOWN entrepreneurs enjoyed a spectacular prosperity through the long coal boom in southern Illinois. Cut off, as we have seen, from direct participation in the coal industry, they had early turned all their energies to the job of servicing the growing community. Under their guidance a series of real-estate booms developed in all parts of the coal field. Building and loan associations sprang up in every village to "help the miners own their own homes." Faced with almost no competition from the coal-company stores, local merchants thrived in the retail trade. The local bankers expanded their activities year after year as the coal industry continued on its long era of expansion.

But the local enterprises, as everyone was later to discover, were even more seriously inflated than the coal industry itself. As the coal industry in Franklin, Saline, and Williamson Counties reached its final peak and turned downward, the structure of local business activity was gradually left with less and less real foundation. For many years the structure was kept intact under increasing strain. Then suddenly, and at the worst possible time, the whole structure crashed, adding new and unforeseen difficulties to the growing crisis of unemployment among the coal miners. Overnight the people found their homes being repossessed, their savings wiped out, their local-government treasuries empty. The communities were suddenly bankrupt.

THE COLLAPSE OF THE REAL-ESTATE BOOM

Real-estate promotion was the first of the boom activities to pass from the scene. Through the long period of prosperity in southern Illinois, coal-town real-estate promotion tended to run ahead of itself.[1] There had been a speculative real-estate boom in 1905, another followed in 1912, and the most hectic of all developed in the wartime

[1] See pp. 13 ff.

years and immediately afterward. Inflation in the coal industry had meant inflation multiplied in real estate. Real estate was not a very solid basis for the local financial structure of the coal community; yet the banks, the building and loan associations, and even the local governments themselves were built upon it. The sudden end of the real-estate boom was thus to have considerable significance in the community.

The End of Real-Estate Promotion

The year 1921 was the last year of the great activity in coal-town real estate and the culmination of the long-range tendency toward inflation. . (See figs. 3–A, p. 12, and 16–A.) The time had come again, as in 1907 and 1913, for a readjustment. The condition to be corrected, however, was far more serious this time than ever before. On top of that, the southern Illinois coal industry had unexpectedly come to the end of its era of growth, and in 1922, for the first time in nearly a quarter of a century, the community looked into an uncertain future. The time had passed when the periodic adjustment in real-estate activity could be left to the faithful growth of the coal industry.

The collapse began with the 1922 strike. Even with a very slight increase in the number of miners employed during 1922, real-estate activity fell off precipitously. In 1923 mine employment rose rapidly, and the year established an all-time record for the number of men at work in the mines in Franklin, Saline, and Williamson Counties. But the upturn in employment during the year scarcely slowed the pace of the downward trend of real-estate activity. When the widespread abandonment of southern Illinois mines really got under way in the middle of the 1920's, real-estate business dropped sharply. By 1926, in spite of the recovery of coal tonnage to wartime levels, real-estate activity had fallen to the lowest point since the depression of 1907 (fig. 16–A).

Ten years were to pass before the full effects of this slump were finally recognized in the community. Meanwhilè, there were straws in the wind, of course. The promotion schemes of the local entrepreneurs, many of whom were caught unawares with new subdivisions on their hands when the decline began in 1922,[2] were brought to a close. The first portentous lists of unpaid taxes, appearing in coal-town newspapers in 1923, showed that the chief delinquents were the

[2] The end of the boom was quite unexpected. Late in 1921 a coal-town newspaper reported: "The great building boom which started here early in the year continues unabated, and today there are probably more houses in course of construction in this city than at any previous time in its history . . . there appears to be no letup in the building activities . . . the people have faith in the [town's] future."

Fig. 16 – INDICES OF LOCAL BUSINESS ACTIVITY IN FRANKLIN,
SALINE, AND WILLIAMSON COUNTIES, 1921–1938

A. NUMBER AND AVERAGE VALUE
OF DEEDS FOR TOWN LOTS

B. ASSETS AND NEW LOANS OF BUILDING
AND LOAN ASSOCIATIONS

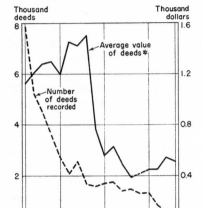

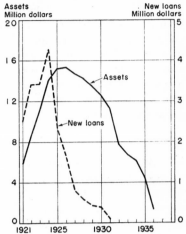

* Williamson County only.

C. BANK DEPOSITS AND POSTAL SAVINGS

D. TAXES EXTENDED AND COLLECTED

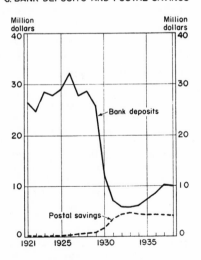

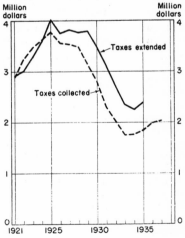

Source: Appendix tables 21, 22, 23, 24, and 25.

WPA 3650

real-estate promoters who had suddenly decided that their outlying town additions were not worth the taxes levied on them by the county.[3] Entrepreneurs who had been engaged in real-estate promotion either took their talents to other communities or, more frequently, turned their attention to their other business interests within the coal field.

But the so-called "silk-shirt era" was just getting under way when the era of real-estate expansion closed; the miners still look back on the period between 1922 and 1927 as the time of the crest of the great coal boom. During this period the miners enjoyed the highest daily wage in the history of the coal field (the $7.50 per day Jacksonville Scale). Jobs and money were still plentiful. In spite of the signs of the gathering storm, the great changes that were taking place in the financial structure of the coal-mining community went unnoted except by a few.[4]

Real-Estate Values in the 1920's

Real-estate *values*, for example, did not decline, although real-estate *transactions* fell sharply after 1922. Indeed, real-estate values continued to rise above the wartime peak, despite the rapid disappearance of their foundation after 1922 (fig. 16–A). During the first period of mine abandonment, from 1923 to 1926, the market value of real estate reached a new record. After 1927, the year in which the actual condition of the coal field first became generally known to the community, values rose again. Not until 1929, nearly a decade after the first clear indication that a deflation was inevitable, did the people of the coal field recognize that the values were being sustained on thin air. With that realization disaster came quickly; during 1929 coal-town real-estate values fell to half the level reached in 1928. In the belated crash the financial structure of the coal field was swept away and the community was reduced to utter bankruptcy.

---

[3] Between 1922 and 1925 the financial condition of several coal towns was disrupted by this unexpected development. In one town, for example, firemen and policemen went without pay periodically for several years, and failure to collect special assessments halted a program of municipal improvements.

[4] The community was somewhat diverted during this period by the vest-pocket civil war between the Ku Klux Klan and the "Knights of the Flaming Circle," which took a score or more lives all told and brought the National Guard hurrying to the coal field every month or so to restore order among the feudists. This was also the period of the fantastic reign of Charlie Birger, gambler and gangster extraordinary, reputed to have committed a dozen-odd homicides in the coal field between 1924 and 1926.

Although the southern Illinois coal field is perhaps most noted throughout the Midwest for these incidents, they appear to have had only an accidental connection with the community itself. They shed no light on the basic development of the coal towns, except that they perhaps reflect the flamboyant recklessness of the last years of the boom.

BUILDING-AND-LOAN ACTIVITY

In 1922 the business of promoting new subdivisions in the coal towns was disrupted; whole blocks of newly platted lots were abandoned to the tax collectors; and the housing boom began to subside. Families were moving out of the coal towns faster than newcomers could take their places. In towns where it had been impossible to rent a house, houses were suddenly plentiful. In Herrin, for example, every fiftieth house was vacant as early as 1923, and with another Herrin mine being abandoned every month or so, vacancies were increasing rapidly. The physical shortage of housing soon disappeared.

One might have expected that the building and loan associations, which had come to the fore during the wartime housing boom, should at this point have begun to slacken their activity. Instead, the close of the era of real-estate promotion actually doubled the building and loan association business. In 1922 new loans issued by the associations climbed to a new record, nearly 1 million dollars above 1921, and this record was repeated in 1923. In 1924 new loans increased again by nearly 1 million dollars and the year set a final record— 4¼ million dollars—for new loans issued in any given year. During the 3-year period (1922–1924) which marked the beginning of the decline of the southern Illinois coal industry, the building and loan associations issued more loans than had been made through two decades of the development of the field (appendix table 23 and fig. 16–B).

The Reasons for the Building-and-Loan Boom

The belated flurry in building-and-loan activity appears to have resulted from several special conditions. In the first place, the new "prosperity" had carried forward new residential building, though not at the frenzied wartime pace; and it had brought hundreds of coal-town workers into the market for homes. Their desire for property and security was strong, and their foresight into the future was not altogether clear. After the Jacksonville Scale was established, a large number of coal-town families had enough income ($1,000 to $1,500 a year) to provide a comfortable living, but not enough to make large cash investments. For such families the associations had a persuasive argument: "Why pay rent when you can buy or build a home on easy terms?"

But the increased purchasing power of the coal-town workers does not provide the full explanation for the activity of the associations. There is evidence to show that those who chose to rent vacant houses were not always able to do so. According to the testimony of numerous miners, it was difficult to find a house to rent anywhere in the coal field during this period, even though many houses were vacant. Instead, purchase through the building and loan associations was urged upon the coal-town residents whether they wished it or not.

Over the course of the two decades after 1900 several local entrepreneurs [5] had slowly accumulated a considerable number of coal-town houses. Meantime, the growth of the coal industry had greatly increased the original value of the property and built up a large paper profit. The wisdom of continuing to hold this property became more and more questionable after 1922. Of course, real-estate values were still high. But taxes on town property had become a sizable item after the war; and in addition, the values built up during the war showed signs of wavering. There were many coal-town property owners who were in no way reluctant to begin closing out their surplus holdings.

Moreover, the building-and-loan transaction had become extremely profitable for persons with real estate for sale. Illinois laws provided that interest on loans from the associations could not be deemed usurious. Through a complicated system of interest, "premiums," and fines, loans made by the associations yielded at times a fantastic return, running as high as 15 percent or more per annum. Persons owning vacant houses were naturally anxious to reap such lucrative returns from their property, and they were not inclined to bargain with prospective renters as long as sales through the building and loan associations were possible.

In any case, the associations flourished in their brief day. In 1921, after 20 years of growth, the coal towns owed the associations more than 5½ million dollars in loans outstanding (appendix table 23). In 1924, just 3 years later, outstanding loans had jumped to more than 13 million dollars. Meanwhile, the community had obligated itself to pay into the associations a total of nearly 1½ million dollars annually in interest and premiums. It had also assumed the obligation to retire through years to come a principal which was inflated far beyond the reasonable value of the property. There were special penalties added to the debt of those who could not make their payments on time. On top of all, many of the borrowers had agreed—without realizing it clearly—to assume the obligations of other borrowers who had bought in the same block of property, in case their payments stopped.

---

[5] A number of miners had also invested their savings in houses which they rented to other miners. Although some eventually accumulated as many as three or four houses, their investments were usually on a small scale. Late in the 1920's most of these little investors began to lose first one house and then another, and during the depression they were reduced to the common level.

The End of the Building-and-Loan Boom

The flurry of building-and-loan activity ended in 1924, 3 years behind the close of the era of real-estate promotion (fig. 16–B). In 1925 the new loans issued by the associations dropped off by nearly one-half. The decline continued through 1926, the last year of the coal field's fading prosperity; and with the beginning of hard times in 1927, new loans fell below 1 million dollars. As far as new business was concerned, the associations had returned to the unimportant position which they had occupied before the war. The community was no longer in the market for the building-and-loan plan.

Through these same years the great majority of the borrowers apparently made their payments faithfully, for the associations continued to prosper in spite of the decline of new loans. From 1925 through 1927 the community was able to pay about 4 million dollars to the associations in interest and premiums and to retire about 7 million dollars in old obligations, reducing the total amount of loans outstanding to 11¼ million dollars (appendix table 23). For a short time, it appeared that the home-loan business had been stabilized, and that eventually the debt would be liquidated, the associations would disappear, and a community of homeowners would result.

The period of stability, however, was brief. Between 1925 and 1927 borrowers were finding it increasingly difficult to meet the payments they had contracted for. As the summertime slump at the mines grew more protracted year by year, the miners began to fall behind in their payments. Sometimes they required most of the following winter to pay off their fines and accumulated interest. Many borrowers, indeed, were unable to catch up during the work season, and each fall found themselves a little further in debt than they were the year before.

There came a time when some workers could not meet their payments at all. As early as 1925 and 1926 mortgage foreclosures on coal-town real estate became common, and the ominous legal notices, "Notice of Publication: In Chancery . . ." began to appear throughout the coal field; common complainants in these notices were the building and loan associations. The real difficulties, however, did not start until after 1927, the year when hard times first set in. At the end of that year borrowers still owed more than 11 million dollars to the building and loan associations. Apparently, however, a number of loans were almost retired, for between 1927 and 1930 borrowers had succeeded in retiring an aggregate debt of nearly 4 million dollars and clearing their title to so much property. After the retirement of these loans the 1930 debt stood at almost 7 million dollars, with an annual interest charge of $785,000. This was a burden which the community could no longer bear.

What happened to the workers who owed for these loans may be illustrated with a few random cases:

1. When Mr. A. first came to the coal field in 1922, he discovered that there was little possibility of renting a house, although numerous houses were available for purchase through the Building and Loan Association. Mr. A. accordingly signed a contract to purchase one of these houses and agreed to pay $1,700 for house and lot. When he took over the house, he understood that five other new occupants were to be tied together with him in a block of six; each of the six was to assist the others in a neighborly way to make payments on their houses. Each member of the block paid monthly "dues" of $22.50.

From 1922 through 1926 Mr. A. kept up his installments and paid in $1,100 on his loan. Shortly before the 1927 strike, recalling that his original debt was $1,700, he took $600 in cash to the association intending to finish paying off the debt. He was told, however, that he still had $1,100 to pay. Undaunted by this thought, he kept up his monthly payments until 1930.

Some time before 1930, one after another of the other five borrowers in his block was laid off at the mines and began to miss payments. Finally, three of the borrowers quit paying altogether. The manager of the association then told Mr. A. that there was no point in continuing to make his payments. Thus he lost every cent he had paid on "his" house, and the house as well. The other five miners in his block suffered the same fate.

2. A certain house in one of the coal towns was valued at $1,500 when it was built before the war. In 1924 it was sold for $1,500 to Mr. B., who kept up his payments until he had paid in $1,500, about half of which went for interest. In 1929 Mr. B. lost the house, and the debt was taken over by Mr. C. Mr. C. kept the house until 1934, when he, in turn, lost the house after paying in $1,000. In 1935 the house was purchased by Mr. D. for $250, to be paid off at $10 per month. Said Mr. D. in 1938, "Now the property is clear except for $900 in back taxes."

3. Mr. E. bought a home title clear soon after the war. In 1927 he contracted a large debt, and in order to pay it off, he obtained a loan of $700 on his home from the local Building and Loan Association. In return, he agreed to pay $12.50 on the premium each month, plus interest on the balance due at 2½ percent monthly.

During the next 2 or 3 years, the mine where Mr. E. worked shut down several times, and during the winter it frequently hoisted only 2 days a week. Mr. E. made his first five payments successfully, but defaulted for the next 5 months. When he resumed his payments, the first six installments went for fines and interest; then for several months he was able to retire the premium at the rate of about $6 a month. In 1929 he was laid off again, and this process was repeated.

The outcome was that in 1931, after paying in about $700, his debt to the association was still slightly more than $700. "Then I just moved out—didn't even wait for them to evict me."

4. Mr. F. moved into one of the coal towns in 1925, and took over a $1,500 house previously occupied by another miner who had moved away. The house had two debts, one to the company which owned the lot, the other to the Building and Loan Association. The previous purchaser had already paid in $1,000 on the first and $480 on the second debt.

Through the checkoff, Mr. F. soon retired the first debt at the rate of $40 a month. He then concentrated on monthly payments of $13.75 to the association. Between 1925 and 1932 he paid in about $1,100 on the house. In 1932 he lost his job, but continued his payments until his money was exhausted in 1933. Then he defaulted but "hung on" to the house. His tenacity was rewarded, for in a few months, "when everything was going bust," the building and loan failed.

"We used to have one of the livest little towns you ever saw."

Abandoned Stores in Zeigler, Ill.

For 4 years he heard nothing of his obligation. But in 1937 he received a letter from a "loan agency" stating that it had bought the assets of the association, and that a debt of $967.63 on the house "must be terminated very soon." Mr. F. estimates that the house is now worth about $200.

House Wrecking

It may be gathered from these incidents that the building and loan associations suddenly found themselves in possession of a large number of repossessed coal-town houses. For a short time, they were able to dispose of these houses to new borrowers. Between 1927 and 1931, however, so many unemployed miners either migrated from the coal field, or doubled up to save on rent and electric lights, that the real-estate market was soon loaded down with hundreds of vacancies. Houses could be neither rented nor sold outright. Least of all could they be closed out under the building-and-loan plan; the miners had become embittered over their losses and were resolved not to enter such an agreement again.

But while property depreciated, taxes went on as before. The building and loan associations were faced with the necessity of selling the repossessed property before tax collectors had taken what little value remained. Many of the vacant houses were being damaged by small boys, or were being taken away board by board to repair the miners' houses. Moreover, the existence of so many vacant houses reduced the value of property that was still occupied, a consideration to which coal-field entrepreneurs have always been highly sensitive.

About 1930 the associations began selling the repossessed property for secondhand lumber. Houses already vacant were closed out in short order to out-of-town buyers who wrecked them and carted the lumber away. When a new vacancy occurred, the wrecking-crew was on hand. Houses in which the dispossessed miners had invested $1,000 to $2,000 were sold for as little as $25 to $50; and town lots that had cost the miners as much as $400 were forfeited to the State by the hundreds. In this way, some of the coal towns lost as much as one-third of their total number of houses.

Local newspapers looked with unconcealed favor on this process. "The sooner that these vacant houses are taken away," said one, "the better it will be for the property that is left. Every time one is pulled down, its value proves to enhance the value of other property." They pointed to the fact that when the repossessed houses were unoccupied, they constituted a "fire hazard"; and on the other hand, when they were occupied by "squatters," they tended to "breed disease and sickness."

However that might be, the fact was that the number of houses in the coal towns diminished more rapidly than the population. If one of the main purposes of house wrecking was to eliminate the surplus of housing, this end was achieved. Within a few years, house wreckers had demolished not only the surplus of housing, but a substantial number of the houses actually needed for the population. Families of the unemployed took to crowding together more than ever, to living in tents, in shanties built on the garbage dump, in chicken houses, in vacant stores. At the end of the era of building-and-loan financing, the problem of insufficient housing had become one of the more pressing difficulties of the southern Illinois coal field.[6]

The disposal of repossessed building-and-loan property to the house wreckers did not save the associations from bankruptcy. As soon as the flow of money into the associations started to waver, the stockholders naturally asked to withdraw their investment. The associations were thus forced to meet obligations for which they had no resources, other than paper profits and depreciated real property. Beginning in 1931 the associations started to fail throughout the coal field. Out of the 35 associations which had been operating at the peak of the home-loan business, only 6 continued in operation in 1936, and the activity of those was confined almost altogether to cleaning up the few loans still outstanding.

THE BANK CRASH

The phenomenal rise of funds deposited in the coal-town banks during and after the World War was succeeded by a period of "stabilization." The establishment of the Jacksonville Scale at the mines did not bring any further increase in bank deposits, but it did allow the banks to hold their wartime gains. In 1923 deposits reached 28 million dollars, then leveled off (appendix table 24 and fig. 16–C).

The Condition of the Banks in the 1920's

There is some evidence that many of the coal-field banks actually had more money than they were able to invest wisely. In any case, a loan policy of unusual leniency appears to have been widely adopted. Some sections of the community found that unsecured "friendship" loans were easy to obtain, and a considerable amount of money went for such purposes.[7] A present-day banker in the coal field reports

---

[6] The 1940 Census count of vacant housing units in Franklin, Saline, and Williamson Counties (preliminary figures) showed that 1.3 percent of the units were not occupied. In Harrisburg (Saline County) unoccupied dwellings were 0.9 percent of the total; in West Frankfort, 0.7 percent. These figures indicate crowding in the extreme; one must search far in the entire country to find evidence of so extraordinary a housing shortage.

[7] An extreme example of this type of loan came to light in the liquidation proceedings of a bank in Johnston City (Williamson County). The bank had loaned $5,000 without security to Charlie Birger, the notorious coal-field gangster. Birger's note became worthless when he was hanged for his misdeeds in 1927. Carstens, Arthur and White, Ina, *A Semi-Stranded Area*, unpublished ms., Federal Emergency Relief Administration, Washington, D. C., pp. 42 ff.

that some bankers during the early 1920's had frequently made loans on real estate up to 150 percent of the value of the property. Even where no such fantastic policy was followed, the appraisal of the value of security offered for loans often tended to be optimistic. For a time this practice of the less cautious bankers appears to have worked successfully enough. As long as the miners kept their money on deposit and the borrowers met their obligations, the interest income of the banks was increased and prosperity reigned.

The banks under more conservative leadership necessarily operated under similar, if less extreme, circumstances. Within the community itself the principal loans were secured either by town and farm real estate or by the notes of local merchants. Although farm mortgages were reasonably safe, loans on town real estate, even if held to only 50 percent of appraised value, were dangerous risks in view of the boom values which prevailed during the 1920's. When mine pay rolls were high, the local merchants enjoyed a spectacular prosperity and their credit was safe. But the merchants depended on credit extended to miners, and credit could easily become bad debts. Other funds not loaned locally were generally diverted to heavy investments in "conservative" bonds; these, too, were vulnerable. Even the conservative banks (except those with their funds in farm mortgages)[8] were in no position to meet a rainy day.

It was not until 1927, however, that the fissures in the coal-town banking structure were first observed. Anticipating a major strike in 1927, the miners had started nearly a year in advance to build up their savings; and when the strike occurred on April 1, 1927, they began on schedule to withdraw their money. Two coal-town bank officials who soon saw that they could not pay the strike withdrawals legitimately, forged some bogus securities for the emergency. Along in the summer of 1927 both bankers were caught and convicted. The community was scandalized, and took careful note of this incident. Three other banks closed during the strike year, but all the rest were able to meet the situation adequately. As soon as the strike was settled, heavy withdrawals stopped (fig. 16–C).

But as time passed, ugly rumors began to circulate. For example, miners at work underground in a mine at Johnston City heard one day in the summer of 1928 that a West Frankfort bank was about to close its doors. Immediately all the miners dropped their tools and rushed into town to get their money. The bank paid off in cash all afternoon. When the president offered a reward for the arrest of the person who

---

[8] Saline County banks turned out to be the only sound banks in the coal field; and while Franklin and Williamson together lost 26 banks, Saline lost only 4. One main reason for the survival of the Saline banks was that the territory they served depended as much on farming as on mining, and hence absorbed the shock of the declining coal industry more easily than Franklin and Williamson.

started the rumor, the run stopped and the bank was saved for the time.

A few months later two Franklin County banks decided to try consolidating their position by a merger. Again suspicion was aroused. Put on the defensive, the new company issued this somewhat incoherent explanation to depositors:

> Service is always a paramount goal of every well-balanced financial corporation. There is a definite and pronounced trend toward an era of consolidations and mergers among financial institutions. Banks, insurance companies, investment companies, and other organizations dealing in money and credit are proceeding on the theory of the old adage—"in union there is strength"—and the credit fabric of the State and Nation is given greater expansive power and elasticity by means of these combinations. With these facts in mind . . . the consolidation . . . has today been perfected and ratified.

Four other mergers and reorganizations were hurriedly put through in the three counties during 1929.

It was too late for patching up the structure. The pinch had come, and the miners were withdrawing the savings they had put away for hard times. To meet these new demands, the banks found their portfolios filled with all too many defaulted notes, real-estate mortgages that could never be repaid, and depreciated bonds.

The Collapse

The Herrin State Savings Bank, after doing business for more than a quarter of a century, finished the year 1928 with nearly half a million dollars on deposit. In 1929 unemployed miners drew heavily on their savings and reduced their accounts to $380,000. Withdrawals continued through the first months of 1930 until finally deposits stood at $275,000. One Wednesday morning early in April 1930 residents of Herrin saw that a typewritten notice had been stuck on the front door, announcing that the bank was undergoing "examination and readjustment." In Johnston City, 6 miles away, the same notice had been posted that morning at the larger of the town's two banks. Before the day was over runs had started on every bank in Williamson County.

Several days later one of the Williamson County newspapers, speaking for the threatened coal-town entrepreneurs, did its bit to stop the withdrawals:

> Professional and business men point out that where money is taken from a bank and hidden in the home, there is danger of total loss by fire, burglary, or robbery, and that at the worst one never suffers total loss if the money is left safely in the bank.[9]

The same issue reported that "confidence in the bank situation was

---

[9] Nearly a year later the newspaper was still pointing up news stories of burglaries with the moral, "Keep your money in the banks."

being restored," but announced that four other Williamson County banks had just closed, bringing the week's total casualties to six. By the end of 1930 the 3 counties had lost 10 more of the 36 banks which operated at the first of the year. Active deposits fell from about 26 million dollars to 12 million dollars, partly because of the funds tied up in the 16 defunct banks and partly because of the continued drain on the stronger banks that managed to survive the year. Throughout 1931 the liquidation proceeded. Williamson County lost another bank and half of its total deposits. Franklin County lost three of its last seven banks, together with almost four-fifths of the deposits with which it started the year. (See appendix table 24.) The last of the large banks in Franklin County—the First National Bank of Zeigler—was saved only by the intervention of the Bell & Zoller Coal & Mining Company, which bought control and hurried funds to Zeigler in time to stop a run on the bank.

At the end of 1932 Franklin and Williamson Counties together had on deposit only 7 cents for each dollar held in 1928. All that remained in Franklin County was the one important bank at Zeigler and three small banks outside the coal towns. Williamson County had two small banks, neither of which had sufficient resources to handle more than a fraction of the county's banking business. Total deposits in the three counties had been reduced from 29 million dollars to 6 million dollars, of which three-fourths was held in the Saline County banks that had weathered the storm. The bank holiday of March 1933 came as something of an anticlimax in southern Illinois.

By 1933 defunct banks in the three counties held 14 million dollars in frozen deposits. Not until 1934 were any substantial payments made on these claims against the banks, and even then the payments were equal to only about one-fourth of the total amount involved. Payments continued, however, through 1935 and 1936 until roughly half of the deposits were repaid. During 1937 most of the receiverships were dissolved,[10] and a final deficit to depositors amounting to approximately 7 million dollars was written off the books.

Postal Savings

When the United States Postal Savings System was first established in coal-town post offices about 1910, local businessmen in the three counties hoped that as long as the foreign born refused to deposit their savings in local banks anyhow, they would at least be willing to trust their money to "the Government's keeping." "It is expected," they said, "that not nearly so much money will be sent out of the country hereafter." Actually, however, the Postal Savings System was

---

[10] In the summer of 1940 a defunct bank in Johnston City, still in the courts, was about to make its first payment to depositors since April 8, 1930.

not popular with the miners. After 2 years of operation, there were only 131 postal depositors in the 3 counties. Even when the World War upset the flow of savings to Europe, postal savings gained little; the miners turned to the local banks instead. All during the 1920's the very existence of the postal system remained largely unrecognized.

It was not until after the bank crash that the miners began to make use of the Postal Savings System; by that time it was too late to salvage very much of their money. During the first year of the crash, bank deposits declined 14 million dollars, but postal deposits increased only 1 million dollars. In 1931 deposits in banks dropped another 5 million dollars, while postal savings increased only about 1½ million dollars. Postal savings did not reach their peak (4½ million dollars) until 1933, a year after the banking structure of Franklin and Williamson Counties had been virtually wiped out. (See appendix tables 24 and 25 and fig. 16–C.)

For whatever reason, the community had placed full confidence in the stewardship of its local entrepreneurs. The one avilable institution which could have helped to cushion the shock was forgotten, and it actually helped very little. The chief function of postal savings was to provide a place of safekeeping for what little money could be scraped together from the ruins of the banks.

BANKRUPT GOVERNMENTS

The increase in the coal-field tax income after 1918 had permitted the expansion of schools, roads, "charities," local improvements, and all the services so urgently needed by the newly grown-up community. These expanded functions required, in turn, still further increases in tax revenue. A new school building, for example, meant that the school district must hire new and better teachers, as well as pay off the interest on the school bonds. In order to hold what gains had been won, the community had obligated itself for further increases in its future tax revenues.

In the early 1920's the job of providing the community with adequate social equipment had still scarcely begun. One improvement suggested another. When a new high-school building had been completed, there was less justification for neglecting the city hall, or the county poor farm, whose condition was a chronic scandal. Road construction was a job for two decades. In the middle 1920's many of the coal towns still had unpaved streets, no central water supply, no adequate sewage system. Counties and townships were required by the State to set up still other functions, such as increased aid to the blind.

Tax Income in the Early 1920's

It was altogether natural, then, that the coal-field tax levy should have risen steadily after the war. In 1919 the tax income for the three counties passed 2 million dollars for the first time; in 1922 it passed the 3-million-dollar mark; and in 1925 it reached nearly 4 million dollars (appendix table 22 and fig. 16–D). But in spite of the increased tax income, local government officials were finding it more and more difficult to make ends meet. In Franklin County, for example, the collapse of real-estate promotion schemes in 1922 had disrupted the finances of several towns, leaving firemen, policemen, and street maintenance workers unpaid. Williamson County had similar difficulties. The extraordinary expenses of the sheriff's and coroner's offices during the Ku Klux Klan civil war threw the county into considerable debt and revealed how precarious its fiscal base actually was.

Experts who examined the county records cautioned the officials as early as 1925 that "strictest economy" would be necessary and recommended the budgeting of accounts, but the problem was too large to be solved in this simple way. A short "economy" drive was launched, however, in 1926, and the tax levy was reduced to encourage this effort. But when the time came actually to cut expenses the local officials could think of no methods more far-reaching than moving the sheriff's offices to the jail to save rent, cutting the "purchase of food supplies for the county farm," and "extreme caution" in "helping paupers, so-called." After 1 year of such economy the levy was raised again.

Unpaid Taxes

If local government officials could not keep their house in order during the last years of the coal boom, they were to face an utterly impossible task when the boom ended. In 1927 all the other difficulties of the local tax bodies were reduced to insignificance by a new and unexpected development: property holders began neglecting to pay their taxes. Collections slipped a little further behind in 1928, and warrants drawn on the local tax funds decreased in value. The need of outside help for the hard-pressed local governments had reached the point of "urgency," according to a private auditor of the counties' affairs.

Tax forfeitures became far more serious in 1929. Warrants issued against the Williamson County general fund were discounted 20 percent. More trouble developed as the unemployed made increasing demands on the meager pauper-relief funds. The tone of the auditor's annual report now carried a note of hopelessness and panic. But this was only the beginning. The schools were hard hit for the first time by the disappointing 1930 school-tax collections, which reduced their revenue by nearly one-fourth. The closing of the banks in

Franklin and Williamson Counties during 1930 tied up a large part of the public money, stopping salaries of teachers and county officials and payment to paupers. In Saline County, where the banks stayed open, the extraordinary expenses for relief drained the local treasuries. Still forfeitures increased. By 1931, even after some of the frozen bank deposits had been released, Franklin and Williamson Counties were unable to borrow in advance on anticipated taxes. In the judgment of the few local banks that still operated, the credit of the local tax bodies had become totally worthless.

After 1931 the whole tax system stalled. The coal companies, of course, continued for the most part to pay their taxes, but they had won sharp reductions in both assessed valuations and levies and had thus cut their tax bill by more than one-third. Large numbers of farmers, particularly those whose land was superior, also kept their taxes clear. But in the towns, where the majority of the taxes were levied, and on the poorer farm land, property owners by the thousands simply stopped paying taxes altogether. Such a large proportion of the population was involved in tax delinquency that the sheriffs were not able to take any action to force collection. Although each newly elected sheriff pledged himself to collect the back taxes of the "well-to-do" delinquents, the job of separating the well-to-do from those truly unable to pay turned out to be impossible, and the various drives for bringing in collections were all dropped after a month or two of threatening publicity.

The spread of tax delinquency led to a general breakdown of most of the functions of the local governments. Pauper-relief resources diminished rapidly, while need increased. The local governments eventually threw up their hands and called on outside help to save the unemployed from starvation. The schools remained open, but teachers were dismissed by the score; buildings fell into disrepair, and the teachers who were retained had to work as long as a full year without pay. School and county warrants were cashed regularly for 50 cents on the dollar and frequently for less. The sheriff of Williamson County refused to serve papers unless his fees were paid in advance:

> And by fee I don't mean county orders; I mean cash. I have 8 thousand dollars in county orders now that I can't get money for, and it takes money for us to buy gasoline to drive all over the county serving papers.

The town of Benton turned off the city lights, cut the police force to 1 underpaid employee (for 8,000 people), stopped work on the streets, and reduced the fire department to the minimum required by the insurance companies. Towns throughout the coal field followed suit. "The town," said a local paper, "has no money with which to pay for the expensive tastes the people cultivated when dollars were literally growing on trees."

The decline of tax revenues was not simply a temporary phase; local officials soon recognized 'that there was no hope, granted the existing tax base, of collecting revenues adequate for the needs of the community. A great deal of the property valuation in the towns had been destroyed by the building-and-loan house-wrecking policy, and the depression had brought a general reduction in valuation and levies on the remaining properties. Many of the townspeople who had forfeited their taxes over a period of years were eventually able to resume payments on a current basis. But by law any tax payments were credited to back taxes, which in many instances were so great that they exceeded by far the value of the property itself. Rather than attempt to clear their property of all back taxes, property holders who might have kept up current taxes paid nothing at all. At one time the local governments attempted to have all back taxes written off the books in order that current taxes could be collected; the Attorney General of the State, however, ruled that the procedure was not legal.

According to the latest figures available, the tax structure of the coal field is still hopelessly shattered. Williamson County Commissioners discovered in 1936 that the clerical cost of carrying back taxes on the records was one-fourth of the total income from the county levy. Taxes were not paid in Williamson County in 1936 on 31 percent of all lands, on 49 percent of personal property, and on 67 percent of the town lots. Coal towns in Franklin and Williamson Counties showed tax forfeitures in 1937 as follows:

Town	Percent of all lots with taxes unpaid
Herrin	71
Johnston City	77
West Frankfort	71
Zeigler	70

Even in Saline County, which remained comparatively solvent through the depression, tax delinquency is serious in terms of ordinary standards. Eldorado taxpayers, for example, were in arrears on 21 percent of the town lots in 1937, and in Carrier Mills the rate of forfeiture was 28 percent.

In order for the community to carry on its functions at all, State and Federal Governments have been called upon to supply an ever increasing part of the necessary money. Local responsibility for unemployment relief broke down before the coal depression was well under way. The three counties were able to contribute only 10 percent toward their direct relief cost during the fiscal year ending June 30, 1939. Old-age assistance, which now costs about 1 million dollars a year, is borne principally by revenues derived outside the three counties. The Federal Government pays the wages of the thousands employed on the work programs. In order to maintain acceptable school standards, the State has been forced to provide a larger and larger share of the school costs; in 1937, indeed, the State paid somewhat over half of the money required to run the schools. Long-postponed local improvements, which are vital to the welfare of the community but which the community itself could not conceivably finance, could not have been carried forward without the WPA.

Chapter VI

ATTEMPTS AT A SOLUTION

BETWEEN 1923 and 1933 the southern Illinois coal field evolved by slow stages from an active, booming mining community to one beset at every turn with deep-seated economic difficulties. Since the general causes of this state of affairs involve the whole bituminous coal industry and are Nation-wide in scope, the community itself has been helpless to halt the decline. Recognizing that the coal depression was beyond local control, the community was forced to turn in upon itself to seek a solution for its growing difficulties. While some of these attempts have met with modest success, they have not contributed greatly to the solution of the basic economic problems of the community.[1]

ATTEMPTS TO CHECK MINE UNEMPLOYMENT

Unemployment of miners in southern Illinois resulted either from the displacement of labor, following the installation of loading machines, or from the abandonment of mines. Coal miners facing unemployment accordingly had two distinct problems, depending upon the prospects of their individual mines. If a mine stood a good chance to continue working, the miners' problem was to keep out the machines. For those mines on the verge of bankruptcy, on the other hand, the problem was to work out arrangements for carrying on operations.

---

[1] We leave out of account here such activities as bootlegging, which residents of up-State Illinois erroneously believed to be one of the principal occupations of unemployed miners. There was of course some illegal liquor traffic in the coal field, but it appears to have been a poor business in the dark days of the depression, for—among other reasons—few could afford to buy.

We also omit the various activities based on the principle that the unemployed might solve their problems by selling magazine subscriptions, collecting coat hangers, cleaning tombstones, making flowerpots out of tin cans, and other "ingenious" attempts to create services which no one wanted.

Attempts to Eliminate the Machines

When southern Illinois coal operators first began to install mechanical loading equipment in 1925 and 1926, no wage scale for the new occupation of operating the machines had been agreed upon. The miners, sensing from the start that the machines would eventually "revolutionize" the southern Illinois coal industry and create widespread technological unemployment, first took their stand against the machines on the question of the wage scale for machine operators.

Miners who load coal by hand work on a tonnage rather than an hourly basis, and the first thought of the miners was that the new loading machines should also be operated under a tonnage wage scale. At the negotiations to fix loading-machine wages in 1926, this position was advanced by the scale committee of the Illinois union. Although the union conceded that the machine rate might be somewhat lower than the prevailing hand-loading scale, the practical effects of its demands would have been the prevention of mechanization in the field. As it developed, however, the operators were pressing for a wage reduction. The eventual outcome was a compromise in which the miners won a renewal .of the prevailing wage and the operators won an hourly wage scale (considerably higher than average) for the loading machines. From this time on, the international and the Illinois union offered no resistance to mechanization as such, but took the position instead that the benefits of the machines should be passed on to the miners through a shorter workday.

The miners at the face, however, frequently had a different view of the matter. They knew from experience that after an operator installed machines, reduced earnings and increased unemployment would inevitably follow. It appeared to them that the way to avoid the effects was to attack what appeared to be the causes. Accordingly, there developed a general antagonism against the machines themselves, leading on several occasions to unauthorized strikes in an attempt to prevent their installation.

In October 1928 some 1,800 miners at New Orient went out on strike to prevent mechanical loading devices from coming into the mine. The miners demanded that if the conveyors were set up, "all employees should be given steady work." The strike, which was not supported by the subdistrict union, was short-lived; within a few days the miners returned to work. A few months later 400 of the 1,800 miners were displaced.

Two years later the Committee for the Elimination of Mining Machinery was formed in southern Illinois to urge that all miners "cease work on loading machines and conveyors." The committee set a strike day and sent speakers to every mine local in Franklin and Williamson Counties to build support. But again the subdistrict union did not sanction the action and the strike was a total failure.

All local action against the machines eventually failed with one exception. Following the 1932 strike two of the larger Saline County operators agreed that no machines would be worked or installed at their mines. Later on, however, this agreement was also lost (though two of the mines covered in the contract were never mechanized because of engineering difficulties). Since 1933 the machines have been accepted as inevitable. Except for sporadic "slowdown" strikes and occasionally a refusal to reopen bankrupt mines on a machine basis, the miners have not since opposed machine loading in southern Illinois.

Attempts To Reopen Abandoned Mines

Mine abandonment, as we have seen, was a far more serious cause of unemployment than the introduction of machine loading. Usually mine abandonment was presented to the miners as inevitable. Many of the larger operators decided to close certain of their mines because of lack of a market, about which the miners themselves could of course do nothing. At other mines the coal territories had been either flooded or completely worked out. There were several small bankrupt mines in southern Illinois, however, which the miners did attempt to keep operating.

A mine crew's wage claims play an important part in the reorganization of defunct mines. Wages are paid in southern Illinois on the basis of 2 weeks' work, but the actual money is not forthcoming until another 2 weeks have passed. When an operator goes into bankruptcy, the miners ordinarily get no notice until "a pay is missed," that is, until their pay for the period ending 2 weeks earlier is defaulted. Meanwhile, the miners have put in $20,000 to $60,000 worth of work. After bankruptcy, claims for the amount defaulted are placed against the receiver, who cannot reopen the mine until he has settled this claim to the satisfaction of the men.

In spite of the miners' wage claims, the receiver ordinarily has the advantage when negotiating for reopening the mine. The miners by this time have usually been unemployed for 6 months to a year and a half,[2] and are anxious to go back to work. Of course they are also very much in need of the month's missed pay. In this situation, the miners have often been willing to make large concessions to get their mine operating again.

In reopening bankrupt marginal mines, one of two plans was ordinarily adopted. Sometimes the miners would draw their missed pay in cash, and then go back to work at what amounted to lower wages. The other plan was to go back to work without wage concessions,

---

[2] Operators planning to "miss a pay" usually do so in February or March, at the beginning of the annual slump. Ordinarily attempts to reopen a defunct mine begin in the fall at the start of the coal season.

either disguised or otherwise, but to make concessions on the missed pay, taking partial payment for full settlement, or agreeing that the debt be paid off a little at a time. In each case it was usually agreed that the mine crew would put in 1 or 2 months' work without pay, cleaning up the mine before reopening.

It is obvious that under each of these plans the miners were really subsidizing marginal operations. Well aware of this fact, they assumed that after a time these mines would be able to stand without help. Actually, however, such a time never came at most of the reopened bankrupt mines, and the miners were eventually faced with the choice of either granting more and more concessions, or of halting their subsidy and closing the mines.

As a result, most of the attempts to open bankrupt mines failed. A mine crew at West Frankfort, which tried to keep its mine operating at all costs, missed a pay each spring for 6 years in succession, then closed down. Most of the crews at bankrupt mines, however, refused to work indefinitely under such conditions. At a marginal mine in Benton, for example, the miners worked for a full year at wages equal to 70 percent of the union scale, then demanded the full scale and closed the mine down rather than continue their subsidy. Another mine crew at Johnston City voted to remain unemployed rather than make an agreement to spend their pay from the reopened mine at the company store. Another mine carrying a debt on two missed pays was closed because the mine crew was unwilling to make further concessions to the operator until 10-year-old wage claims were paid.

In addition to granting concessions to marginal operators, the miners on various occasions attempted to take over bankrupt mines and to operate them cooperatively. Failure greeted each of these ventures. The equipment available for cooperative mining was usually inadequate; the miners encountered other difficulties when they attempted to market their output; and at times the plan was disrupted by quarrels among the cooperators. When royalties and jobbers' fees had been paid, the miners frequently found that they had been working for less than half of full union wages. After struggling along for a season or so, the miners let their leases pass to private operators.

Sharing the Work at the Mines

The miners' attempts either to eliminate coal-loading machinery or to reopen bankrupt mines failed to check in any real measure the growth of unemployment in the southern Illinois coal field. The local problem was thus soon reduced to one of ameliorating the hardships of unemployment. Except for some meager unemployment benefits, the miners' efforts in this direction consisted mainly of the adoption of the policy of sharing work at the mines when a reduction of crew became necessary. Displacement of labor by loading machines has been cushioned at every mechanized mine in southern Illinois by the use of "divided time." The policy was accepted by the miners to be the lesser of two evils, and it has long been written into the union contract.

In spite of obvious advantages, the policy did not increase actual employment and hence did not help to solve the general problem of unemployment in the coal field. Frequently, divided time has entailed considerable hardship for the miners. When the mines on divided time were not working regularly, the policy reduced the earnings of the greater part of the working crew to a level below subsistence standards, and on occasion it actually increased the total relief load. Such a situation occurring in the summer of 1938 helped to raise the WPA and relief rolls to a record peak for the three counties. (See fig. 20, p. 133.)

Divided time, moreover, took care of only a very small proportion of the displaced miners. It did not, for example, help miners laid off after a mine was abandoned. Although some of the younger workers from an abandoned mine belonging to a company with other mines working were sometimes rehired, company-wide share-the-work plans were never an established practice; and workers not actually needed at other mines were not reemployed.

Divided time is now largely a thing of the past. At one time the mechanized mines in southern Illinois had hundreds of surplus men dividing time with the rest of the crew. Many of them were eliminated after the 1932 strike. Divided time was subsequently extended as new machines were installed, but by 1941 it had almost "worked itself out" through deaths and resignations. In June 1940 the surplus men dividing time in the 3 counties had been reduced to only 66 workers.[3]

The "Gopher Holes"

Nearly all of the coal mined in southern Illinois is produced at shipping mines,[4] large-scale operations which load coal for railway shipment to Chicago, St. Louis, and throughout the Midwest. Alongside the larger operations there has always existed a small makeshift coal-mining industry catering to the truck and wagon trade of near-by farmers and townspeople. When the larger coal industry began to fail, one of the paradoxical results was a rapid expansion of the smaller submarginal industry.

---

[3] See footnote 10, p. 32.

[4] In 1926 the shipping mines produced 98 percent of the coal output of the three counties; and in 1938, after the expansion of local mining, the shipping mines still produced 97 percent of the total output.

The gopher holes, which make up this smaller industry, are extremely poor producers. The coal seam they work consists mainly of leavings which were too thin and poor to attract the operators who first started large-scale mining in southern Illinois two generations ago. The seam averages only 3 to 5 feet in thickness where the gopher holes operate, so that mining and underground haulage is difficult. Because of the meager capital of the operators, none can afford to sink a slope more than 50 or 75 feet deep; hence the mines are all located in the poor-grade coal near the outcrop.[5] The primitive equipment of the mines usually consists of a couple of discarded pit cars from a larger mine, a few hundred feet of cable, a salvaged automobile motor for hoisting the coal, and a tipple made of scrap lumber. Most of the gopher holes have no undercutting machines, and practically all loading is done by hand. Many do not even have storage space at the tipple and cannot load or hoist unless someone is waiting at the tipple to buy a load of coal.

Before 1929 the function of the gopher holes was merely to fill small local orders which the shipping mines did not care to handle; during this period gopher holes employed in their best years only 120 to 180 miners as against a peak of 36,200 in the shipping mines. After 1928, however, the development of hard roads in southern Illinois expanded the possible market of the local mines to include a radius of 100 miles, and they began in a small way to compete with the shipping mines.[6] Handling a low-grade coal, the small mines had to deliver coal in their new market at a price far below that of the larger mines. Although a part of this difference was made up through cheap trucking costs, coal from the local mines sold for half the price of deep-vein coal at the tipple, and sometimes less. This difference had to be absorbed through lower and lower wages at the local mines. The difficulties of the local mines were further increased by bitter competition among themselves.

In spite of these conditions the number of gopher holes began to increase after 1929. As unemployment grew more and more critical, the wages and working conditions in the gopher holes became less unattractive to the miners. Makeshift tipples began to appear in every hollow along the outcrop. Unemployed miners and their sons

[5] The entire gopher-hole industry is strung out east and west along the southern fringe of the No. 5 seam, which outcrops in the center of Williamson County and the south of Saline County. There are no gopher holes in Franklin County, where the overburden runs from 300 to 600 feet.

[6] The local mines in Williamson and Saline Counties now sell most of the coal used in southern Illinois as far as the Ohio River and in southeastern Missouri in the vicinity of Cape Girardeau. They seldom truck as far as St. Louis, however, because they cannot compete with the local mines in St. Clair County, Ill., just across the Mississippi from St. Louis.

rm Security Administration (Rothstein).

"An old engine, a piece of cable, and a stick of wood or two—that's all you need."

A Gopher Hole Near Marion, Ill.

would come out from town, lease a few acres of coal, and begin digging the slope themselves. In a few weeks they would start hoisting 5 or 10 tons of coal a day, which they would sell to the trucks for whatever it would bring. Sometimes a farmer in need of ready cash would start digging on his own land, and eventually hire a half dozen neighbors and relatives to help load out the coal. A few local enterprisers went into business on a more elaborate scale with undercutting machines, Diesel hoists, screening equipment, and a mining crew of as many as 40 men.

In 1929 there were only 25 local mines, employing 151 men, in Saline and Williamson Counties. By 1932 the number of mines had increased to 75, and employment jumped to 444 miners, who loaded out 154,000 tons of coal for the year. In 1939 there were 106 local mines in the 2 counties, employing a total of 741 men. Tonnage in 1939 had increased to 547,000 tons, about equal to the output of one moderate-sized shipping mine in the coal field (appendix table 9).

In a few instances the rapid increase in the number of local mines clearly benefited the unemployed miners in southern Illinois. Several of the larger mines employ 25 to 40 men each, and maintain a wage scale considerably above relief standards, though somewhat below the union scale at the shipping mines. A few farmers have also raised their annual incomes by sinking small mines on their own land, thus supplementing summertime work on the farms with wintertime work in the mines.

By and large, however, the gopher holes have not had any appreciable effect upon the unemployment problem of the coal field. For every new job created at the gopher holes, 20 jobs were being eliminated from the shipping mines. Moreover, a large number of gopher-hole miners scarcely make a living at their new occupation. Because the mines sell only to the domestic trade within a region where winter weather is mild, the work season includes no more than 5 fall and winter months each year, and the average time worked a year is about 120 days. Daily wages in some of the more primitive mines run as low as $1 a day or less, and seldom go higher than $4 a day. Many of the miners are not self-supporting during the work season, let alone during the 7 idle months of the year.

ATTEMPTS TO BRING IN INDUSTRY

Residents of the southern Illinois coal field have long been aware of the precariousness of the area's economic base. Not very long after the first mines were sunk, local businessmen came to realize that the coal industry had its shortcomings. The panic of 1907 fell hard in southern Illinois, and even in the good years when the industry was growing steadily long periods of summertime unemployment were common. While local newspaper editors were computing in 1910 that the coal industry in the three counties would last another 7,369 years, they had already realized that coal alone would never make a stable community. Typical newspaper comments were:

> The mines are not the stable, every-day employers of labor which a town must have in order to grow..
>
> Diversified industries are sadly needed as the community at present is very much in the position of having all its eggs in one basket.

It was agreed that new industries would have to be attracted; if they would not come of their own accord the community would have to offer inducements. After some years of fruitless waiting, the second of the alternatives appeared to be the only hope.

What the Coal Field Had To Offer

Investors looking for a place to build a factory had no compelling reason for choosing the southern Illinois coal field. True enough, the district did have certain advantages. As one local newspaper put it:

> Much has been said relative to [this community's] excellent railroad or shipping facilities, its geographical location, its abundance of suitable factory land, its wonderful fuel advantages, and its water and electric possibilities.

But these advantages were not unique. Good railroad connections, for example, could be found almost anywhere east of the Mississippi and north of the Ohio Rivers, and abundant "factory land" is in itself hardly an attraction for manufacturers. Cheap fuel was obviously a talking point, but was a real advantage only if everything else were equal.[7]

Local publicity also made much of the central geographical location of the coal field. Actually, however, a glance at the map will show that its location is not particularly favored. Herrin is closer to Memphis than to Chicago, and closer to Atlanta than to Des Moines. It is at the edge and not in the center of the great midwestern market. A manufacturer looking for central location would have no reason to select southern Illinois in preference to St. Louis, Indianapolis, or any one of a dozen other established industrial centers lying north of the coal field.

As for water "possibilities," the statement quoted made a virtue of a handicap. One of the difficulties in attracting industries to the coal field has been the lack of a dependable water supply. Periodically, severe droughts strike southern Illinois, closing the mines and even hindering the operation of the railroads. The "possibilities" of

---

[7] Fuel expenditures form a very small part of manufacturing cost, amounting to only "2.8 percent of the gross value of products manufactured." Bureau of the Census, *Fifteenth Census of the United States, Manufactures: 1929*, Vol. I, U. S. Department of Commerce, Washington, D. C., 1933, p. 158.

storing water for the dry season were present, although it was not until 1939 that they were realized. The United States Department of Agriculture in cooperation with the WPA has recently completed the first of a series of storage reservoirs in southern Illinois which will now assure an abundant year-round water supply.

Cheap wages are a familiar claim of areas which advertise to bring in outside industry. "Docile" and "contented" labor—as the euphemism of the copywriters puts it—is a substantial attraction for prospective investors, and the regions which lay claim to an open-shop tradition have not been modest about saying so. Southern Illinois promoters could never make such a claim persuasively; they have always had great difficulty convincing investors that low wages might be expected anywhere within the coal field.

Even though investors were frequently assured that no attempt would be made to organize any new industry, the possibility of future collective bargaining still existed as long as the miners' union continued to set the example. Almost anywhere outside of the closed-shop coal field the chances of eventually having to come to terms with employees were less. Most investors thus preferred to go elsewhere. The substantial industries which have been established in southern Illinois are all located in such towns as Chester, Metropolis, Centralia, and Mount Vernon, at a discreet distance from the coal towns.

It was believed in the coal field that the advantages and disadvantages could be brought into closer balance if local subsidies to new industry were thrown into the scale. Subsidies, however, were difficult to raise. Early episodes involving gifts to unreliable manufacturers had burned many fingers; and few people were anxious to repeat the experience, particularly when the mines were booming and prosperity seemed assured. When the long coal depression had begun, the idea of subsidies was revived, but although there was plenty of desperate enthusiasm at that time the scheme never seemed to work.

"Land a Factory"

The campaign to bring new industries to the coal field was crystallized in two extended drives, each involving mobilization of public support to raise money for subsidies. The first of these drives, beginning in 1912 and lasting until the beginning of the wartime coal boom, was precipitated by a lull in the local real-estate business following a prewar slump in the coal industry.[8] The "plan" involved in this

---

[8] A real-estate-promotion firm with "important offices" in Birmingham, Ala., and Huntington, W. Va., played an important part in these prewar schemes, conducting sales in Benton, Christopher, West Frankfort, Harrisburg, and Eldorado. This firm was described in local newspapers as "a large operator in the location of factories and the sale of real estate in connection therein."

drive, which was engineered by local real-estate promoters, aimed to raise a subsidy fund painlessly through the sale of lots in new subdivisions.

One town made contacts with a St. Louis stove manufacturer who wished to move to southern Illinois "on account of the cheap fuel facilities." In order to provide other inducements, a local real-estate dealer subdivided 150 lots in a section of town called "Factory Heights" and advertised that all money from the sale of lots above the actual cost of the land would be used to build a factory and railroad switches for the stove works. The purchase of the lots thus became a civic duty. It was also made clear that the lots would soon be worth "more than is now asked."

At first these ventures went off successfully. Within a few days 270 lots were sold at $200 each. The town had raised enough money for the stove factory and for an automobile factory as well. "There is scarcely a man or woman," said a local newspaper, "who is not proud to have these skillful manipulators of mother earth among us to attract the commercial industries this way." In due time both the stove and automobile factories were installed and operating with a crew of about 100 men.

But difficulties began to develop almost immediately. A pump factory which had signed an agreement to move to the coal town suddenly refused to carry out its agreement. The stove works ran for 2 years, then shut down. After changing hands many times the machinery was removed and the building was eventually given over to swallows and bats. The automobile factory closed down after turning out one automobile, and the factory building was given in quick succession to a watch factory and a skating rink, and then burnt down. High hopes turned to disillusionment. When the town was offered a shoe factory in 1918 for a $100,000 bonus, it declined, saying, "This town is not handing out any hundred-thousand-dollar packages."

In another town, three real-estate dealers formed a "development company" and set out in 1913 to raise $100,000 for bonus money to bring in a glove, a piano, and a farm implement factory. Through the sale of city lots a total of $57,000 was pledged in a few months. Results were not soon apparent, however, and the drive began to lag. When the glove factory was eventually landed, the development company was unable to pay the bonus promised. Local citizens took over the development company and through straight contributions they were able to pay off the debt to the glove factory and erect a building for the piano factory as well. At this point the piano manufacturer reneged, leaving the town with a vacant building on its hands. •Eventually the glove factory closed down also. After this experience, the local newspaper remarked bitterly:

> The episodes of [a promoter], of factory fame . . . have served to knock [this town's] sounding board out of tune. . . . Enthusiasm and the cold stern reality of raising several thousand dollars are considered to be two entirely different things.

For more than a decade the idea of subsidizing local factories was dropped. The failure of the prewar drives for new industry had been discouraging to those who had paid out money for subsidies without getting any result. Meanwhile, the wartime coal boom had arrived, and prosperity based on coal alone seemed assured. Along about 1925, however, the first effects of the decline of the coal industry began to be felt, and the coal towns once more realized that new industries would be needed to absorb the workers who were rapidly being displaced from the mines. It was a sign of the times that women's literary societies began to present programs like this:

> Creosoting Plant, by Mrs.————————
> Brick Plant, by Mrs.————————
> Ice Cream Plant, by Mrs.————————
> Music

In vain the State Chamber of Commerce warned that "a concern that asks a bonus to locate a plant in your city is not worthy of coming." After 10 years of quiet the slogan, "Land a Factory," was in desperation again raised throughout the coal field.

In 1926 one of the coal towns began to negotiate for a factory with a manufacturer of pillowcases and sheets. The company's expansion plan, which involved the sale of $25,000 in stock to local people, was investigated by the town's booster club and pronounced sound. The company set up local offices and issued publicity emphasizing the fact that 30 girls would be employed and that money contributed would "be an investment rather than a subsidy." Trustees to protect the community's interest were appointed. But the sale of stock turned out to be difficult, and soon the campaign was forgotten.

A neighboring coal town was more successful. Through the cooperation of all civic organizations, the town was able to erect a $35,000 brick building to house its "new textile industry." Miners and business people alike contributed time and money for the building. The manufacturer who agreed to occupy the building was also given gentlemanly guarantees by local unions that his workers would not be organized. "We knew that times were hard and if we tried to organize, he wouldn't have come at all." Late in December 1926 the plant was installed with 56 machines "busily sewing and cutting various sizes of underwear."

Meanwhile, the towns around the edge of the coal field began to land factories at an impressive rate. In 1928 an open-shop town just outside the coal field paid $50,000 for a glove factory. A town to the north of the coal field had raised $125,000 for a shoe factory; to the south it was reported that a rayon factory had been landed. Local newspapers informed the people in the coal towns that 35 factories had located in southern Illinois between November 1927 and April 1929. Speaking before a coal-town audience, a field representative of the State Chamber of Commerce predicted that "southern Illinois would become the center of the manufacturing world within the space of a few years." He urged the enthusiastic local Chamber of Commerce to "pull for new industries" on the basis of its "excellent transportation" and its "super power system."

The growing pressure of unemployment and the success of the campaigns for factories in near-by towns brought the coal field's second drive for outside industry to a climax in 1929. "The industrial fever," said a newspaper, as drives were launched throughout the coal field, "has taken hold of the people in this section of the State." The record of the campaign waged by one of the towns shows how desperately new industry was pursued.

"Sink or Swim"

The town began to bargain in February 1929 with an Ohio overall manufacturer who promised employment for 150 to 200 people, provided the town raised $85,000 for the plant. After a railroad offered a free site for the factory, a local improvement association set out in March to raise the money required. The drive started off well enough. Carpenters offered to donate labor on the building, and other workers pledged a substantial part of a year's wages. The project was endorsed by 13 unions, 3 lodges, and 3 banks. The newspaper carried a full list of contributors, together with frequent warnings and exhortations:

> This overall factory drive is a fight for our very existence.
> Some years ago the people of [this town] set about to build up a live city and succeeded as long as the coal mining industry was thriving. Work in the mines is not so good now. What of the future? What of the day when this country's last mine has hoisted its last ton of coal, far distant as that day may be?

As the drive progressed, it was rumored that a near-by town had made the overall manufacturer a better offer. The association responded by urging local citizens to hurry with their pledges.

> Shall this be another "Tale of Two Cities," one checked by a disloyal few and sliding back into obscurity, the other welcoming opportunities and building to greater heights?
> Shall [we] fail?
> It's now or never, sink or swim.

All through the summer the drive continued. When the manufacturer telegraphed, "Must have contract completed June 15," the association redoubled its efforts. There was open criticism of a "disloyal few, including a few businessmen or concerns" who did not support the drive wholeheartedly. June 15 passed, and the manufacturer impatiently granted more time. Early in the fall of 1929 it was announced that money was still coming in. Optimism continued as architects began to prepare the blueprints for the factory building. The same type of campaign was pursued throughout the coal field. Late in 1929 a local newspaper summarized the status of drives going on simultaneously in five coal towns:

[One town] is making a bid for a factory and held a meeting this week to consider a proposition tendered them. . . . The proposition is a pants factory, which will employ 150 persons.

[Another town] is about to close up their overall factory proposition. . . .

[A third town] is open-minded and willing to "talk turkey" on most any sort of an industry the community could handle.

[A fourth town] is dickering with a stove factory [to occupy the vacant building erected in the 1913 drive].

The citizens of [a fifth town] have taken kindly to the overall factory and the general committee is working hard to sell the required amount of stock to secure the factory. . . .

These industries are a much needed thing in order to take care of the rapid accumulation of surplus labor.

This summary appeared on October 23, 1929, the week of the stock-market crash. It was the last optimistic note; within a few weeks all hope of bringing factories to the coal towns was gone. The drive in the one town to raise $85,000 for an overall factory reached the halfway mark late in 1929. On November 15 it was reported that bids for the factory building would be asked "in a few days." But the bids were never opened and the campaign quickly died. In the town which sought to raise $40,000 for another overall manufacturer, the quota was eventually reported filled. On November 20, however, it was discovered that another $2,000 was needed for moving expenses. The last $2,000 could not be raised, and this campaign was also soon forgotten. The less advanced drives were simply dropped.

As the depression came on, residents of the coal towns learned that industries were as hard to keep as they were to get. The most substantial result of the second campaign for industry was the underwear factory which opened in the coal field in 1926. This plant continued to operate until the first years of the depression. Then one morning in 1931 people passing the factory noticed that the machines were all gone. The manufacturer, remembering that the residents of the town had put $35,000 into the factory building, had departed quietly during the night. Another coal town lost a grocery chain's large central warehouse, which moved unexpectedly to a town beyond the coal field in order to take advantage of the offer of a free new building and "escape the influence of the trade unions."

After the fiasco of the 1929 land-a-factory adventures coal-town people reconsidered the wisdom of schemes to entice reluctant manufacturers by means of either subsidies or acquiescence in substandard wages.[9] For a period of 10 years, they also lost all their enthusiasm for campaigning; and it was not until late in 1939 that efforts to land outside industry could be formally organized again. The new organization, called "Southern Illinois, Inc.," approaches the problems of the community soberly. It offers no subsidies; it seeks to bring only "sound industries that belong in southern Illinois"; it cautions the people to expect no miracles, for "to assume that success is assured is foolish," and results will only come "if Southern Illinois, Inc., is permitted to carry on a permanent, dogged, persistent, and determined campaign."

The following list of the industries, aside from coal mining, agriculture, and the services, which existed in the three counties in 1935 illustrates how completely the campaigns for industry have failed.[10]

Meat packing, wholesale	3 plants
Nonalcoholic beverages	3 plants
Flour and grain mill products	1 plant
Coke-oven products	1 plant
Saddlery, harness, and whips	1 plant
Concrete products	1 plant
Clay products	1 plant
Wood preserving	1 plant
Explosives	1 plant

The average employment of all these plants, plus a number of bakeries, printing plants, ice and ice-cream factories, was 396 persons. Not one of the factories once campaigned for so ardently appears within the list.

BACK TO THE FARM [11]

Southern Illinois is one of the few areas in the United States in which important coal deposits occur below a prairie-land surface.

[9] In 1936 a significant development was reported in a coal town outside the three counties which were included in this survey. This town had landed a garment factory employing a large number of women. But "trouble started when a woman organizer is said to have been led to the outskirts of the town and told not to return." Whereupon, "unrest at the plant . . . ensued to the point that manufacturers finally told . . . businessmen that the situation would have to be handled or the company would establish elsewhere." A near-by Missouri town promised the garment manufacturer a new building if he would move all of his plants there.

[10] Bureau of the Census, *Industrial Market Data Handbook of the United States*, Domestic Commerce Series No. 107, U. S. Department of Commerce, Washington, D. C., 1939.

[11] Data for this section were obtained from the Census of Agriculture for 1900, 1910, 1920, 1930, and 1935, Bureau of the Census, U. S. Department of Commerce, Washington, D. C.

Unlike the declining coal fields in the cramped Appalachian valleys, southern Illinois thus appeared to offer the possibility of resettling displaced coal miners on the land. But this "solution" also encountered serious difficulties. Although a return to subsistence farming helped to cushion the shock of wholesale mine unemployment, the land offered no real solution to the problems of the coal field.

Farming in the Three Counties Before 1930

In 1900 Franklin, Saline, and Williamson Counties were dependent almost solely upon farming. Under their early agricultural economy the three counties had not prospered. Much of the soil of the southern Illinois prairies was extremely poor. In 1900 the production of corn per acre in Franklin, Saline, and Williamson Counties was less than half that of Corn Belt counties 150 miles to the north. Tax assessors in the three counties put the average value of farm land plus improvements at $3 per acre. Coal promoters who began arriving in southern Illinois around 1902 were impressed with the poor quality of the farm land, and before the existence of coal became generally known, they were able to buy up top and bottom for as little as $10 an acre.[12]

Further, the land had been divided into relatively small plots. Instead of the 160-acre units which prevailed in the rich farm district to the north, the farms in the three counties were principally divided into plots of 80 acres or less. With agriculture in the three counties based upon such small units of poor soil, the size of the farm population in 1900 was close to the maximum which could be supported on the land. Before the large-scale development of coal began, the district was well on its way to becoming what would be called today a "rural problem area."

In 1900 the population of the 3 counties was 69,156 persons, most of whom were directly or indirectly dependent upon 9,130 farm enterprises. With the sudden increase of mine employment during the next decade, population rose rapidly and reached 101,245 in 1910. During this period the mines not only attracted workers from the districts beyond the coal field, but from the unprofitable farms near by as well; local farmers welcomed this chance to escape from poor land. Some of the farm land was absorbed by the growing coal towns, and the consolidation of the great blocks of coal lands had further encouraged the movement off the farms. By 1910 the number of farms operated in the 3 counties had decreased by 1,179, the number of hogs had decreased from 95,917 to 52,018, and 34,529 acres of farm land had been taken out of cultivation.

[12] There is a legend that one of the promoters secured title to a block of farm land—together with the coal—from a widow in exchange for a silk dress.

The wartime coal boom beginning in 1915 accelerated these tendencies. By 1920 the population of the 3 counties had risen to 156,738. Despite high wartime food prices and a tremendous increase in the value of farm products in the three counties, the high mine wages continued to make inroads into farm activity. During the decade ending in 1920 another 873 farms disappeared and another 37,255 acres of farm land were taken out of cultivation.

The beginning of the coal depression in the 1920's failed to stop the farm-to-mine trend. Even as employment in the mines began to fall, the land became no more attractive. By 1930 the number of farms had decreased to 6,746 and during the decade of the 1920's a total of 57,333 acres of farm land in the 3 counties were turned back to scrub-oak forest.

The Depression

After 1930, however, the movement off the land was summarily halted. For the first time in 30 years the miners of Franklin, Saline, and Williamson Counties turned back to the land to take their last stand against privation. The size of farm population increased rapidly. In 1930 the farm population of the 3 counties had been 31,136; by 1935 it had increased to 34,949. The 1935 Census of Agriculture reported, in addition, that 3,834 persons who had not been on farms in 1930 were living on farms in the 3 counties in 1935. These newcomers to farms formed 11.0 percent of the 1935 population in the three counties, as against 6.0 percent for Illinois and 6.3 percent for the United States. Said a local newspaper in 1932:

> Many who were on farms before the fat years of the last decade are willing to return to a surer but perhaps not such a fancy living. . . . We think this is the wise thing to do. Every man and his family, barring sickness, can get by on the farm.

But common sense was not altogether on the side of the back-to-the-land movement. The newspaper which thought that the unemployed would have a "surer living" on the land also made this discovery:

> There are ten prospective renters to one farm in [this] vicinity . . . and there are no farms for rent.

Actually, land was by no means plentiful. Some of the farm land had been ruined by mineral salts in the water pumped from the mines. Some had been ruined by the strip mines, which leave behind a wasteland where not even weeds will grow. The good farm land which occurs in several parts of the three counties was of course already occupied. It was not available to the unemployed, who had no money to buy it; and it could have absorbed additional workers only if the existing small farms were further subdivided.

"Them shovels sure mess this country up."

Strip Mine Near Carterville, Ill.

The idle land presented other difficulties. Much of it was obviously worthless. Many blocks of idle farm land owned by the coal companies were mortgaged to bondholders and could not be sold without involving legal difficulties more costly than the value of the land itself. Coal-company land was nearly always available to renters, but it was peculiarly unadaptable to a tenancy system. Most of the land was so badly run down that it could not be farmed until soil-building crops had been plowed in for several years. Renters who had no assurance that they could hold a plot after it had been improved were naturally reluctant to go to such trouble and expense. Whenever coal-company land was rented, it was usually planted to corn year after year, and the poor land rapidly became more and more sterile.

Those who were able to secure plots of land after 1930 achieved a dubious advantage. Between 1930 and 1935 the number of farm enterprises in the 3 counties increased by 1,518. Of these, 517, or more than one-third, were farms of only 3 to 9 acres; an additional 351 new farms contained 10 to 19 acres; and 430 of them consisted of 20 to 49 acres. Only 220 of the new enterprises contained 50 acres or more. According to local county agents, a farmer in the three counties requires at least 80 acres of land before he can become a self-sufficient producer; less than 80 acres provides only for different levels of subsistence farming. In terms of this standard, approximately nine-tenths of the new depression farms were enterprises on which an independent living was not possible. While many of these subsistence farms raised the living standards of families with income from other sources, they provided no real substitute for declining industrial activity.

The Possibilities for a Return to Farming

Many local businessmen in the coal field insist that the salvation of the community lies in the development of agriculture. In a limited sense there is some truth in this contention. Working miners who have not already begun subsistence farming could frequently improve the family diet and at the same time save on their grocery bills by raising garden products, pigs, cows, and a few chickens. It is also true that if the surface land held by the coal companies could be released, a number of self-sufficient farm enterprises could be created, adding slightly to the productive wealth of the three counties.

But neither of these developments would solve the problems of the workers now dependent upon public assistance. Unemployed families without gardens could improve their condition by raising a part of their own food. But a garden does not provide a living, and the need for relief would still persist. On the other hand, farming on any more ambitious scale—even subsistence farming—requires some capital in the form of buildings, equipment, and stock. Judging from the present hand-to-mouth existence of the unemployed families, there is little possibility that they could take advantage of new land should it be made available.

Those local residents who continue to hope that farming in itself will solve all the problems of the coal field have not studied carefully the predicament of their community. In 1930 the average annual farm income per farm inhabitant in the three counties was $192, far below the average for the United States as a whole, and equal to only one-fourth of the farm income of the more fertile counties in the Corn Belt north of the coal field. Although the productivity of the soil in the three counties can and should be increased by careful management,[13] it does not appear likely that the land can absorb large numbers of additional workers without further impoverishment of the entire rural population.

---

[13] Southern Illinois, Inc., advocates the improvement of local agriculture along these lines:
1. Reduction of waste land.
2. Encouragement of dairy and livestock farming.
3. Revitalization of fruit farming by better marketing.
4. Encouragement of part-time farming for coal miners.

Chapter VII

MIGRATION

SCHEMES FOR turning back the clock of technological change, for creating new jobs in the crannies of the declining coal industry, or for bringing in altogether new industries, would appear to be a roundabout approach to the unemployment problem in southern Illinois. Supposedly, an easier approach—or at least the one that the facts about the coal field always bring first to mind—might be the migration of unemployed workers away from southern Illinois. Theoretically, an unsupported population, left behind in a community where the dominant industry has appreciably declined, should under "normal" conditions make its own automatic adjustment. What could be more natural than that workers no longer needed in one place should move to another place where—theoretically, again—they would be needed?

Unfortunately, so nice an adjustment seldom results from the play of automatic forces even under the most favorable circumstances, let alone in the midst of universal unemployment. Shifting industry ordinarily leaves behind a number of stragglers. Lumbering in the cutover district of the lower Michigan peninsula, for example, began declining as early as 1895. With the automobile industry rising only 200 miles away, with three decades of general prosperity prevailing outside the cutover district, and with all the displacing effects of the World War, the district did indeed lose a substantial part of its population. Despite its losses, however, the district has to this day continued to hold more population than it can support. In a declining community there are those disadvantaged residents who will choose a lower economic status where they are settled in preference to the uncertainties of migration.

In the southern Illinois coal field this disadvantaged and immobile group included most of the population remaining in the community in 1939. It must be remembered that the effects of the Illinois coal depression were first felt in 1923 and have been critical since 1927. If migration were destined to make an automatic adjustment of the

107

coal field's unemployed population, it should have shown tangible results within nearly two decades. There has been, of course, some population movement from the coal field since the decline first began, and among certain age groups the movement has been heavy. But one need only glance at the figures showing present unemployment in the southern Illinois coal towns to judge how inadequate a solution migration has actually provided.

LOCAL FORCES AFFECTING EMIGRATION

It is well known that a people's tendency to migrate depends not only on the pressure of economic adversity, but also upon its chances for betterment elsewhere. In the midst of a general depression, opportunities for finding work outside one's home community are, of course, restricted in the extreme. As general unemployment increases and as the labor demand grows more and more selective, a family's chances of successful migration turn more and more directly upon its characteristics and resources. In Franklin, Saline, and Williamson Counties, the characteristics and circumstances of the people make migration more than ordinarily difficult.

Occupational Experience

The chief occupational problem connected with migration from southern Illinois is that of displaced hand loaders from the mines. Other problems exist, of course. Coal-field youth, for example, in seeking to establish themselves where job opportunities are greater, have doubtless been handicapped by lack of training for any favored occupation. In spite of the advantage of their youth, many of their attempts at emigration have ended in failure and have eventually brought the youth back home again to the depressed area. The disadvantage faced by untrained youth is not peculiar to southern Illinois, however, and need not concern us at this point. The problem of southern Illinois service workers—half of the experienced labor force in the three counties—who fail to find work elsewhere is likewise a general one.

As for the coal miners, their past record of adaptability is often overlooked. There was a time when coal miners were welcome enough in other industries. Before the World War, indeed, miners moved so easily into the Gary, Ind., steel mills that the coal operators had to consider special steps to hold their working force in southern Illinois. Miners point out that the shift from hand loading to machine loading in southern Illinois mines in the late 1920's brought such drastic changes in technical operation that they seemed to have been working in two different industries. Yet, wherever age and physical strength permitted, hand loaders took up their strange new tasks without great difficulty. It is true that miners often find outdoor work distasteful and even unhealthful, since work underground at a constant year-round temperature makes them highly sensitive to the extremes of summer and winter temperatures on top; they accordingly take up farm occupations with some reluctance. But miners would not, as miners, be at any special disadvantage in competing for a variety of jobs for which no long apprenticeship is required.

At the same time, there is no doubt that old-time hand loaders displaced from the mines would face difficult odds if they attempted to find work outside the coal field. Age and isolation both weigh heavily against them. The special skills of hand loaders—drilling, timbering, laying track, the ability to judge a dangerous roof, and other skills so necessary in mining—are generally useless outside the mines and offer no advantage in seeking work elsewhere. And when millions of workers are out of jobs, failure to offer special qualifications becomes a critical factor.

The People

Three main population sources supplied practically all the workers for the growing southern Illinois coal industry. First in importance were the near-by countryfolk, usually farmers and their sons who left submarginal farms for day wages in the coal mines or jobs in the growing coal towns. Among all the family heads residing in the coal towns in 1939, 62 percent were born within the State of Illinois.[1] The great majority of the native Illinois workers were born either in Franklin, Saline, or Williamson Counties or in the other 20 southern Illinois counties which comprise "Egypt." Next in importance were the foreign born—Italians, Poles, Croatians, Ukrainians, Czechs, Lithuanians, Hungarians, etc.—who came in great numbers until the beginning of the World War. Foreign-born workers still comprise 15 percent of the family heads in the southern Illinois coal towns, and in 1930 every fifth person in the three counties was either foreign-born or of foreign-born or mixed parentage. The third great source of labor was the hill country lying south of the "little Egypt" area: Tennessee, Alabama, and particularly western Kentucky, where the migrants had frequently worked in coal mines. Natives of this region made up 13 percent of the family heads living in the coal towns in 1939 (appendix table 26).

---

[1] This distribution is of course affected by the age of the family heads, since the migrants' children who are family heads would in many cases have been born in Illinois. Among the older generation, however, Illinois natives still predominated. Of all family heads 40 years of age or over in 1939, Illinois was the source of 50 percent, foreign countries 20 percent, the western Appalachians 20 percent, and other sources 10 percent.

The nature of these population sources is significant to the general problem of mobility in southern Illinois. Two of the principal groups, the natives of the area itself and the migrants from Kentucky and the western Appalachians, are not a cosmopolitan population, in the first generation at least. In education, dialect, family traits, religion, and numerous folkways, southern Illinois is a clearly defined region, a region homogeneous with the western Appalachians and altogether unlike central and northern Illinois. In spite of the broadening influence of large-scale industry, the miners' union, and the recent popularity of education, the past culture of the region still persists. As far as social patterns are concerned, Chicago and even St. Louis (only 100 miles away) are in another world. The native and the Kentuckian coal miner have social ties in southern Illinois that are powerful indeed. The suggestion that job opportunities might be more plentiful up-State will often bring forth such comments as these: "Well—this country's always been my home"; or "Why my kinfolks are all round about here." In short, most of the older native-born residents of the coal field like their own community best. Opportunity elsewhere must be real opportunity to outweigh their natural desire to stay at home.

The foreign born and their families have no such deep social roots in the community itself. On the contrary, their integration has been traditionally hampered by local prejudice, which is only now disappearing thanks to years of common schooling among the second generations. The foreign group tends to be tied to the coal field by other circumstances, however. Many among the older generation migrated directly from Europe to southern Illinois, and they are as unfamiliar with the country beyond the coal field as the natives themselves. Lacking helpful outside contacts, even with their own nationals in Chicago, their mobility is made extremely difficult by the universal provincial prejudice which makes the "alien" unwelcome in every community where he is not known. Of course these immobilizing forces fall with considerably less burden on the children of the foreign born.

The Settlement of the Coal Towns

Although southern Illinois was first settled nearly 100 years ago, the coal towns themselves are new. Nome and Juneau, Alaska, were grown-up towns when cows still pastured in what are now the business districts of the coal towns. Earlier chapters have pointed out that when the rapid development of Franklin, Saline, and Williamson coal began in 1902, the three counties were poor and isolated farm communities supporting only a fraction of their present population. Herrin and Eldorado had about 1,500 residents each in 1900, and Carrier Mills had nearly 500. Johnston City was a sleepy villlage of about 800. Zeigler and Bush did not exist. West Frankfort, now the largest coal town in southern Illinois, was only a crossroads store. The total population of the 7 selected coal towns was 4,200. After making allowance for changing city limits and adjusting the census figures [2] accordingly, the approximate population increase appears as follows:

1900	4, 200
1910	19, 000
1920	41, 000

The coal boom between 1900 and 1910 thus brought a fourfold increase in coal-town population, and the World War decade more than doubled the 1910 population.

Further increases in the coal-town population continued until 1923, the peak year for employment at the mines.[3] And even after 1923 migrants still moved into the coal towns, though the movement no longer balanced the losses of the population leaving. A special survey of out-of-State family heads living in West Frankfort and Herrin in 1939 showed these proportions entering the coal field during the different periods of its development:

Date of entering Franklin, Saline, and Williamson Counties	Percent of all family heads born outside Illinois
Before 1904	12
1904–1913	29
1914–1918	22
1919–1923	18
1924–1928	8
1929–1939	11

These figures are substantially influenced by mortality among the groups migrating earliest. If these migrants had moved at about the same age and at the same rate during each period, the later groups would show greater representation than the earlier. Migration was thus at its peak between 1904 and 1919; and the movement into the coal field after 1919, while it did exist, dwindled to little significance.

Other things being equal, the population of new communities often tends to be highly mobile in response to economic pressure; and as these figures show, the coal towns are obviously newly settled. One

[2] See Bureau of the Census, *Fourteenth Census of the United States: 1920*, Population Vol. I, U. S. Department of Commerce, Washington, D. C., 1921. The census actually reported population as follows: 4,218; 17,709; and 37,248. Adjustment must be made for Zeigler, which existed in 1910 but was not incorporated. In estimating the 1920 figure, Johnston City and West Frankfort population must be increased by about 4,000 persons to allow for persons in outlying sections which were incorporated into the 2 towns shortly after 1920.

[3] See fig. 17, p. 114. Children of school age in the three counties increased 20 percent between 1920 and 1923.

striking feature of timing in the settlement of the coal field should, however, be noted. The settlers came principally in two waves, the first wave responding to the original coal boom—1904 to 1913—and the second arriving during the World War years. The last wave had been settled about 10 years when the need for emigration first presented itself in the late 1920's. Presumably, the later group, more than the earlier arrivals, would have found emigration a solution to their problems as the mines closed down, and apparently a considerable number of them did indeed move elsewhere in the late 1920's and early 1930's. But a large group of migrants had arrived before 1910, and had been settled for a full generation when the decline started. Within that time most of this earliest group would have grown old and put down social and economic roots making migration extremely difficult.

Money for Moving

As time passed, all these forces retarding emigration were overshadowed by another force even more compelling. During the early stages of the coal depression in the middle of the 1920's, miners thrown out of work were usually able to finance a move and to support themselves in a new community if they found no work immediately. As the depression grew more severe, however, the reserves which might have been used earlier for migration were slowly exhausted. At one time an unemployed miner had numerous ways of scraping together enough money to get out of the coal field: he could mortgage his house or sell the equity he had earned, he could draw his savings out of the bank, he could sell his building-and-loan shares. A few years later most of these nest eggs had vanished. His home was repossessed, his savings either spent for groceries or tied up in defunct banks, his building-and-loan shares worth only so much secondhand lumber.

By 1934 a considerable part of the entire coal field population was no longer able to stay off relief, let alone to travel about the country in search of nonexistent job opportunities. Even the Oklahoma refugee has his secondhand automobile, some money for gas, and the prospect of a job—such as it is—a few hundred miles down the road. But hundreds of southern Illinois families, and the very ones which would presumably gain most from migration, have for years had literally no reserves left for moving.[4] Residence requirements for relief have reinforced this disadvantage.

This factor, again, immobilized families and older workers more directly than youth. Even after 1934 underprivileged coal-field youth without family responsibility could still travel to the North in search of work. Some of the youth found jobs, particularly in the

---

[4] See pp. 51–52.

automobile factories at Flint and Detroit and in the Chicago service industries. But many others hastily returned home to the coal towns when their jobs ended or their money ran out. Youth's only advantage has been greater freedom to search the distant labor markets for work. Obviously, when jobs cannot be found, youth are stranded in the coal towns just as older workers are.

A STRANDED POPULATION

The coal field's unemployed workers have been isolated from more favored labor markets, have had no special occupational advantages when they did seek work elsewhere, have had peculiar social ties to their community, and have long ago exhausted the reserves which might have financed migration. In the face of such difficulties, automatic migration could scarcely have made any great contribution toward solving the coal field's unemployment problem. The result of these frictions is a stranded people. Their story is briefly told in figure 17, which relates the yearly trend in population—as reflected in the Franklin, Saline, and Williamson school census [5]—to the trend in coal-mine employment in the three counties.

Between 1918 and 1923, years which brought to a close the long era of expansion in the southern Illinois coal industry, population change was strikingly responsive to economic change. New jobs in the mines were being created each year, and population flowed into the coal field, keeping pace with the growth of employment. But after 1923 the situation changed rapidly (fig. 17). Even during the years when there was still a chance to find jobs beyond the coal field, Franklin, Saline, and Williamson Counties were already showing the chief characteristic of a stranded area: a decline in employment without a corresponding drop in population.

With the general depression and the drying up of job opportunities outside of southern Illinois, the population of the coal field became increasingly "redundant" in relation to available work. In spite of mass unemployment, the disastrous strike of 1932, and several years of inadequate relief, no great exodus occurred. Between 1929 and 1933 mine employment fell 36 percent, but school-age population in 1933 was only 14 percent less than it had been in 1929.

Even with the beginning of Nation-wide recovery after 1933 the maladjustment in southern Illinois was further increased, though at a somewhat slower pace. The number of miners employed in the three counties in 1938 was 18 percent below the number employed in 1933; the school-age population declined only 6 percent during the

---

[5] Although the annual school census (population aged 6 to 21 years) is not a perfect measure of total population changes, its 1920–1940 trend for the three counties did not differ widely from the total population trend shown in the decennial census itself.

Fig. 17 – POPULATION OF SCHOOL AGE AND MEN EMPLOYED
AT SHIPPING COAL MINES IN FRANKLIN, SALINE,
AND WILLIAMSON COUNTIES, 1918-1938

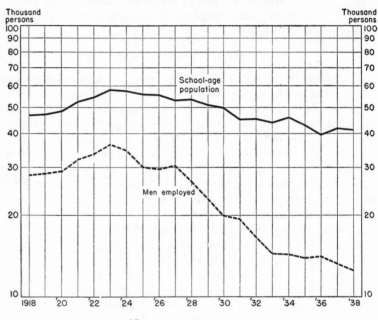

Source: Appendix tables 2 and 27.   WPA 3651

same period. Thus it was that southern Illinois in 1939, after 16 years of this trend, presented the record of long-time unemployment and chronic poverty described earlier in this report.

The Record of Depression Mobility

The school-age population trend shown in figure 17 gives only a general year-by-year picture of population losses in the southern Illinois coal field during the past two decades. Data for a more detailed analysis of significant population changes are provided in the decennial United States Census figures for 1920 and 1930, and in the special 1939 census of population conducted in seven southern Illinois coal towns by the Division of Research, WPA.

There were approximately 41,000 persons living in the 7 coal towns at the time of the 1920 Census. This population, which was still being rapidly increased by migration to the coal field, showed the expected traits of a frontier people. For example, males greatly outnumbered females; there were 111.4 males for every 100 females in the 4 towns for which census data on sex are available,[6] and in individual towns the ratio ran as high as 116.9. An equally remarkable characteristic of the population was its youth. In Herrin (the only town for which age was reported in sufficient detail for computation) the average age of the 1920 population was 22.6 years, as compared with an average of 27.3 years for the State of Illinois as a whole.

Population Changes Between 1920 and 1930

As was noted in the preceding section, the coal-field population continued to increase between 1920 and 1923 and thereafter it began to decline. By 1930, 7 years after the turning point in the fortunes of the southern Illinois mines and 3 years after the critical period set in, the population of the 7 coal towns was still 41,000 persons. Under the most favorable conditions for emigration, the size of the population had thus merely returned to approximately the 1920 level.[7]

The ebb and flow of migration during the decade had brought marked changes in the composition, if not the size, of the population. The sex ratio fell from 111.4 males per 100 females in 1920 to 105.6 in 1930. In part, of course, this change resulted from the natural tendency for births to draw the sex ratio toward 100 over a period of time. But in even greater part, the smaller proportion of males in 1930 appears to have resulted from the emigration of many unattached men, ordinarily the most mobile group in any community, who departed for greener fields as the pressure of unemployment grew more intense. The relative ages of the people changed substantially, too. The average age for Herrin (the one place where comparison is possible) increased from 22.6 years to 26.5 years during the decade. The sudden slowing down of immigration after 1923 had helped to raise the average age, since it checked the influx of younger workers with their children. Moreover, the persons who began to leave the coal towns subsequently were not a cross section of the entire population, but tended to be concentrated in the younger age groups.[8]

---

[6] The four towns were Eldorado, Herrin, Johnston City, and West Frankfort.

[7] Total emigration during the decade was of course somewhat more than was required to cancel immigration, since the natural population increase was likewise canceled. In the 7 towns there were approximately 4,800 births in excess of deaths during the decade.

[8] Migration from Herrin between 1920 and 1930 was greatest for those who were 10 to 14 years old in 1920 (20 to 24 in 1930). Altogether, 37 percent of this group left Herrin during the decade. Migration was least among those 45 years and over in 1920 (55 and over in 1930); this group lost only 17 percent during the decade. These figures are based upon a comparison of expected survivors from the 1920 population with actual residents in 1930.

Population Changes Since 1930

The theoretical desirability of migration from the coal towns was scarcely a debatable question after 1930, when large sections of the people came to realize that the community could no longer support its population. At the same time, the obstacles to migration had become many times more formidable than ever before. If the miners and their sons had good reason for hesitating to try their fortunes outside the mine district before 1930, they had much better reason afterward, even though the local situation had itself become rapidly worse. The choice of the unemployed between migration and staying put after 1930 was accordingly made under excessive pressure from both directions. Under such circumstances, how would a population react?

The most striking fact about the behavior of the coal-town population under these conflicting forces was the small size of its population decrease. The population of the 7 selected coal towns in 1930 had been 41,373 persons. During the next 9 years there were presumably 2,606 births in excess of deaths in the 7 towns.[9] Without any emigration, the expected population of the towns should have been 43,980 persons in 1939. Actually, however, the 1939 population was 38,208 persons. The net emigration from the coal towns was therefore 5,772 persons. Nine years of depression migration thus removed no more than one-eighth of the people from the community. Moreover, because of natural population increase, the actual population loss was considerably less, amounting to only 3,165 persons, about one-thirteenth of the 1930 population.[10] Spontaneous migration from the coal towns since 1930 has not run an altogether one-sided race against natural population increase (fig. 18).

---

[9] This estimate is based on the assumption that the birth and death rates in the seven towns were the same as in the three counties as a whole. The county data are derived from reports of the Illinois Department of Public Health.

[10] This loss (7.6 percent) was unevenly distributed among the seven coal towns. Zeigler and West Frankfort lost heaviest (20.9 and 13.3 percent, respectively), doubtless because of the dismissal of members of the Progressive Miners of America, who were strongest in these two towns, after the 1932 strike. Johnston City, the hardest hit of the larger towns, lost all of its mines after 1930, but only 10.1 percent of its population. Herrin, kept active by its large retail trade, lost 1.0 percent. Eldorado, Carrier Mills, and Bush each actually gained population during the 9 years (3.2, 4.4, and 9.2 percent, respectively). These gains resulted from natural population increase and a small influx of near-by farmers and unemployed and in no way indicate the existence of favored havens within the depressed area. Bush, for example, gained proportionately more population than any other of the seven towns. Yet 80 percent of Bush's gainful workers were unemployed in 1939!

Between 1930 and 1940, the three counties lost 6.6 percent of their population; Franklin County losses were 13.3 percent and Williamson lost 4.2 percent. Saline County actually gained 0.9 percent during the decade.

Fig. 18 – GAIN OR LOSS IN POPULATION OF 7 SOUTHERN ILLINOIS
COAL TOWNS, 1930-1939

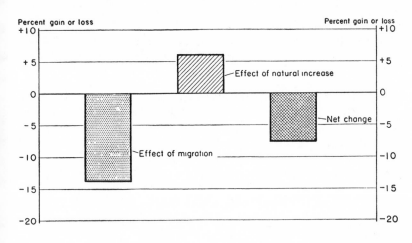

WPA 3652

Changes in age composition of the population during the 9-year
period were especially striking. In 1930 persons 45 years of age and
over constituted 20 percent of the total population in the coal towns
studied. In 1939, however, the proportion had risen to 28 percent.
The average age of the population increased similarly, from 26.9 years
in 1930 to 29.2 years in 1939, substantially above the 1930 average
for both Illinois and the United States as a whole. In the space of
less than one full generation, the coal-town population had passed
from a relatively youthful composition to a relatively aged one.[11]

So rapid an evolution in age composition between 1930 and 1939
resulted from three forces. One of these was natural aging. In 1920
the coal towns, still newly settled communities, were heavily weighted
with young couples who had recently migrated to the booming coal
field. As the boom subsided, the influx of young people was halted.
In the course of 20 years these persons have of course grown old,
filling the once thin ranks of the older age groups. The second influence was a drop in the number of births, following from a decrease in
the number of women of childbearing age and from a decrease in the
reproduction rate itself. Finally, depression migration reduced the
number of young, mobile persons faster than the number of older
persons in the population.

---

[11] In Herrin, the one town for which 1920 figures are available, the proportion
of persons 45 and over was as follows: 1920, 13 percent; 1930, 21 percent; 1939,
29 percent.

Age Differentials in Migration

The influence of these three forces may be partially disentangled when the effect of migration on the different age groups is isolated; that is, after calculating the number of 1930 residents expected to survive to 1939 and comparing the result with the actual 1939 population.[12] The results of this method, as presented in figure 19, show a wide variation in mobility according to age.

Fig. 19- GAIN OR LOSS IN POPULATION ATTRIBUTABLE TO MIGRATION, BY AGE GROUP, 5*SOUTHERN ILLINOIS COAL TOWNS, 1930-1939

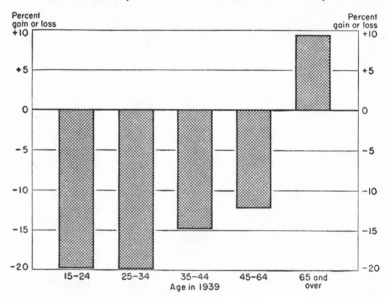

*1930 data for Bush and Carrier Mills are not available.

WPA 3653

[12] To ascertain the proportion of the 1930 coal-town population groups which would survive to the 1939 census, it is necessary to apply survival rates to the 1930 population. From United States life tables it is possible to obtain the proportion of persons at any one age who are expected to be alive at any specified later age. Thus, out of 1,000 white males born, 905 are alive at age 10–14, and 885 at age 19–24, according to 1930 mortality experience in the United States. The ratio of these numbers is .98. This is the "survival ratio" of white males aged 10–14 over a period of 9 years. Similar ratios were calculated for the other age-sex groups.

These ratios then permit an estimate of the number of persons surviving to 1939 from the 1930 population. The estimated survivors, in turn, may be compared with the number of persons enumerated in the WPA survey of the labor market in four cities (see footnote 2, p. 26) to determine the influence of mobility, Thus, if 3,000 persons aged 20–24 were expected to survive, and only 2,400 persons were actually enumerated, the population loss through migration for the age group would be estimated at 20 percent.

After 1930 migration clearly offered special possibilities to coal-field youth. On the one hand, their economic status in the coal field was less favored than that of any other age group of able-bodied workers. Most of the young workers reached maturity after the expansion of mine employment had stopped, and they had no prospect of finding jobs in the mines until the great surplus of experienced jobless miners had been eliminated.[13] At the same time, they were in a better position to risk the hazards of migration; they had in many cases no family responsibilities, and they could be more easily trained to fit the job requirements of distant employers. In addition, the youth alone had access to the Army, the Navy, and the CCC, each of which stimulates migration. The older workers, on the other hand, held whatever mining jobs were available, and hence were as a group less severely stricken by unemployment. Those older workers who were unemployed stood little chance of successful migration because of their age and their training in a semiobsolete occupation.

Accordingly, youth migrated most readily. Every fifth person between the ages of 6 and 25 years in 1930 (15 to 34 in 1939) had left the coal towns without being replaced by incoming population in the same age group.[14] The persons who were 26 to 35 years old in 1930 migrated somewhat less readily, and in the next older group, migration took less of a toll still. The number of those who were 56 and over in 1930 (65 and over in 1939) actually increased as a result of migration during the 9-year period (fig. 19).

Birth-Rate Changes

It is impossible to derive migration estimates for children whose ranks were filled by births after the 1930 Census. It is known, however, that the absolute number of persons under 15 years of age declined 29 percent during the 9-year period. There is little doubt that a considerable part of this decrease resulted from emigration. But emigration was not the only cause.

Through aging and emigration, the number of women of child-bearing age (20 to 44 years) declined somewhat after 1930,[15] reducing

---

[13] See pp. 34, 41.

[14] The emigration of the younger persons during the 9-year period was particularly heavy in Johnston City, West Frankfort, and Zeigler. Zeigler lost through migration 51 percent of its male population aged 20–24 in 1939, and 41 percent of its females in the same age group. In the group aged 25–29 years in 1939, Johnston City lost 50 percent of its males and 38 percent of its females. West Frankfort lost through emigration 32 percent of both males and females aged 20–29 in 1939.

[15] There were 7,473 females aged 20–44 in the 5 larger coal towns in 1930. By 1939 the number had declined to 6,766, a drop of 9 percent.

the number of persons born within the coal towns. More important, the reproduction rate among the women who remained fell off noticeably between 1930 and 1939. In 1930 the ratio of children under 5 years of age to each 1,000 women aged 20–44 in the 5 larger coal towns was 443, exactly that required to hold the population size stationary if local death rates were equal to the average United States rates. By 1939, however, the reproduction ratio had fallen to 385 children under 5 years of age per 1,000 women of childbearing age. Should reproduction persist at the decreased rate, the first full generation maturing after the decline began would suffer a natural decrease of 13 percent.[16]

PROSPECTS FOR FUTURE MIGRATION

The various local frictions which hinder migration from southern Illinois would ordinarily tend to become stronger, rather than more relaxed, as time passes. Emigration in the late 1920's was probably made easier by the fact that one considerable part of the coal-town population was made up of newcomers who had been settled only a few years when unemployment first became serious in 1927. By 1939, however, even this last wave of settlers had lived for at least 20 years in the coal field, and the earlier wave had been settled for upwards of 30 years. Now that the coal towns are no longer new towns, mobility is not so easy. The aging of the unemployed workers also decreases the chances of migration; if displaced hand loaders were occupationally handicapped 10 years ago, their handicap has been multiplied now that they are 10 years older. Likewise, year after year of continued depression would have reduced whatever reserve resources the unemployed might—by some miracle of good management—have kept intact.

Above all, it is probable that those unemployed who had the greatest likelihood of successful migration would have been the first to leave the coal field, in a static depressed situation migration would naturally be expected to decline over a period of time. If relatives in Chicago, or a friend in Detroit, or a former employer in Moline were interested in helping a family leave southern Illinois, they would probably have done so within the past 12 years, or not at all. Similarly, surplus workers whose skills would be in demand elsewhere would be expected to migrate shortly after their predicament became clear, or not at all. Only two groups would appear to be an exception to this tendency: those who may in the future be thrown out of work for the first time, and unemployed youth coming of working age. As for the rest of the distressed population, an unemployed coal miner's comment well

---

[16] See *Population Statistics, 1. National Data,* National Resources Committee, Washington, D. C., 1937, p. 50, for data on reproduction ratios calculated to maintain a stationary population without migration.

describes their plight: "Everybody that was able to get out left a long time ago."

Putting together two facts—first, that emigration throughout more than a decade of intense distress has not appreciably reduced the total population of the coal towns, even though the early years of this period coincided with the last years of Nation-wide "prosperity"; and second, that emigration hereafter is likely to be more difficult than in the past—we may infer that expected migration will hardly solve the problems of the southern Illinois coal field, in the near future at least. This judgment must of course be qualified to allow for a possible employment boom beyond the coal field. A Nation-wide labor shortage would assuredly draw off many of the youth and the surplus middle-aged workers, and might indeed end unemployment in southern Illinois.[17] But pending such a development, the coal field's surplus workers are in large part likely to stay where they are.

Over a long stretch of time, the readjustment of coal-field population to economic opportunity is somewhat more probable. It is true that at present births outnumber deaths in Franklin, Saline, and Williamson Counties and this relationship may be expected to continue for some time to come. Since 1930, however, the birth rate has fallen sharply, and in several generations the resulting population decline will have become appreciable. The continued emigration of youth will make substantial inroads in population size over a period of time, and will at the same time further reduce the number of births. In the long run the problem might largely solve itself. But as J. M. Keynes has said, "In the long run we shall all be dead."

---

[17] Since this was written, there has been an increase in the emigration of young southern Illinois workers to defense centers. Meantime, however, the War Department has announced plans to construct a huge ordnance plant near Herrin. It is said that the plant will employ 6,000 workers by 1943. If the British experience means anything, the opening of these jobs will bring a large number of former residents back to the coal field, where they will run considerable risk of being stranded again when the emergency has passed.

Chapter VIII

RELIEF

DEPRESSED AREAS represent a tremendous loss to the national economy. In terms of wasted man power, of depressed living standards, of bleak and hopeless lives, the incalculable costs mount year after year. There are also not insignificant costs in terms of public expenditures. The depression of the southern Illinois coal field has led to an extraordinary expenditure for public assistance. For the past 4 years an average of well over one-third of the entire population in Franklin, Saline, and Williamson Counties has been on the rolls of the various public-welfare programs, and twice the proportion rose to one-half. Between 1933 and the middle of 1939 the cost of relief had run to a sum equal to more than half the assessed valuation of the property in the coal field—mines, railroads, farms, and town real estate combined.

At the beginning of the depression the local coal-field communities attempted to meet their relief needs on a purely local basis. But before very many months had passed, relief costs had exhausted all the available resources, both public and private, within the communities; and still the people were hungry. Some time later the State of Illinois took over partial responsibility for meeting the coal field's relief needs; but it too was prepared to carry no more than a small part of the full burden, at least not without slighting the needy in other sections of the State. An adequate recognition of the urgency and extent of the relief problem in the coal counties came only with the beginning of Federal aid. Today, with the Federal Government still furnishing the greater part of the funds for relief in the stranded area, the problem is of concern not only to the residents of the coal field itself, but to the country at large.

TRADITIONS IN LOCAL RELIEF

Franklin, Saline, and Williamson Counties have been familiar with both chronic and recurrent poverty from the earliest development of

123

the coal mines. In a community dominated so completely by a single fluctuating and hazardous industry, the position of the working population was never secure. Strikes and suspensions at the mines have been recurrent, and the shadow of destitution during the long slumps in the coal market were an inescapable part of every miner's experience. Mine accidents took a heavy toll in dead and injured each year, leaving widows and crippled workers without means of support. Even in the best days of the coal boom, the regular quotas of the aged, widows, and the blind without families to support them was a continuing problem.

For nearly 30 years the responsibility for giving help to the unfortunate was distributed in the community according to a long-standing tradition. The local unions, for example, took the misfortunes of the working miners as their particular province. When a miner was killed, other miners gave money to help his family, knowing well that their own family might be the next to be stricken. Or if a miner was sick or injured, the union locals helped him until he recovered. For many years the heavy cost of mine accidents fell entirely upon the locals, and even after the union forced an accident compensation law through the Illinois Legislature, the miners were still called upon from time to time to help other unfortunate miners. The job of providing relief during strikes was largely a responsibility of the locals, sometimes borne in part by contributions from the district and international union. The locals were also expected to contribute heavily to the sentimental charities organized on occasion by the local booster clubs; and they were the mainstay of the drives to raise money for such special emergencies as relief of victims of the tornado which swept across the coal field in 1925.

The great absentee coal operators naturally took little interest in these special difficulties of the coal towns. Their attitude toward the unemployment of miners had been clearly stated in 1914 when an operator, in answer to a request from the Governor of Illinois that he do something to "relieve the suffering" of the unemployed, announced: "We are selling no coal and therefore to operate the mines would be a dead loss. We can do nothing until . . . people begin to buy coal." In later years a few of the local operators made some effort to help a dozen or so workers who were out of jobs, and a few would sometimes donate coal to the needy. But for all practical purposes, the operators contributed nothing except their taxes.

The small businessmen in the community played an important but frequently forgotten role in relieving the strains of the predepression era. Connected closely with the miners through family and personal ties and at the same time dependent upon the miners' good will for their trade, the little merchants were obligated to carry the miners through recurrent shutdowns and strikes. When the mines reopened these debts were repaid—unless the miners in debt lost their jobs, in which case the merchants, of course, lost heavily. Other businessmen confined their charity to passing out Christmas baskets to "deserving" families, to donating coal, and to assisting in other standard civic-club activities.

Pauper-Relief Standards

Theoretically, townships and counties carried the responsibility for the rest of the community's relief needs. The basic temporary relief throughout Illinois was township pauper relief, administered by an elected official in each township. The philosophy behind township relief was that only the "worthy" deserved charity, and that even so, help should never be given until a family was utterly destitute. As elsewhere in the United States, the able-bodied unemployed were considered to be outside its scope. Township relief was administered in such a way as to attach the maximum of shame and degradation to the recipients,[1] so that families hesitated to "go on the town" until they had sunk below the point of caring about local attitudes. Expenditures for town relief thus stayed at a bare minimum.

The county governments carried on several relief activities. A county pauper fund, administered according to the same low standards that governed township relief, was used to supplement the funds available to the township supervisors. About the time of the World War the three counties set up what appears to have been, all things considered, a remarkably advanced system of aid to the blind, providing $30 a month to recipients. A mothers' "pension" system, introduced at about the same time, was supposed to take care of widows with children, but the funds provided were so limited and the standards so low that the system was not of great benefit. Some idea of how the system operated may be gathered from the following 1927 report of the Williamson probation officer:

> There has been a big demand for help from the [Mothers' Pension] Fund. The larger number of these requests have been from mothers who are absolutely up against it. . . . During the past quarter there have been 20 applicants for the pension; of this number it has been necessary to add 6 to the list. . . . Of the number refused, 5 have been grandmothers . . . The law states that the pension is for the natural mother. Three have been refused because of their characters. . . . The additional 6 were refused help as they had sufficient income.
>
> Conditions as a whole show the pensioners are trying to overcome whatever handicaps they have been placed under. While the attitude of a few is not the best, as a group they are appreciative. The probation officer regrets that there have been as many additions necessary as have been made.

In spite of its high-sounding name, the mothers' pension was only another form of pauper relief.

---

[1] The law required that the names of all recipients should be published every 3 months.

Finally, the counties were responsible for maintaining the poor farms. These primitive institutions were designed mainly for the care of the aged and disabled without families, although it is on record that at one time the Saline County poor farm had inmates as young as 14, while in Williamson County all applicants for pauper relief were once sent to the poor farm. Whether under the care of contractors or of county employees, poor farms were an admitted disgrace to the community—but a disgrace that no one seemed particularly anxious to remove. Indeed, whenever county officials became alarmed over increasing deficits, their first thought was to cut down on the food allowed the inmates at the poor farm.

The county supervisors' records abound with such reports as these:

> We visited said poor farm July 1 and found the building in very bad shape, doors broke, plastering falling off, stair way post broken out, brick missing in walls. Patients were in very good shape except one very old gentleman . . . whose bed was not as it should be—he being paralyzed, the flies tormenting him almost to death.

In 1 county the supervisors discovered on an annual visit that 13 inmates were sleeping in 1 room; whereupon it was recommended that "inmates that are sick and broken out with sores be removed and separated from the others whose condition is better." No real improvements were made, however. Years later the supervisors again became alarmed, declaring that "the condition of the buildings on the County Farm . . . is such that proper care cannot be given . . . and is a discredit to the citizens of this County." But as late as 1930 a State inspector reported finding:

> . . . a good jail and a home for the dependent aged that is a disgrace to the county. There is no plumbing in the buildings and no bathing facilities. Heating and water systems are both inadequate . . . no fire extinguishers . . . bedding and mattresses worn out . . . . Inmates are given barely enough food to exist on. In addition, the food is of poor quality and poorly prepared. . . . When one of the aged residents dies he is buried on the farm with no marker for his grave. This might be expected in an institution where so little respect is shown for the living.

Predepression standards of poor relief in the coal field were not particularly high.

Predepression Relief Expenditures

It is not possible to discover how much money was actually spent for relief by the local unions in the predepression years, although it is clear that the total must have been considerable. During the 1927 strike alone the locals spent at least $50,000 for "bean orders," and apparently their regular relief expenditures over a period of time were sizable. It is likewise difficult to learn much in detail about the extent of private charity. It appears, however, to have been insignificant except for the charity represented by bad debts on grocers' ledgers. Pauper relief, aid to the blind, and mothers' pensions in the townships and counties, on the other hand, have left sufficient record to permit reasonably reliable estimates of their extent and significance in the last years of the 1920's (appendix table 28).

Aid to the blind, which was administered according to relatively high standards [2] in the coal field, makes a useful basis for judging the full program of public assistance provided by the three counties. Ordinarily, aid to the blind should be one of the least costly parts of a well-rounded program of public assistance, for the simple reason that the incidence of blindness is low compared with the incidence of economic difficulties. Between 1925 and 1929, however, aid to the blind made up an obviously disproportionate part of the total assistance expenditures of the southern Illinois townships and counties; over the entire 5-year period payments to blind pensioners amounted to 36 percent of all public-assistance costs. The blind received roughly double the relief granted to mothers during the period, and about three-fourths of the total cost of both the poor farms and outdoor pauper relief.

Of course, the first part of this period overlapped the last years of the coal boom, when the need for pauper relief was not extraordinary. But in the last part of the 5-year period unemployment had become increasingly severe in the coal field. During these years the disproportion between aid to the blind and the other forms of relief actually increased. In 1929, when the great coal depression in southern Illinois had reached an advanced stage, exactly half of the public-assistance expenditures went for aid to the blind, while the other half was divided among mothers' aid, outdoor pauper relief, and the poor farms. The unemployed, in short, were not provided for in the philosophy that governed pauper relief; and as their numbers increased, they were expected to look elsewhere for assistance.

Actually, the township and county officials were clearly unable to provide unemployment relief, aside from all considerations of their attitude toward assistance. Even to carry on under the traditional system became a more and more difficult task after 1927. By 1930 the counties were petitioning the State to relieve them of mothers' pensions and aid to the blind; when their request was rejected, they began to pay recipients on these programs in more or less worthless county warrants. In the face of the deepening crisis at the coal mines, the local governments were utterly helpless. During the entire 5-year period, 1925–1929, the townships and counties had been hard pressed to raise $229,000 for pauper relief. Had they been required to carry the cost of relief during the depression, they would

---

[2] The word "relatively" bears emphasis. The Williamson supervisors in 1929 referred to the payment to blind pensioners—$1 a day—as a "paltry sum"; and one could scarcely quarrel with this judgment.

have had to raise more than 100 times this sum for the period 1933–1937. The total amount spent for pauper aid from 1925 through 1929 would have lasted exactly 8 days at the peak of the relief load in the coal field during the summer of 1938.

THE DARK DAYS

The history of relief in the coal field after 1929 follows, on an intensified scale, the well-known pattern that prevailed in nearly every community in the United States, except that every difficulty was multiplied manyfold. For a period of about 4 years at the beginning of the depression (1929 to 1933), the unemployed in southern Illinois had practically no real assistance from any quarter. The townships and counties were paralyzed financially, and could extend only the most meager assistance or none at all. In 1931 the township tax levies for the poor were either used up immediately (as in most of the Saline townships where tax anticipation warrants were still salable) or else yielded no return worth mentioning. The State of Illinois was not prepared—on the basis of either philosophy or funds—to take upon itself responsibilities that had been the special province of the smaller governing units for nearly 100 years. The union locals at the abandoned mines had exhausted their treasuries within a few months after the layoff, and were unable to give further aid to their members. Still the people were being reduced to dire want, and something had to be done.

Early in the crisis the coal towns attempted to meet the needs of the unemployed with community chest drives. One town in Saline County started a drive to raise $8,000 late in 1930, announcing that the greater part of the money collected would be used for direct relief to the "deserving" needy. The money for this purpose was to be raised by contributions of 1 day's pay from businessmen and the active mine locals. Another Saline coal town had a more ingenious plan:

> [We] will raise a community fund by donations and by public events, such as a charity basketball game between high school and alumni players, and by finding employment for all that can be placed in various industries.

In another town a community fund was started with money donated by the union locals. In still another, the drive was led by the Church Benevolent Association, which collected money, clothes, and coal for distribution and started a woodyard in which relief workers were given the value of all wood sold. The Associated Charities in another town opened a commissary in a vacant store for distributing clothes and groceries to the unemployed.

These organizations were hopelessly snowed under in a very short time. The drive to collect 1 day's pay brought in about one-third of the quota in both 1930 and 1931, netting about $2,500 each year for the care of 300 to 400 destitute families. The Associated Charities in a second town had almost no money at all; late in 1930 it had $26 to spread among 42 families, and it was eventually reduced to paying 20 cents a week to families in extraordinary need. After the failure of its 1931 drive another town announced hopelessly:

> The funds cannot be stretched to the necessary point. . . . After close calculation the board decided the minimum it would take to provide for the needy. . . . To date the board has one-fourth that amount. . . . The board is at a loss to know what to do.

Early in 1931 the State of Illinois stepped into the relief picture in an unusual way. The Governor of Illinois had conceived the idea of collecting unemployment-relief money by soliciting a day's pay each month from all the employees on the State pay roll. In the course of a year a total of $183,000 was raised in this manner for distribution throughout the entire State of Illinois. Out of this sum Franklin, Saline, and Williamson Counties were allotted $25,000 to be distributed to the needy through the various community funds in the coal towns, and through the American Legion, the Knights of Columbus, the Elks, and other organizations specified by the State employees. But these reinforcements from outside the coal field were scarcely sufficient to allow the community funds to hold their own; for as the depression deepened, contributions from the mine locals and other groups within the coal towns dwindled rapidly.

The relief given out by the community funds usually stopped at the city limits of the larger coal towns. In the smaller mine camps and company towns a periodic dole of Red Cross flour was practically the only relief available, and these communities quickly found themselves in extremely desperate circumstances. The American Society of Friends, after making a survey of these districts in 1931, agreed to set up kitchens at the semirural schools in order to provide undernourished miners' children with a least one good meal a day. Twelve Quaker school kitchens were opened in the outlying mine towns in Williamson County and in a few months the program was extended to Franklin and Saline Counties. Theoretically, the rest of the needs in the semirural mining communities was supposed to be carried by township pauper relief, although everyone knew that there was no pauper-relief money.

In the early spring of 1932 relief committees described their predicament in these terms:

Franklin County—

> Practically all local public and private resources are exhausted. . . . The contributions of State employees are nearly at an end. The investigation indicates that help must be provided from outside the County in order to provide a minimum of subsistence. . . .

Saline County—

> There are 13 townships in this County and distress is reported from each one of them. Local resources in each township are practically exhausted. . . . Local agencies are bankrupt.

Williamson County—

> There is the possibility in three [out of 12] townships of raising a little further money from township taxes. Voluntary funds in the County are completely exhausted.· . . . The American Friends Service Committee is very anxious to withdraw. . . . The American Red Cross states that it cannot continue supplying funds. . . . [3]

The Illinois General Assembly eventually recognized that the $200,000 a year provided by the Governor's semiofficial unemployment fund was not adequate for the problem at hand. On February 6, 1932, the General Assembly set up the Illinois Emergency Relief Commission and appropriated 20 million dollars for relief.[4] Of the 10 million dollars made available to the IERC at once, 96 percent was allocated to Cook County. Six weeks later, after frantic telegrams from the southern Illinois coal field, the IERC allocated funds for 2 months' needs to Franklin, Saline, and Williamson Counties— to the amount of $31,800. With this grant the IERC continued to insist "strongly" that the counties and townships should realize the "necessity" for using local funds "both public and private" instead of coming to the State for money. But the time had come when this advice no longer had much meaning to the coal field. By the end of 1932 the townships were able to carry only 10 percent of the relief cost, while private charity paid for 13 percent; the IERC carried the rest.[5] During the following year the local contribution declined to almost zero.

---

[3] *First Interim Report*, Illinois Emergency Relief Commission, Chicago, April 15, 1932, pp. 14–15, 29–30, 33.

[4] See Glick, Frank Z., *The Illinois Emergency Relief Commission*, University of Chicago Press, Chicago, 1940.

Glick gives an excellent account (p. 26) of the stormy sessions of the Assembly during the weeks when the bill to create the IERC was under debate. At one point in the House the bill failed to receive the two-thirds majority necessary to make the measure immediately effective. Whereupon the Speaker of the House "broke his own policy of not speaking to a measure," and said:

"There is grave danger now. The Federal Government has already issued the orders necessary to curb disorder if it arises. . . . The armories are under guard now."

Later in the day the two-thirds majority was mustered. Several downstate members changed their votes, with such statements as:

"There isn't going to be any blood on my hands tonight. I'm going to vote for this bill and sleep with a clear conscience. This is war. This is hell."

"If I am facing political death, let me die doing the right thing."

[5] *First Annual Report*, Illinois Emergency Relief Commission, Chicago, 1933, p. 128. In other downstate counties local contribution carried 61 percent of the cost of unemployment relief in this period.

Even with State help—and with Federal Reconstruction Finance Corporation help shortly afterward—the local authorities were hard-pressed to keep the relief system intact. After the first IERC grant in April 1932, the Franklin County committees were still able to pay families only $2 a week (in commodities), and in the town of Benton relief families got $1.38. Standards in Williamson County were apparently no better. In Saline, the county committee was able to give the largest families $1.48 a week, and in May 1932 the expenditure was cut to 76 cents. In December 1932 the three counties were paying families on relief as follows: Franklin County, $1.57 a week; Saline County, $1.73 a week; and Williamson County, $1.67 a week.[6] By December 1933 the average weekly relief for families had risen to only $2.74. Not until the summer of 1934, with the beginning of the Emergency Work Relief Program under the FERA, did the weekly relief income of families rise as high as $5 per week in the coal field.

How the unemployed survived the dark days between the layoff and the beginning of adequate relief in 1934 is something of a mystery. The hardships of every American community during this period are a familiar story; in the coal field—where the depression started earlier and ran a more virulent course—these hardships were multiplied many-fold.[7] The Red Cross flour distribution and the Quakers' school-lunch program, meager as they were, came to have tremendous importance as a last bulwark against hunger. At a parochial school in 1 town, undernourishment was so extreme that when a kitchen was opened to provide 1 solid meal a day, 150 children gained an average of nearly 2 pounds each within 1 month. The IERC warned in 1933 that the inadequate relief prevailing throughout most of little Egypt "is bringing on an increase in respiratory diseases and nervous conditions." The Commission testified further that the eventual cost of medical care for the undernourished "will no doubt be many, many times greater than the cost of sufficient food." [8] In a survey of relief needs in Saline County in 1933 it was discovered that at least 50 homeless men had been sleeping in the open fields for months. In Franklin County deaths from exposure and starvation were reported.[9]

[6] *Ibid.*, p. 55. This was the period of the famous 1932 coal strike. The strikers' relief needs placed a particularly heavy strain upon the inadequately financed relief system in the coal field.

[7] Franklin County reported a higher rate of unemployment in the 1930 Census than any other county in the United States. Williamson and Saline Counties were not far behind.

[8] *First Annual Report*, Illinois Emergency Relief Commission. p. 62.

[9] Walker, Wilma, "Distress in a Southern Illinois County," *The Social Service Review*, Vol. 5, No. 4, December 1931, pp. 558–581. The author of this article concluded: "One shudders . . . at the thought of [the coming] winter and no food in a community where their own resources are absolutely drained." Yet, *2 more years* were to pass before adequate outside aid was provided.

In the face of this predicament families adopted a variety of desperate measures either to keep off relief (the stigma attached to "paupers" was still strong as late as 1934) or to supplement the relief they received. The coal-town newspapers for the period reveal the community's constant preoccupation with the job of securing food— "not delicacies," it was explained, "but hardy food such as flour and beans." Defunct-mine locals busied themselves with setting up commissaries and soup kitchens, stocked by small contributions from the active locals or with partly spoiled food collected about town. Gardening, which had been somewhat neglected during the coal boom, became one of the most important pursuits in the communities where idle land was available; and indeed, home-grown vegetables kept many a family from going hungry. Several communities, reduced eventually to foraging for food, sent expeditions to the farm districts north of the coal field to beg something to eat.

These years of inadequate relief resulted not only in immediate suffering, but also in the destruction of the last reserves of a large part of the working population. Miners who still had credit at the neighborhood stores continued to run up bills as long as possible—with the result that scores of little businessmen were wrecked by accumulated bad debts, and credit ceased to exist. Even after the collapse of the banks and building and loan associations, most of the families had a few possessions which could be sacrificed in the emergency. Some had houses to sell, money in the postal savings, automobiles, radios, or a few odd pieces of furniture. Piece by piece this property disappeared. When their possessions were gone, the families started tightening their belts and foregoing the things they had always thought of as necessities. "Doubling up" began, on houses, on parts of houses, on electric lights, on water. Or the lights were disconnected and the old kerosene lamps brought out, water was shut off and leaky wells put back into service. More often than not this retreat led at last to the relief rolls, but only after the families had been pauperized.

The communities' relief needs after 1933 accordingly increased out of proportion to the further increases in unemployment. Meanwhile, the coal field gradually settled down to the realization that the siege of unemployment would not be lifted for years to come. With this realization, the old emergency-relief payments, designed to fill a family's stomachs with beans and bread for a month or so, could no longer be justified. The time had come for changes which both the local community and the State itself were helpless to initiate.

PUBLIC ASSISTANCE AFTER 1933

The story of relief in Franklin, Saline, and Williamson Counties after 1933, traced in figures 20, 21, and 22, is in brief a story of progressively increasing need and increasing case load.

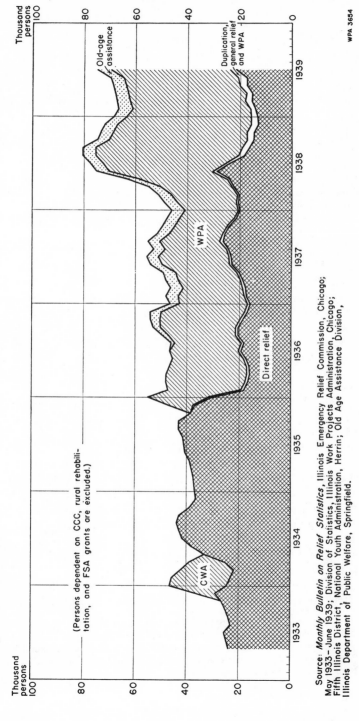

Fig. 20—PERSONS DEPENDENT ON PUBLIC ASSISTANCE IN FRANKLIN, SALINE, AND WILLIAMSON COUNTIES
April 1933 – June 1939

Source: *Monthly Bulletin on Relief Statistics,* Illinois Emergency Relief Commission, Chicago;
May 1933 – June 1939; Division of Statistics, Illinois Work Projects Administration, Chicago;
Fifth Illinois District, National Youth Administration, Herrin; Old Age Assistance Division,
Illinois Department of Public Welfare, Springfield.

Extent of Dependency

The close of the era of the dole late in 1933 found about 25,000 persons dependent upon direct relief in the 3 counties (fig. 20). With the initiation of the Civil Works Administration late in the year, dependent persons increased rapidly to 44,000. The CWA absorbed about as many needy workers from outside the direct-relief rolls as from the rolls themselves; and when the CWA was liquidated, a large number of newly assigned CWA workers applied for direct and work relief on the FERA program. With Federal aid supporting the coal field's relief system, the number of needy persons under care in the 3 counties stood at the 40,000 mark in June 1934, and the distress described in the preceding section was considerably relieved.

The June 1934 relief load included more than one-fourth of all the residents of the three counties,[10] indicating a relief problem of crisis proportions. As time passed, dependency on relief in the coal field rose steadily above this mark. By the end of 1935 every third resident of the coal field was dependent on public assistance; and late in 1936 the proportion rose again, to 36 percent. In the summer of 1937, with Nation-wide industrial production at the highest point since 1929, relief intensity in the coal field rose to still another record. A year later (July 1938), when the coal field's assistance load reached its greatest peak, 54 percent of the people in the three counties were dependent on either direct relief, WPA, or old-age assistance for their living (fig. 21).

Not only the relief-load peaks, but the wintertime troughs [11] as well, were rising throughout this period. The lowest relief intensity in the winter of 1933–34 was 18 percent of the total population of the three counties, but the following winter the relief load did not fall below 24 percent. During the next 3 years the winter load rose steadily, so that more than 30 percent of the population was still dependent on public assistance at the lowest point during the winter of 1937–38. In the winter of 1938–39 the proportion of the total population dependent on public assistance did not fall below 44 percent during any month. Those who still required aid at the year's peak of mine activity had expanded over a period of 6 years to include a substantial part of the entire population of the coal field.

The growth of the relief load in the three counties after 1933 did not reflect immediate changes in mine employment (although the number

---

[10] In computing the population base, actual population change between 1930 and 1940 was distributed evenly throughout the decade.

[11] The most active employment season in Franklin, Saline, and Williamson Counties comes between October and March, when the demand for coal is greatest. Midsummer is the dullest season.

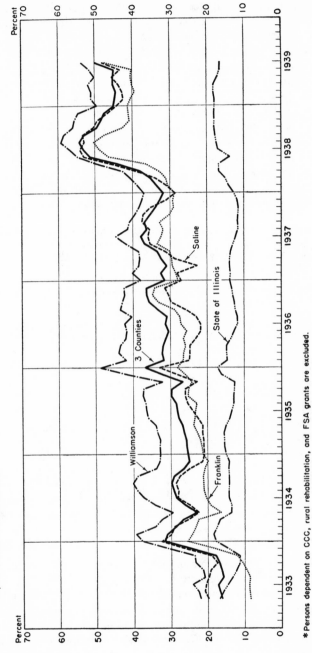

Fig. 21 – PERCENT OF POPULATION DEPENDENT ON PUBLIC ASSISTANCE* IN FRANKLIN, SALINE, AND WILLIAMSON COUNTIES AND IN ILLINOIS

April 1933 – June 1939

* Persons dependent on CCC, rural rehabilitation, and FSA grants are excluded.

Note: Population changes 1930–1940 have been distributed.

Source: See fig. 20.

WPA 3655

of working miners did decrease during this period) so much as the cumulative effects of the slow exhaustion of the community's last reserves. Between 1926 and 1932 the annual pay roll of the coal mines fell 80 percent. Yet it was not until after 1933 that the relief load began to shown an appreciable increase. Years of trying to live on insufficient income had brought a large part of the population to the threshold of relief, and the least economic adversity—or even the continued delay of "recovery"—brought a new quota of exhausted and needy families to the relief rolls. Thus it was that 1933 and 1938 were both 8-million-dollar pay-roll years at the coal mines; yet the number of persons dependent on relief in 1938 was nearly triple the number in 1933. The dark days of inadequate relief had sown a harvest which subsequent assistance programs were to reap in full measure. (See appendix table 29 and fig. 22.)

Fig. 22—ESTIMATED ANNUAL COAL-MINE PAY ROLL AND ANNUAL EXPENDITURES FOR PUBLIC ASSISTANCE IN FRANKLIN, SALINE, AND WILLIAMSON COUNTIES, 1925–1938

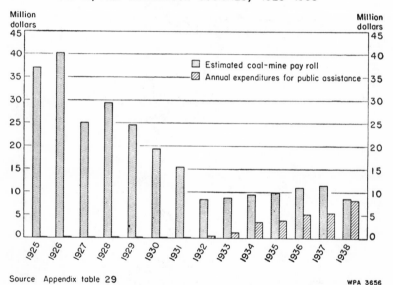

Source Appendix table 29

WPA 3656

The money put into circulation by the public-assistance agencies came to play an increasingly important role in holding the economic life of the coal community together. As late as 1933 dwindling mine pay rolls were still virtually the only primary source of wealth within the coal field. By 1938, however, the public-assistance programs had not only taken under care far more workers than were employed at the mines, but were also paying into the community a sum nearly equal to the annual mine pay roll itself. During 7 separate months in the summers of 1937 and 1938, public-assistance payments actually exceeded mine pay rolls. The coal field had indeed become, by 1938, a community with two industries instead of one; but the second industry was relief.

Types of Dependency and Assistance in the Coal Fields

The relief population in Franklin, Saline, and Williamson Counties has been made up of three principal types of dependents. To begin with, there are the so-called "nondepression" relief recipients. The growth of the southern Illinois relief rolls after the close of the CWA led to the discovery of widespread chronic dependency for which no public assistance had ever before been provided. During the early months of 1934 Williamson County reported 659 cases (exclusive of widows and the blind) on relief for reasons not directly related to the depression—that is, for such reasons as old age, chronic illness, mental or physical handicaps. In the 3 counties combined there were 1,471 such cases.[12]

Although these nondepression needs, once recognized, were great enough to have swamped the old pauper-relief system,[13] they of course accounted for only a small number of the persons receiving relief. In Franklin County 13 percent of the 1934 relief load (exclusive of widows and the blind) was dependent for "reasons other than unemployment"; and the Saline and Williamson rolls showed that 10 percent were nondepression cases. When old-age assistance under the Federal Social Security Act [14] was initiated in Illinois in 1936, it took under care the majority of all persons 65 and over—one of the principal nondepression dependent groups living in the coal field. In terms of the *total* public-assistance program, however, old-age assistance still occupied a distinctly minor place in Franklin, Saline, and Williamson Counties. (See fig. 20, p. 133.)

Two different types of jobless relief dependents are indicated in figure 20. Each summer, when the coal mines ordinarily slow down operation for the seasonal slump, the number of persons receiving

[12] *Monthly Bulletin on Relief Statistics*, Illinois Emergency Relief Commission, Chicago, Vol. 1, Nos. 6 and 9, June and September, 1934.

In Williamson County, where the IERC conducted special research on the relief rolls at this period, only 1 case out of about each 25 opened was "known to a relief agency" before 1930. But in two up-State counties with the same proportion of "nondepression" cases in the total load, every eleventh case had been "known to a relief agency" before 1930. These figures are further evidence of the backwardness of public assistance in the coal field before 1930.

[13] The pauper funds provided by the townships and counties between 1925 and 1929 could have carried no more than one-sixth of the "nondepression" needy who turned up after adequate relief became available in the coal field.

[14] Aid to the blind and aid to dependent children (mothers' pensions) in the three counties are not administered under the Federal Social Security Act, but are still carried by the counties (1939).

public assistance tends to rise sharply until the beginning of winter activity reduces the rolls once more. In the summer of 1934, for example, about 7,000 persons were added to the rolls between June and August but had left the rolls by November. Although partly obscured by the beginning of new assistance programs, the same tendency was noticeable in 1935 and 1936. It became particularly striking in 1937 and 1938, when 11,000 to 14,000 newly dependent persons remained on the rolls only for the duration of the summer slump.

Recently the responsibility for meeting these strictly seasonal needs was shifted in part from the regular direct- and work-relief systems to the Illinois unemployment-compensation program. Miners who put in reasonably full time during the fall, winter, and spring, but who were unemployed in the summer, became eligible for benefit payments under this program on July 1, 1939, and were therefore ineligible for work relief. About 1,500 workers in the 3 counties, practically all of them miners, were transferred from the WPA rolls to unemployment compensation during the first month of the new program,[15] and the number of persons dependent on WPA was accordingly reduced by about 5,000. In future summers unemployment compensation will substantially flatten the seasonal peak in the coal field's relief load.

But relief needs arising out of seasonal unemployment at the mines were never a very large part of the total welfare problem, as figure 20 shows. In March 1937, the busiest month in the southern Illinois coal industry for nearly a decade, 47,000 persons were still dependent upon public assistance in the 3 counties. The peak of mine activity during the 1939 season left 66,000 persons dependent on the welfare programs. Except for a minority of persons in families without an employable member, this stubbornly persistent relief load is made up of the able-bodied long unemployed, from both mine and service industries, and their dependents. The fundamental public-assistance problem in the three counties is thus not so much to provide for emergency, temporary unemployment nor for the long-time welfare needs of the helpless, as to create a substitute industry to employ workers cast off by a rapidly changing industry. The basic and by far the most important type of public assistance in the stranded area is accordingly work relief.

---

[15] Seasonal unemployment was particularly serious in the summer of 1939. Out of 9,500 men who had worked in the coal mines during the winter months, about 9,000 filed claims for unemployment benefits in the first month of the new program, according to the estimates of local unemployment compensation officials.

During the first benefit-year of Illinois unemployment compensation, workers registered at the Harrisburg, Herrin, and West Frankfort offices were compensated for 67,705 weeks of unemployment, and apparently their payments would have amounted to between $500,000 and $750,000. See Illinois State Department of Labor, Division of Placement and Unemployment Compensation, *Illinois Employment Security Review*, Springfield, Vol. 1, No. 1, July 1940.

"Just WPA going on now."

Main Street, Cambria, Ill.

Work Relief

The inadequacy of the dole was not a theoretical question in southern Illinois. Three years of grocery-order relief, of soup kitchens and hand-me-down clothing at the beginning of the depression had reduced a large part of the unemployed to such poverty that active purchasing power among the relief population had virtually disappeared. As a result, scores of merchants became superfluous during the era of relief in kind and were driven to the wall. Extended idleness among active workers on the dole had taken its toll in demoralization as well as in poverty. In the meantime, the program of public improvement in the community had been halted and the existing social equipment had fallen into disrepair for lack of necessary workers. The only immediate solution for these critical problems was a broad drive to substitute public jobs for idleness, a wage income for grocery orders.

The first broad program of work relief [16] came with the initiation of the Federal-sponsored Civil Works Administration in November 1933. Within a few weeks the CWA had put more than 6,500 unemployed persons to work on public projects in the 3 counties, and CWA pay checks—averaging about $15 a week in the coal field—gave many of the unemployed the first real money they had seen in years. When the CWA was liquidated in April 1934, the job of providing work relief was turned back to the State relief commission, operating under the Federal Emergency Work Relief Program. By the middle of the summer of 1934 about one-third of the coal-field relief families with employable members were assigned to work relief, and by winter the proportion had risen to two-thirds. Unlike the CWA, the new work-relief program based its monthly wage on a relief budget, with certain adjustments to allow for the purchase of food on the open market, for transportation, etc. On this basis, the State program continued to operate until stabilized work-relief machinery was established by the WPA in October 1935.

The greater share of the coal field's employable needy were assigned to the WPA by January 1936, and the program rapidly became one of the principal sources of income and employment within the stranded community. During the first 4 years of operation WPA provided jobs for 7,000 to 15,000 unemployed workers and supported a total population of 23,000 to 55,000 persons. The WPA pay roll has varied from 4 million dollars to 6 million dollars a year. Operating on such a scale, the program solved—in part at least—the graver relief problems inherited from the early years of the depression. The poverty and

[16] The able-bodied unemployed had long been required to "work out" their township orders on the public roads but this system could scarcely be called work relief. "There is the question," said a coal-town newspaper in 1932, "of how much work a man could be expected to do for 76 cents worth of groceries a week."

distress among the relief population was appreciably relieved. With free buying power restored to the unemployed, local business revived; and the store space left vacant during the era of the dole gradually began to fill up. Idleness in good part disappeared. Finally, the community was enabled to construct and to repair needed public facilities.

The list of the WPA's physical accomplishments in the three counties is an impressive record in itself. It shows, for example, that WPA workers had improved 1,311 miles of rural roads and 459 miles of coal-town streets up to June 1939 (not counting projects begun but not yet completed). For thousands of rural inhabitants of the community, the road program meant accessibility to town and school over all-weather roads for the first time since the countryside was settled a hundred years ago; for town residents it opened up scores of miles of needed streets which had never before been usable in winter weather. In Williamson County WPA workers helped to build three huge storage dams, enabling the community to develop its first public recreation site and to make its first real attack upon the perennial problem of disastrous summertime water shortages. The list of completed projects includes among other items such work as the construction of 3 playgrounds, a swimming pool, 2 community buildings, 5 parks, 2 athletic fields, and 5 schools; the improvement of 2 libraries, 2 gymnasiums, 4 parks, and 46 school buildings; the complete renovation of 2 courthouses; the construction and repair of 112 miles of ditches for draining malarial marshes, 6 miles of sewers, and 15 miles of water mains. As a first step toward combating the high incidence of typhoid fever in the coal field, the WPA launched an extensive program of sanitary engineering.

The professional and service activities of the WPA have also been of great value to the stranded community. The women on the sewing and canning projects, for example, have produced a large quantity of clothing and food for distribution to relief families. The WPA school-lunch projects have more than ordinary importance in helping undernourished children, and the existence of the home-nursing program to aid the sick and disabled has meant the prevention of needless suffering among hundreds of unfortunate families. White-collar WPA workers have carried through a complete accounting of delinquent taxes in the three counties and thus collected the first facts about one of the coal field's most serious problems. The WPA recreation centers established in nearly all the coal towns have provided the only available diversion for thousands of persons from both employed and unemployed families.

All these projects, plus those conducted by the National Youth Administration, have utilized otherwise idle labor to bring solid benefits to the people of the community. Some, like the sewing projects and the home-nursing program, have helped to alleviate immediate distress. Projects like Crab Orchard Dam and the NYA student-aid program have provided a basis for future attempts to eliminate chronic unemployment in the stranded area. But most of all, the WPA has improved the community—through roads, schools, parks, recreation, drainage systems, sewage systems, water systems—and made the southern Illinois coal field a more modern, healthful, and pleasant place to live in.

Chapter IX

CONCLUSIONS

FRANKLIN, SALINE, and Williamson Counties are a small part of the total problem of depressed areas in the United States. The introduction of the report pointed out that the southern Illinois coal field is only 1 among a large number of separate depressed areas existing before the national defense program was initiated; and that while the 3 southern Illinois counties contain 140,000 people, all the depressed areas combined have a population of about 13 million. However important the story of southern Illinois may be, it is less significant in itself than as an instance of the larger problem.

RECENT PUBLIC POLICY

The experience of the southern Illinois coal field suggests that attempts to solve the problems of all the depressed areas on a purely local basis are foredoomed. The interplay of Nation-wide forces created the depressed areas, and neither subsistence farming, handicraft industry, locally initiated "land-a-factory" drives, nor ingenious "make-your-own-job" schemes can basically alter their situation. One can scarcely avoid the conclusion that a national approach offers the only hope for a solution. In Great Britain this conclusion is accepted, but in the United States it is not.

American Policy

The United States has never attempted a broad and deliberate approach to the highly specialized problems of the depressed areas. In the distressed agricultural areas, it is true, a great deal of valuable reconstruction work has been done through the encouragement of scientific farm practices, through the soil-conservation and rural-electrification programs; in the Tennessee Valley these programs blanket a large and important region. At times an effort has even been made to remove farm families from hopelessly poor soil; the

143

Farm Security Administration, for example, has recently moved several hundred stranded families from submarginal land in the Cookson Hills of eastern Oklahoma. These programs are only the beginnings of an approach to the total problem of distressed farm communities. As for the nonagricultural depressed areas, their very existence as a special problem has received very little official recognition. With a few isolated exceptions,[1] they have been covered by the same measures—both emergency and long-term—devised to deal with the altogether different unemployment problems of less disrupted areas. Officially, no great distinction is made between the unemployed coal miner in Herrin and the unemployed automobile worker in Detroit.

The Work Programs

In terms of immediate problems, it is true, no distinction is called for. The work programs, by far the most important of the over-all relief measures, have properly placed first emphasis upon the relief of distress and the performance of socially useful work; upon the prevention of suffering, and at the same time, the preservation of the morale and skills of the unemployed. This emphasis obviously applies no less reasonably to depressed areas than to the rest of the Nation. The first two jobs of the work programs in depressed areas have necessarily been to feed and clothe millions of destitute people and to prevent deterioration of work habits. This fact must always be kept foremost in mind.

Beyond these two immediate purposes, the work programs have on record other substantial benefits to the depressed areas. Through the creation of purchasing power, they have rescued the communities' trade and service industries. They have made possible long-needed local improvements which many a bankrupt depressed area would otherwise never have enjoyed. They have also completed a number of projects designed to aid in rebuilding a community's economic base. The program to salvage Key West by turning it into a winter resort is perhaps the most famous of these, and there have been scores of projects designed to provide a depressed community with power, better transportation, and the like, in the expectation that new supporting industries would then be attracted. The Crab

---

[1] The principal exception was a small-scale experiment in "government communities" administered under the FERA, the Division of Subsistence Homesteads of the Department of the Interior, and the Resettlement Administration. In 1935 there were about 7,000 persons living in 41 of the communities. Originally the experiment aimed at enticement of factories into nonagricultural derelict areas, but eventually it narrowed down to a program emphasizing adequate housing and part-time farming for industrial workers.

Incidentally, it was planned to build one of these communities at West Frankfort. Ill., but the plans never materialized.

Orchard Lake project in the southern Illinois coal field was planned with a like purpose.

But with all these accomplishments, there are still serious difficulties involved in the application of the general administrative rules of the work programs to the peculiar problems of the depressed areas. The work programs operate, for example, within the concept of modified local responsibility. A community in need of a Federal work project is presumed to be solvent, at least to the extent of contributing, as sponsor, a fair share toward the total project cost. In a depressed community this theory breaks down. By 1940 score upon score of depressed and bankrupt American communities were finding increasing difficulty in making the required sponsors' contributions for urgently needed work-program projects.

The principle of "legal residence" grows out of the same concept. The work programs delegate to each local community the selection of persons eligible for employment. Almost universally, the local community requires a person to prove that he is a "resident" of the community before he is certified for employment. This procedure tends to freeze "surplus" workers within the depressed areas.[2] Unemployed workers who might readily be absorbed into a more active labor market have no way of reaching it, since their right to work-program employment and all other public assistance stops automatically if they leave home. And those who do take the chance are promptly sent home again, "where they belong," if their migration is not successful.

The work programs also operate within the limitations of a short-time, emergency perspective—necessarily so, in view of their short-term appropriations.[3] This perspective makes it difficult for the work programs to pursue a broadly planned approach to the problems of the depressed areas. Careful consideration cannot always be given to such significant long-time needs as retraining the unemployed from obsolete trades or assisting migration from communities which can never be revived. Projects are confined largely to building roads, schools, and other social equipment which, though needed, can never in themselves relieve the basic economic plight of the distressed communities. Even when there are more basic projects—

---

[2] It is sometimes said that public assistance itself freezes a "surplus" population. This is a somewhat loose way of expressing two entirely different ideas: (1) that legal residence requirements, associated with public assistance but not necessarily essential to it, tend to prevent mobility; and (2) that if public assistance is stopped, needy families will often be driven in desperation to set out upon the road in search of food and shelter.

[3] One manifestation of this emergency point of view is the so-called "18-months rule," which requires that WPA workers be terminated (with certain exceptions) after 18 months of continuous employment on the program. Whatever effects this ruling may have generally, it obviously works the greatest hardship upon the unemployed in depressed areas.

such as those of the Key West reconstruction program—the approach is sometimes piecemeal and indirect, leaving the desired results to be hoped for rather than assured.

British Policy [4]

More than a decade ago the government of Great Britain first recognized the special nature of the problem of the depressed areas; and between 1928 and the beginning of the war in 1939 it administered special measures for their relief. Although the analogy between British and American depressed areas must not be pressed too far,[5] the history of the British programs does provide certain experience applicable to America. Their failures are particularly revealing.

Transference

The British measures have provided for two separate attacks on unemployment in the depressed areas.[6] In 1928 the government initiated the first of these, called "industrial transference," a program for encouraging and assisting migration from the depressed areas to the places where unemployment was less severe. This approach was based on the belief that concentrated unemployment is a "worse evil" than the same amount of unemployment distributed evenly throughout the country.[7] In addition, it was believed that an "unsatisfied

---

[4] See Dennison, S. R., *The Location of Industry and the Depressed Areas*, London: Oxford University Press, 1939; Goodrich, Carter and Others, *Migration and Economic Opportunity*, Philadelphia, 1936, pp. 565 ff; Greene, Lee S., "State Policy in the British Depressed Areas," *Social Forces*, Vol. 18, No. 3, March 1940, pp. 558–581; annual reports of the Commissioner for the Special Areas in England and Wales, London, 1935–1938; annual reports of the Commissioner for the Special Areas in Scotland, Edinburgh, 1935–1938; *Minutes of Evidence Taken Before the Royal Commission on the Geographical Distribution of the Industrial Population*, London, 1938, pp. 237 ff.

[5] There is no close British analogy for either the extremely isolated American depressed areas or for our depressed agricultural areas. But the British experience in depressed coal-mining regions, for example, is obviously pertinent.

[6] We leave out of account the interesting checkered career of public works in the British depressed areas. From 1925 to 1928 the British Government made grants to the stricken communities for the purpose of public works within the areas. Some question was raised, however, about the propriety of building up the social amenities of communities whose future was uncertain. In 1929 emphasis was accordingly shifted to schemes for employing depressed-area workers to build public works in prosperous areas. In 1931 the public works program was largely abandoned. With the passage of the Special Areas Act in 1934, public works schemes were again initiated in the depressed areas, with particular stress laid upon housing and those public works related to sanitation and public health. See Greene, *op. cit.*, p. 342.

[7] Sir William Beveridge expressed this point of view as follows: "From a national point of view a condition of 40 percent of unemployment in one district and 4 percent in another calls for redress rather than argument." Quoted in Goodrich, *op. cit.*, p. 590.

demand" for labor actually existed in the more active areas, and that adequate labor mobility would not occur automatically.[8]

Even in relatively good times the transference program encountered great difficulties. Immobilizing forces were not* easy to overcome, even with payment of moving expenses and the offer of jobs in the new location. Parents were reluctant to see their children go away. Persons with property refused to leave it. Homesickness was a major obstacle to successful transference. As for the jobs provided in the transference scheme, one can scarcely conclude that they were generally satisfactory when nearly half the youth, and more than one-third of all the transferred workers, eventually came home again to the depressed areas. After 1931, as general unemployment spread through the more prosperous sections of England, there was a new problem: the "receiving areas" raised such strenuous objection to transference that the tempo of the program was slowed down (though by no means halted) for several years.[9] But over the course of a decade some headway was made. Between 1927 and 1938 some one hundred thousand workers were permanently transferred to localities outside the depressed areas, so that the program did produce a minor reshuffling of the population.

Inducements for Investors

The second method of attack on depressed-area unemployment was encouragement of private industrial expansion within the areas themselves. In 1934 Parliament approved the Special Areas Development and Improvement Act, empowering two Special Areas Commissioners to initiate steps for reviving selected depressed communities' in South Wales (coal), the Tyneside (coal), Durham (coal), Cumberland (coal and shipbuilding), and Southwest Scotland (shipbuilding and heavy industry).[10] The Commissioners were to publicize the industrial

---

[8] In 1928 this argument ran as follows: "The existence of local unemployment does not make it unnecessary or uneconomic to bring in labour from other areas. It is quite normal to find simultaneously in the same area unemployment and an unsatisfied demand for labour . . . In districts where the level of unemployment is low, those who remain unemployed may be of less than the average employment value . . ." *Report*, Industrial Transference Board, 1928, p. 19. Quoted by Dennison, *op. cit.*, p. 171.

[9] "There are cases where the local authorities and everybody else regard it [transference] as a menace. For example, when Luton had its great influx of labour it began to put up danger notices and to advertise that it did not want people coming in at that pace because it did not know what was going to happen. There are prosperous areas, selfish areas, which have set their faces against the introduction of labour even though they could very well have supported additional labour. It is not always an easy thing to bring them in." *Minutes of Evidence Taken Before the Royal Commission on the Geographical Distribution of the Industrial Population*, p. 262.

[10] Numerous derelict areas were omitted out of consideration for administrative difficulties.

opportunities of the areas and to interest prospective investors by means of "appeal and persuasion." They were to set up "trading estates," i. e., groups of factory buildings for lease to manufacturers, and to improve the industrial facilities of the areas by making light, heat, and power available for industry. In 1936 provision was made for supplying capital loans to investors; and in 1937 the act was amended to permit the Commissioners to offer also small subsidies in the form of tax exemptions, rent payments, and the like.

Almost total failure greeted the Commissioners' initial attempts to carry out the purposes of the act through "appeal and persuasion." Shortly after the 1934 act was approved, one of the Commissioners circularized 5,829 firms asking whether they were prepared to consider establishing plants in the special areas. Three-fourths did not reply; 1,313 gave "an unqualified negative answer," and only 12 stated that they were prepared "to consider" the question. The Commissioners soon concluded that "there is little prospect of the special areas being assisted by the spontaneous action of industrialists now located outside," and they urged the provision of such real inducements as were made available in 1936 and 1937.[11]

A new set of problems arose when the Commissioners were finally empowered to offer concrete inducements to new industry. Not that inducements failed to bring forth many willing investors; indeed, "the demand" for them, it was observed, "far exceeds the supply." One difficulty was that the sum of money made available for inducements was small,[12] and the number of new jobs thus created could not diminish unemployment appreciably. But small-scale as the program was, it nevertheless aroused immediate opposition from competing unsubsidized manufacturers in both the prosperous and the depressed areas. This opposition forced the Special Areas Commissioners to restrict the offer of inducements to "noncompeting" industries only, and in turn prevented the expansion of the program beyond laboratory-experiment proportions. The Commissioners were struggling with this dilemma when the war began in September 1939.

THE HEART OF THE PROBLEM

Whatever small benefits the two British depressed-area measures may have achieved, they had hardly scratched the surface of the total problem by the beginning of the war. Both the transference and inducement programs, it must be remembered, operated mainly in a period of general depression. It is easy to imagine that subsidized

---

[11] Dennison, *op. cit.*, p. 165.

[12] Between 1937 and 1939 total commitments for tax exemptions, rent payments, and the like amounted to about $750,000. Capital sums loaned amounted to 7½ million dollars in the Government venture, plus 10 million dollars through the private Nuffield Trust.

new industry could revive the depressed areas, or that their unemployment could be dissolved by finding jobs for the stranded workers in another area. But when industry is contracting everywhere, and when every community, even the most prosperous, has a labor surplus, these schemes are little more than an elaborate system for robbing Peter to pay Paul. The general problem of the depressed areas is finally insoluble in the midst of a Nation-wide depression.

In better times the seriousness of the depressed-area problem will, of course, diminish, but there is little chance that it will automatically dissolve. Characteristically, the depressed areas were no more able to attract new industry during the years before the depression set in than afterward. A new era of industrial expansion will likewise pass many of them by.[13] Spontaneous migration has also turned out to be an unreliable solvent for pockets of surplus labor, even in good times. The southern Illinois coal field was accumulating a "redundant population" all through the last half of the 1920's, a period when the conditions for spontaneous emigration were presumably ideal. In the future, stranded workers will probably experience increasing difficulty in finding job opportunities elsewhere; for a decade of intense depression has put new handicaps in the way of successful emigration from the depressed areas.

The Depressed Areas in the National Defense Program

When more active times arrive, therefore, careful consideration is due the special plans devised to aid the depressed area's victims, either through encouragement of industrial expansion in the depressed areas or by "guided migration" of surplus workers toward the active areas. The conditions necessary for the operation of both plans will probably come into existence in the evolution of the national defense program; and it is to be expected that each plan will then have its own enthusiastic advocates. It should be recognized, however, that neither plan can be put into action without involving hidden dangers.

The Two Special Plans: What They Involve

Theoretically, the more desirable plan would be encouragement of industrial expansion inside the depressed areas. If the proposed industries were to be permanent, or if they should offer a reasonable chance of post-emergency conversion into permanent industries on a sound economic basis, this sort of program could indeed be recommended without reservation. It is not likely, however, that any great

---

[13] Some of the depressed areas have traditionally been disadvantaged by competition with low-wage, nonunion areas. In any future period of industrial expansion, this disadvantage will have been diminished by the operation of the Fair Labor Standards Act and the National Labor Relations Act.

part of the new defense industries will be either permanent or convertible. If not, the policy of locating them inside the depressed areas, despite obvious immediate advantages, would eventually bring new difficulties. Such a policy would bring "home" again a large number of workers who had already left the areas. It would also hold within the areas workers who might otherwise have willingly moved to jobs elsewhere. The temporary boom would thus end with the problems of the depressed areas multiplied.

Guided migration, the alternative plan, also appears to offer limited possibilities for betterment of the depressed areas—or rather, of the people now living in the depressed areas—particularly those living in areas where industrial expansion is clearly out of the question. The predicament of the southern Illinois labor force suggests that such a plan would involve a minimum of four steps: a training program for both inexperienced youth and "obsolete" older workers; a system for allocating jobs in the prosperous areas to applicants from the depressed areas; provision of travel money to enable entire families to move to the new jobs; and a waiver of legal-settlement regulations to prevent the forced return of families to the depressed areas if they should need relief at their new residence.

There are two main objections to this type of program. One of them, originating within the depressed areas themselves, stresses the aftereffects of large-scale migration from a community: the younger workers are drained away; social patterns are disturbed; established property values decline; local businessmen lose trade; the taxing power of the community deteriorates; excess labor supplies, held in reserve for seasonal work, are lost. It seems obvious, however, that such objections would be of little weight if set against the successful resettlement of otherwise surplus workers.

The second and more serious objection is that a guided-migration program endangers labor standards in the receiving areas. It is pointed out, for example, that the scheme for "guiding" farm workers from the depressed areas of eastern Oklahoma into the Southwest contributed a substantial part toward the difficulties that developed among California and Arizona migratory workers in the late 1930's.[14] Unless carefully administered, such a scheme could always be abused by employers who would be tempted to recruit workers indiscriminately as a source of cheap labor. The only answer to this objection is that a guided migration must presuppose the existence of actual, bona fide shortages, and *that the plan must be held in abeyance when no labor shortages exist.*

---

[14] See Brown, Malcolm and Cassmore, Orin, *Migratory Cotton Pickers in Arizona,* Division of Research, Works Progress Administration, Washington, D. C., 1939, pp. 68–75.

Long-Time Problems

Whatever temporary effects the national defense program might have upon the depressed areas—with or without the administration of the two special plans—defense activity will not likely result in the permanent solution of the depressed-area problem. Moreover, the depressed areas will likely be the last to benefit from defense activity.[15] Thus, questions relating to public assistance, local improvement of depressed areas, and migration are certain to recur.

Public Assistance

Until the depressed areas are permanently dissolved—that is, presumably for a long time yet to come—their population will continue to require extraordinary amounts of public assistance. One may judge from the predicament of the unemployed in southern Illinois what consequences would follow if this need were neglected. Since the problem is basically one of a great and long-accumulating surplus of highly employable workers, the responsibility for meeting their need falls principally upon the Work Projects Administration. But the areas place extra responsibilities upon all the other public-assistance programs as well.

A double-edged assistance problem is rapidly coming to maturity in the depressed areas. On the one hand, exceptional need persists, or is at best only temporarily relieved. But the ability of the depressed communities to keep up their end of relief costs is progressively weakened. If a general deterioration of depressed-area assistance is to be avoided, those States which have not already done so should make provision for assuming an increasing share of public-assistance costs which cannot be met by bankrupt local communities. And where the State itself is unable to assist the people of its depressed areas, increased Federal responsibility should be anticipated.

Local Improvements

There is a common feeling that the construction of roads, schools, recreational and social facilities, and similar local improvements in the depressed areas is somehow wasteful. "Why build up a doomed community?" it is asked. "The improvements will be worthless when

---

[15] Among the defense contracts signed by the Government between June 1940 and January 1941 only 1½ percent directly involved the depressed areas. Their "average share," in terms of population, would have been seven times greater. Moreover, the contracts they had received were concentrated in a very few counties. Three counties held 46 percent of all the depressed-area defense contracts; 15 other counties held an additional 41 percent; and 40 other counties held the rest. About 450 of the depressed counties had no primary defense contracts whatever.

the people move away." And true enough, there are within the depressed areas many hopelessly derelict communities where extensive local improvement would simply be time and money wasted. By and large, however, this point of view dangerously oversimplifies the predicament of the depressed areas.

It is quite incorrect to assume that a large emigration from the depressed areas is necessarily in prospect; slow population losses and depopulation are two entirely different things. The southern Illinois coal field and many another American depressed area are going to be well populated for generations to come. It thus appears to be somewhat unreasonable to expect that the depressed-area population should forego the use of needed local improvements for an indefinitely long time.

Regional Conservation and Development

In some American depressed areas economic development has been held in check by past failure to develop some potential advantages. In some—notably in the agricultural and lumbering areas—economic collapse has inevitably followed in the wake of wasteful exploitation of resources. It goes without saying that where such conditions exist, public policy should aid in recovering and developing the missing factors.

The reforestation and soil-conservation programs, the projects for converting depressed areas into recreation centers, and the great power developments like the Tennessee Valley Authority have had such a purpose. Their proved achievement shows the possibilities of this type of approach to the problems of similar areas. There is merit, for example, in the suggestion that a "little TVA" be developed in southern Illinois, based upon low-cost power derived from coal. Obviously, however, such schemes should not be expected to produce substantial, permanent results overnight.

Spontaneous Migration

"Unguided" migration is continually draining a small part of the population away from the depressed areas. It is, of course, true, as this report has pointed out at some length, that during the 1930's people were not leaving the depressed areas fast enough to keep pace with local economic disintegration, nor even to cancel the local excess of births over deaths in most of the areas. But except for a few areas, people did move out in sufficient numbers at least to offset the influx of newcomers. And in Great Britain at the height of the transference program, spontaneous migration was quietly removing two workers from the depressed areas for every worker removed by the elaborate transference machinery.

Without this small spontaneous movement, the depressed-area problem in America at the end of the 1930's would have been somewhat more grave than it actually was. In the southern Illinois coal field, for example, one would have expected to find half the workers unemployed in 1939, supposing no emigration between 1930 and 1939, instead of the 41 percent actually reported. There seems to be little doubt, further, that this spontaneous movement is successfully terminated in the great majority of cases; indeed, spontaneous migration usually will not go forward (except in special situations) without good chances for successful termination—hence its slow pace.

It follows that barriers and frictions which unnecessarily retard the slow, free migration of workers from the depressed areas are likely to operate against the public interest. Such immobilizing forces are many and diverse, and they range from border blockades and the more harsh legal-settlement laws to the failure of bankrupt local communities to provide their youth with an average level of training. To eliminate the existing barriers wherever possible and, more important still, to prevent the establishment of new ones would appear to be about as fruitful an attack on the depressed-area problems as the most alert and complex "guided-migration" scheme.

This does not mean that spontaneous migration from the depressed areas is always good in itself. The greatest mischief is done when people are forced to migrate "spontaneously" without good chances for successful resettlement, even though their home communities may be utterly derelict. Migrations growing out of inadequate public assistance, irresponsible labor recruiting, and the like are a serious national problem. The mass hardships of one such recent migration have already fired the public's indignation. Similar incidents are always latent in neglected depressed-area situations.

Appendixes

TABLES

Appendix A

TABLES

Table 1.—Number of Shipping Coal Mines Opened, Abandoned, and in Operation in Franklin, Saline, and Williamson Counties, 1900–1939

Year	Mines opened	Mines abandoned	Mines in operation	Year	Mines opened	Mines abandoned	Mines in operation
1900	2	2	14	1920	9	4	93
1901	5	2	17	1921	10	3	99
1902	5	1	20	1922	5	3	101
1903	7	4	26	1923	5	13	103
1904	10	—	32	1924	5	17	95
1905	5	2	37	1925	2	11	80
1906	11	2	46	1926	2	1	71
1907	12	2	56	1927	2	14	72
1908	10	2	64	1928	2	6	60
1909	4	2	66	1929	1	9	55
1910	2	2	66	1930	2	2	48
1911	5	3	69	1931	2	5	48
1912	3	4	69	1932	1	3	44
1913	5	2	70	1933	2	5	43
1914	3	5	71	1934	4	5	42
1915	1	—	67	1935	5	5	42
1916	3	2	70	1936	6	5	43
1917	6	3	74	1937	—	5	38
1918	16	4	87	1938	3	3	36
1919	4	3	87	1939	2	4	35

Source: Illinois Department of Mines and Minerals, *Coal Report of Illinois*, annual, Springfield, 1900–1939.

Table 2.—Men Employed at Shipping Coal Mines in Franklin, Saline, and Williamson Counties, 1900–1940 [1]

Year	Men employed			
	Total	Franklin	Saline	Williamson
1900	1,548	—	182	1,366
1901	2,206	—	203	2,003
1902	2,635	—	249	2,386
1903	3,292	—	424	2,868
1904	3,789	—	321	3,468
1905	5,119	413	396	4,310
1906	6,685	696	984	5,005
1907	8,968	1,342	2,069	5,557
1908	11,621	1,918	3,427	6,276
1909	13,428	2,732	4,066	6,630

See footnote at end of table.

157

Table 2.—Men Employed at Shipping Coal Mines in Franklin, Saline, and Williamson Counties, 1900–1940 —Continued

Year	Men employed			
	Total	Franklin	Saline	Williamson
1910	14,391	2,630	4,081	7,680
1911	16,136	3,736	3,868	8,532
1912	17,592	4,472	4,659	8,461
1913	19,875	5,314	5,408	9,153
1914	20,441	6,452	4,832	9,157
1915	20,470	7,798	4,129	8,543
1916	21,876	8,606	4,768	8,502
1917	24,497	10,511	4,745	9,241
1918	27,990	11,618	6,468	9,904
1919	28,240	11,855	6,253	10,132
1920	28,878	12,261	5,876	10,741
1921	31,781	14,264	6,049	11,468
1922	33,126	14,840	5,861	12,425
1923	36,199	16,231	7,114	12,854
1924	34,641	15,816	6,816	12,009
1925	29,957	15,007	5,373	9,577
1926	29,500	14,543	5,802	9,155
1927	30,178	15,234	6,148	8,796
1928	26,405	14,259	4,869	7,277
1929	22,724	12,287	4,594	5,843
1930	19,661	10,670	4,246	4,745
1931	19,044	10,064	4,392	4,588
1932	16,205	9,441	3,947	2,817
1933	14,459	7,900	3,854	2,705
1934	14,365	8,407	3,733	2,225
1935	13,092	6,907	3,870	2,315
1936	13,309	7,697	3,915	1,697
1937	12,465	6,795	3,985	1,685
1938	11,843	6,611	3,577	1,655
1939	11,057	6,504	3,195	1,358
1940 [1]	10,200	6,700	2,450	1,050

[1] Figures for 1940 are preliminary.

Source: Illinois Department of Mines and Minerals, *Coal Report of Illinois*, annual, Springfield, 1900–1939.

Table 3.—Production, Capacity,[1] and Average Number of Days Worked at Shipping Coal Mines in Franklin, Saline, and Williamson Counties, 1900–1940

Year	Production (thousand tons)	Capacity (thousand tons)	Days worked	Year	Production (thousand tons)	Capacity (thousand tons)	Days worked
1900	1,262	1,460	242	1921	27,754	40,276	193
1901	1,740	2,166	225	1922	22,673	45,620	139
1902	2,219	2,938	211	1923	27,276	47,334	161
1903	3,047	3,779	226	1924	26,693	48,981	153
1904	3,326	4,213	221	1925	26,315	44,259	166
1905	4,264	5,200	230	1926	28,625	41,560	193
1906	4,886	7,034	194	1927	18,518	44,160	117
1907	7,807	9,557	229	1928	22,859	38,457	166
1908	9,459	12,170	218	1929	24,163	35,674	190
1909	11,110	15,404	202	1930	19,687	32,535	169
1910	10,985	16,896	182	1931	14,579	31,726	129
1911	10,757	18,269	165	1932	11,273	29,165	108
1912	15,161	20,826	204	1933	11,076	27,348	113
1913	17,416	22,793	214	1934	11,840	25,704	129
1914	18,126	24,289	209	1935	13,140	26,219	140
1915	18,337	27,541	186	1936	15,744	25,308	174
1916	21,428	28,876	208	1937	15,951	25,815	173
1917	25,448	29,842	239	1938	12,774	25,829	138
1918	29,266	32,288	254	1939	14,210	26,968	148
1919	25,930	34,112	213	1940	14,833	(2)	(2)
1920	25,389	38,757	183				

[1] Capacity is computed as the average daily output of all mines operating during a given year multiplied by 280. The hypothetical full working year is considered to be 280 days.
[2] Not available.

Source: Illinois Department of Mines and Minerals, *Coal Report of Illinois*, annual, Springfield, 1900–1939.

Table 4.—Average Hourly Earnings of Hand Loaders in Bituminous Coal Mining in Principal Producing States, Selected Years, 1919–1933

Year	Average hourly earnings of hand loaders					
	Illinois	Indiana	Kentucky	Ohio	Pennsylvania	West Virginia
1919	$0.889	$0.875	$0.686	$0.761	$0.753	$0.778
1922	1.127	1.094	.704	.893	.672	.841
1924	1.003	1.034	.646	.791	.682	.764
1926	.976	1.040	.579	.752	.651	.710
1929	.791	.865	.547	.545	.542	.591
1931	.800	.869	.489	.440	.485	.486
1933	.558	.577	.317	.293	.296	.326

Source: Bureau of Labor Statistics: *Hours and Earnings in Anthracite and Bituminous Coal Mining, 1919–1920*, Bulletin No. 279, 1921; *Hours and Earnings in Bituminous Coal Mining, 1922, 1924, and 1926*, Bulletin No. 454, 1927, *Hours and Earnings in Bituminous Coal Mining in 1929*, Bulletin No. 516, 1930; and *Wages and Hours of Labor in Bituminous Coal Mining*, Bulletin No. 601, 1934, U. S. Department of Labor. Washington, D. C.

Table 5.—Bituminous Coal Production in the United States by Principal Producing States, 1910–1939 [1]

[Amounts in millions of tons]

Year	Bituminous coal production							
	United States	Illinois	Indiana	Ohio	Pennsyl-vania	West Virginia	Ken-tucky	All other States
1910	417	46	18	34	151	62	15	91
1911	406	54	14	31	145	60	14	88
1912	450	60	15	35	162	67	16	95
1913	478	62	17	36	174	71	20	98
1914	423	58	17	19	148	72	20	89
1915	443	59	17	22	158	77	21	89
1916	503	66	20	35	170	86	25	101
1917	552	86	27	41	172	86	28	112
1918	579	89	31	46	179	90	32	112
1919	466	61	21	36	151	79	30	88
1920	569	89	29	46	171	90	36	108
1921	416	70	20	32	116	73	32	73
1922	422	58	19	27	113	80	42	83
1923	565	79	26	41	172	108	45	94
1924	484	68	21	30	131	102	45	87
1925	520	67	21	28	137	122	55	90
1926	573	69	23	28	153	144	63	93
1927	518	47	18	16	133	145	69	90
1928	501	56	16	16	131	133	62	87
1929	535	61	18	24	144	139	60	89
1930	468	54	16	23	124	121	51	79
1931	382	44	14	20	98	101	40	65
1932	310	33	13	14	75	86	35	35
1933	334	37	14	20	79	94	36	54
1934	359	41	15	21	90	98	39	55
1935	372	45	16	21	91	99	41	59
1936	439	51	18	24	110	118	48	70
1937	446	52	18	25	111	119	47	74
1938	349	42	15	19	78	93	39	64
1939 [1]	393	46	17	20	92	108	43	67

[1] Figures for 1939 are preliminary.

Source: Bureau of Mines, *Minerals Yearbook*, annual, U. S. Department of the Interior, Washington, D. C., 1937–1940.

Table 6.—Production at Shipping Coal Mines by Method of Loading, Franklin, Saline, and Williamson Counties, 1927–1939

[Amounts in thousands of tons]

Year	Production at shipping coal mines				
	Total	Underground mines			Strip mines
		Loaded by hand	Pit-car loader	Mobile loader	
1927	18,518	17,556	117	240	605
1928	22,859	19,444	1,662	1,101	652
1929	24,163	15,058	6,082	2,273	750
1930	19,687	9,871	6,348	3,035	433
1931	14,579	5,165	5,779	3,417	218
1932	11,273	3,455	4,215	3,308	295
1933	11,076	3,591	2,832	4,301	352
1934	11,840	4,529	3,458	3,466	387
1935	13,140	3,903	4,302	4,139	796
1936	15,744	4,161	4,492	6,040	1,051
1937	15,951	2,832	4,224	7,614	1,281
1938	12,774	1,655	2,755	7,068	1,296
1939	14,210	747	365	11,678	1,420
	Percent distribution				
1927	100	95	1	1	3
1928	100	85	7	5	3
1929	100	63	25	9	3
1930	100	51	32	15	2
1931	100	35	40	23	2
1932	100	31	37	29	3
1933	100	32	26	39	3
1934	100	39	29	29	3
1935	100	30	33	31	6
1936	100	26	29	38	7
1937	100	18	26	48	8
1938	100	13	22	55	10
1939	100	5	3	82	10

Source: Illinois Department of Mines and Minerals, *Coal Report of Illinois*, annual, Springfield, 1927–1939.

Table 7.—Men Employed, Capacity, Output per Man-Day, and Percent of Output Loaded by Machinery at the 21 Mechanized Shipping Coal Mines [1] in Franklin, Saline, and Williamson Counties, 1926–1938

Year	Men employed	Capacity (thousand tons)	Output per man-day (tons)	Percent of total output loaded by—		
				All machines	Pit-car loaders	Mobile loaders
1926	15,334	21,610	5.5	—	—	—
1927	15,799	23,437	5.7	2	*	2
1928	15,339	22,657	5.7	10	5	5
1929	13,937	22,014	6.1	40	29	11
1930	12,744	21,522	6.4	59	40	19
1931	12,803	21,146	6.3	75	46	29
1932	11,860	19,884	7.6	77	40	37
1933	10,179	18,014	7.3	82	35	47
1934	9,861	17,050	7.0	70	33	37
1935	9,554	18,215	7.7	75	36	39
1936	9,905	19,403	7.9	83	36	47
1937	9,830	20,772	8.5	88	32	56
1938	9,691	21,117	8.5	91	26	65

* Less than 0.5 percent.

[1] The following mines which installed mechanical loading equipment after 1926 and which operated during 1938 are included: Franklin County—Bell and Zoller Coal and Mining Co. No. 1; Bell and Zoller Coal and Mining Co. No. 2; Chicago, Wilmington, and Franklin Coal Co. No. 1; Chicago, Wilmington, and Franklin Coal Co. New Orient; Franklin County Coal Corp. No. 5; Franklin County Coal Corp. No. 7; Old Ben Coal Corp. No. 8; Old Ben Coal Corp. No. 11; Old Ben Coal Corp. No. 14; Old Ben Coal Corp. No. 15; Peabody Coal Co. No. 18; and Valier Coal Co. No. 1; Saline County—Peabody Coal Co. No. 43, Peabody Coal Co. No. 47, Rex Coal Co. No. 2, Wasson Coal Co. A, and Wasson Coal Co. No. 1; Williamson County—Consolidated Coal Co. New Monarch, Franco Mining Co., Freemen Coal Mining Co., and Seymour Coal Mining Co.

Source: Illinois Department of Mines and Minerals, *Coal Report of Illinois*, annual, Springfield, 1926–1938.

Table 8.—Bituminous Coal Produced per Man-Day in the United States and in Underground and Strip Mines in Franklin, Saline, and Williamson Counties, 1900–1939

[Tons]

Year	Bituminous coal produced per man-day			
	United States	Franklin, Saline, and Williamson Counties		
		All mines	Underground mines	Strip mines
1900	3.0	3.5	3.5	—
1901	2.9	3.7	3.7	—
1902	3.1	4.3	4.3	—
1903	3.0	4.2	4.2	—
1904	3.2	4.0	4.0	—
1905	3.2	3.7	3.7	—
1906	3.4	3.9	3.9	—
1907	3.3	4.1	4.1	—
1908	3.3	4.0	4.0	—
1909	(1)	4.2	4.2	—
1910	3.5	4.4	4.4	—
1911	3.5	4.3	4.3	—
1912	3.7	4.5	4.5	—
1913	3.6	4.3	4.3	7.5
1914	3.7	4.5	4.5	10.5
1915	3.9	5.0	5.0	15.0
1916	3.9	4.9	4.9	13.5
1917	3.8	4.7	4.6	15.7
1918	3.8	4.4	4.4	12.6
1919	3.8	4.5	4.5	—

See footnote at end of table.

Table 8.—Bituminous Coal Produced per Man-Day in the United States and in Underground and Strip Mines in Franklin, Saline, and Williamson Counties, 1900–1939—Con.

[Tons]

Year	Bituminous coal produced per man-day			
	United States	Franklin, Saline, and Williamson Counties		
		All mines	Underground mines	Strip mines
1920	4. 0	5. 0	5. 0	14. 8
1921	4. 2	4. 7	4. 7	4. 9
1922	4. 3	5. 1	5. 0	9. 6
1923	4. 5	4. 9	4. 9	12. 4
1924	4. 6	5. 3	5. 3	4. 7
1925	4. 5	5. 4	5. 3	12. 3
1926	4. 5	5. 3	5. 3	10. 4
1927	4. 6	5. 5	5. 4	19. 2
1928	4. 7	5. 6	5. 4	24. 3
1929	4. 9	6. 0	5. 9	24. 7
1930	5. 1	6. 2	6. 1	27. 9
1931	5. 3	6. 2	6. 2	11. 8
1932	5. 2	7. 3	7. 3	11. 1
1933	4. 8	6. 9	6. 8	14. 6
1934	4. 4	6. 2	6. 1	15. 8
1935	4. 5	6. 9	6. 6	17. 1
1936	4. 6	7. 8	7. 5	23. 2
1937	4. 7	8. 5	8. 3	12. 3
1938	4. 9	8. 8	8. 2	23. 1
1939	(1)	9. 4	8. 9	22. 7

[1] Not available.

Source: Bureau of Mines, *Minerals Yearbook*, 1936, 1939, and 1940, U. S. Department of the Interior, Washington, D. C.; and Illinois Department of Mines and Minerals, Coal Report of Illinois, annual, Springfield, 1901–1939.

Table 9.—Production and Men Employed at Local Coal Mines in Saline and Williamson Counties,[1] 1900–1939

Year	Production (thousand tons)	Men employed	Year	Production (thousand tons)	Men employed
1900	19	114	1920	81	185
1901	14	67	1921	71	160
1902	19	61	1922	73	139
1903	19	70	1923	53	107
1904	16	93	1924	75	124
1905	16	49	1925	48	109
1906	30	101	1926	56	137
1907	34	102	1927	57	165
1908	69	76	1928	73	177
1909	33	139	1929	63	151
1910	57	109	1930	89	236
1911	44	115	1931	92	307
1912	40	79	1932	154	444
1913	46	84	1933	167	506
1914	56	110	1934	225	630
1915	67	151	1935	269	697
1916	50	134	1936	392	785
1917	67	125	1937	474	729
1918	67	148	1938	412	733
1919	87	138	1939	547	741

[1] Franklin County has no local mines.

Source: Illinois Department of Mines and Minerals, *Coal Report of Illinois*, annual, Springfield, 1900–1939,

Table 10.—Population, Labor Force, Employed Workers, Unemployed Workers, and Workers on Work Programs, by Sex, 7 Southern Illinois Coal Towns

Item	Total	Bush	John- ston City	Carrier Mills	Herrin	West Frank- fort	Zeigler	Eldo- rado
All persons	38,193	643	5,351	2,231	9,608	12,725	3,017	4,618
Male	19,294	325	2,743	1,143	4,759	6,483	1,555	2,286
Female	18,899	318	2,608	1,088	4,849	6,242	1,462	2,332
Labor force [1]	15,707	218	2,127	867	4,088	5,226	1,227	1,954
Male	12,246	187	1,682	675	3,133	4,095	1,004	1,470
Female	3,461	31	445	192	955	1,131	223	484
Percent of population in labor force	41	34	40	39	43	41	41	42
Male	63	58	61	59	66	63	65	64
Female	18	10	17	18	20	18	15	21
Employed workers	9,209	44	857	477	2,522	3,257	775	1,277
Less than 30 hours' work in census week	3,465	21	266	174	1,016	1,173	366	449
30 hours' work or more in census week	5,700	23	578	298	1,505	2,070	408	818
Hours not ascertainable	44	—	13	5	1	14	1	10
Percent of labor force employed less than 30 hours in census week	22	10	13	20	25	22	30	23
Unemployed workers [2]	6,498	174	1,270	390	1,566	1,969	452	677
Male	4,857	148	1,012	284	1,140	1,506	330	437
Female	1,641	26	258	106	426	463	122	240
Percent of labor force unemployed	41	80	60	45	38	38	37	35
Male	40	79	60	42	36	37	33	30
Female	47	84	58	55	45	41	55	50
Unemployed workers on work programs	3,369	119	850	229	928	661	243	339
Male	2,679	109	706	180	711	529	199	245
Female	690	10	144	49	217	132	44	94
Percent of unemployed workers on work programs [3]	52	68	67	59	59	34	54	50
Male	55	74	70	63	62	35	60	56
Female	42	38	56	46	51	29	36	39

[1] Persons employed in private industry, persons on work programs, persons seeking work, and persons only temporarily out of the labor market during the "census week," a specified week immediately before enumeration.
[2] Workers who had no jobs in private industry during the census week.
[3] Includes WPA, NYA, CCC, and other Federal emergency programs.

Table 11.—Usual Occupation of Employed and Unemployed Workers in 7 Southern Illinois Coal Towns

Usual occupation	Total labor force	Employed workers	Unemployed workers	
			Number	Percent of labor force
Total	[1] 15,705	9,209	6,496	41
Without usual occupation	3,401	657	2,744	81
With work experience [2]	2,730	657	2,073	76
Without work experience [2]	671		671	100
With usual occupation	12,304	8,552	3,752	30
Farmers and farm workers	175	51	124	71
Forestry workers	19	7	12	63
Coal mine workers	4,920	3,228	1,692	34
Operators, managers, and officials	64	57	7	11
Foremen and inspectors	256	212	44	17
Surface workers	473	398	75	16
Face workers	2,912	1,601	1,311	45
Hand loaders	1,290	451	839	65
Other face workers	1,622	1,150	472	29
Hoisting and haulage workers	1,215	960	255	21
Manufacturing and mechanical workers	1,716	1,039	677	39
Brickmasons, carpenters, electricians, painters, and plasterers	595	316	279	47
Operatives (except in building trades)	266	102	164	62
Other manufacturing and mechanical workers	855	621	234	27
Transportation and communication workers	952	563	389	41
Chauffeurs and truck and tractor drivers	445	230	215	48
Railroad workers	234	176	58	25
Road and street laborers	79	9	70	89
Other transportation and communication workers	194	148	46	24
Tradesworkers	1,763	1,515	248	14
Bankers, brokers, money lenders, and insurance agents	76	72	4	5
Retail dealers	572	529	43	8
Salespersons	792	647	145	18
Other tradesworkers	323	267	56	17
Public and professional service workers	1,027	876	151	15
Domestic and personal service workers	1,041	726	315	30
Restaurant workers	258	185	73	28
Servants	349	180	169	48
Other domestic and personal service workers	434	361	73	17
Clerical workers	691	547	144	21

[1] Excludes 2 workers whose usual occupations were not ascertainable.
[2] Includes both private and emergency-work-program employment.

Table 12.—Industry of Usual Occupation of Unemployed Workers, by Sex, 7 Southern Illinois Coal Towns

Industry of usual occupation	Unemployed workers					
	Number			Percent distribution		
	Total	Male	Female	Total	Male	Female
Total	[1] 6,486	4,848	1,638	100	75	25
Without usual occupation	2,744	1,693	1,051	42	26	16
With work experience [2]	2,073	1,326	747	32	21	11
Without work experience [2]	671	367	304	10	5	5
With usual occupation	3,742	3,155	587	58	49	9
Agriculture and forestry	162	160	2	2	2	*
Coal mining	1,780	1,779	1	28	28	*
Manufacturing and mechanical	612	490	122	10	8	2
Transportation and communication	356	348	8	5	5	*
Trade	300	218	82	4	3	1
Public and professional service	233	103	130	4	2	2
Domestic and personal service	299	57	242	5	1	4

* Less than 0.5 percent.

[1] Excludes 12 workers whose industries of usual occupation were not ascertainable.

[2] Includes both private and emergency-work-program employment.

Table 13.—Industry of Usual Occupation of Employed and Unemployed Workers, by Age Group, 7 Southern Illinois Coal Towns

Industry of usual occupation	Labor force				Employed workers				Unemployed workers			
	Total	Under 25 years of age	25–54 years of age	55 years of age and over	Total	Under 25 years of age	25–54 years of age	55 years of age and over	Total	Under 25 years of age	25–54 years of age	55 years of age and over
Total	[1] 15,682	3,848	9,393	2,441	9,199	1,606	6,211	1,382	6,483	2,242	3,182	1,059
Without usual occupation	3,400	2,063	1,097	240	657	393	234	30	2,743	1,670	863	210
With work experience [2]	2,729	1,509	1,004	216	657	393	234	30	2,072	1,116	770	186
Without work experience [2]	671	554	93	24					671	554	93	24
With usual occupation	12,282	1,785	8,296	2,201	8,542	1,213	5,977	1,352	3,740	572	2,319	849
Agriculture and forestry	225	56	111	58	63	8	37	18	162	48	74	40
Coal mining	5,567	260	3,964	1,343	3,789	227	2,811	751	1,778	33	1,153	592
Manufacturing and mechanical	1,355	251	920	184	743	124	534	85	612	127	386	99
Transportation and communication	895	170	612	113	539	73	392	74	356	97	220	39
Trade	2,010	459	1,308	243	1,710	376	1,117	217	300	83	191	26
Public and professional service	1,254	316	801	137	1,021	217	682	122	233	99	119	15
Domestic and personal service	976	273	580	123	677	188	404	85	299	85	176	38

[1] Excludes 25 workers whose ages or industries of usual occupation were not ascertainable.

[2] Includes both private and emergency-work-program employment.

Table 14.—Labor Force and Unemployed Workers in 7 Southern Illinois Coal Towns, by Age Group

Age group	Total	Bush	Johnston City	Carrier Mills	Herrin	West Frankfort	Zeigler	Eldorado
Labor force_____	[1] 15,696	218	2,124	867	4,085	5,223	1,226	1,953
Under 25 years_____	3,857	66	568	245	966	1,290	253	469
25–54 years_____	9,396	130	1,214	513	2,464	3,128	783	1,164
55 years and over_____	2,443	22	342	109	655	805	190	320
Unemployed workers_____	[2] 6,494	174	1,267	390	1,566	1,968	452	677
Under 25 years_____	2,249	58	424	138	576	688	133	232
25–54 years_____	3,184	97	625	196	785	921	219	341
55 years and over_____	1,061	19	218	56	205	359	100	104
Percent of labor force unemployed_____	41	80	60	45	38	38	37	35
Under 25 years_____	58	88	75	56	60	53	53	49
25–54 years_____	34	75	51	38	32	29	28	29
55 years and over_____	43	86	64	51	31	45	53	33

[1] Excludes 11 workers whose ages were not ascertainable.
[2] Excludes 4 unemployed workers whose ages were not ascertainable.

Table 15.—Employment Status of Families in 7 Southern Illinois Coal Towns

Employment status of families	Total	Bush	Johnston City	Carrier Mills	Herrin	West Frankfort	Zeigler	Eldorado
All families_____	12,477	181	1,652	714	3,231	4,125	982	1,592
Without workers_____	1,102	17	148	93	281	357	48	158
With workers_____	11,375	164	1,504	621	2,950	3,768	934	1,434
Some workers with private employment_____	7,373	43	687	384	1,983	2,603	640	1,033
No workers on work programs_____	6,910	32	607	343	1,862	2,480	616	970
Some workers on work programs_____	463	11	80	41	121	123	24	63
No workers with private employment_____	4,002	121	817	237	967	1,165	294	401
No workers on work programs_____	1,368	23	157	63	236	657	92	140
Some workers on work programs_____	2,634	98	660	174	731	508	202	261
Percent distribution								
All families_____	100	100	100	100	100	100	100	100
Without workers_____	9	9	9	13	9	9	5	10
With workers_____	91	91	91	87	91	91	95	90
Some workers with private employment_____	59	24	42	54	61	63	65	65
No workers on work programs_____	55	18	37	48	57	60	63	61
Some workers on work programs_____	4	6	5	6	4	3	2	4
No workers with private employment_____	32	67	49	33	30	28	30	25
No workers on work programs_____	11	13	9	9	7	16	9	9
Some workers on work programs_____	21	54	40	24	23	12	21	16

Table 16.—Duration of Unemployment Since Last Full-Time Job of Workers in 7 Southern Illinois Coal Towns

Months since last full-time job	Workers unemployed							
	Total	Bush	John-ston City	Carrier Mills	Herrin	West Frank-fort	Zeigler	Eldo-rado
Total	¹ 4,386	132	819	252	979	1,401	337	466
12 months or less	1,268	21	260	73	255	426	67	166
13–24 months	605	12	101	45	163	181	30	73
25–36 months	289	6	66	16	57	91	9	44
37–48 months	308	9	86	29	62	88	11	23
49–60 months	198	9	36	20	51	48	9	25
61–120 months	1,275	53	208	41	272	431	188	82
121 months or over	443	22	62	28	119	136	23	53
	Percent Distribution							
Total	100	100	100	100	100	100	100	100
12 months or less	29	16	32	29	26	30	20	36
13–24 months	14	9	12	18	17	13	9	16
25–36 months	7	4	8	6	6	7	3	9
37–48 months	7	7	11	12	6	6	3	5
49–60 months	4	7	4	8	5	3	3	5
61–120 months	29	40	25	16	28	31	55	18
121 months or over	10	17	8	11	12	10	7	11
Average ² months since last full-time job	38	71	33	31	39	37	74	24

¹ This figure excludes 1,981 unemployed workers who had never had a full-time job, 1 whose employment status was unknown, and 130 whose duration of unemployment was not ascertainable.
² Median

Table 17.—Duration of Unemployment of Workers in 7 Southern Illinois Coal Towns, by Industry of Last Full-Time Job

Industry of last full-time job	Workers unemployed								Average[1] months since last full-time job
	Total	12 months or less	13–24 months	25–36 months	37–48 months	49–60 months	61–120 months	121 months or over	
Total	[2] 4,384	1,267	605	289	307	198	1,275	443	38
Agriculture	184	52	31	13	28	19	38	3	33
Forestry	17	2	6	2	1	1	4	1	†
Coal mining	1,850	336	153	112	140	79	818	212	68
Manufacturing and mechanical	728	251	159	49	33	28	147	61	21
Transportation and communication	361	112	55	27	35	20	84	28	31
Trade	479	185	91	39	32	14	80	38	20
Public service	56	27	7	3	3	2	11	3	14
Professional service	155	59	15	10	8	6	36	21	29
Domestic and personal service	554	243	88	34	27	29	57	76	17

Percent distribution

Industry of last full-time job	Total	12 months or less	13–24 months	25–36 months	37–48 months	49–60 months	61–120 months	121 months or over	
Total	100	100	100	100	100	100	100	100	
Agriculture	4	4	5	4	9	10	3	1	
Forestry	*	*	1	1	*	1	*	*	
Coal mining	42	26	25	39	46	40	64	47	
Manufacturing and mechanical	17	20	26	17	11	14	11	14	
Transportation and communication	8	9	9	9	11	10	7	6	
Trade	11	15	15	13	10	7	6	9	
Public service	1	2	1	1	1	1	1	1	
Professional service	4	5	3	4	3	3	3	5	
Domestic and personal service	13	19	15	12	9	14	5	17	

Percent distribution

Industry of last full-time job	Total	12 months or less	13–24 months	25–36 months	37–48 months	49–60 months	61–120 months	121 months or over	
Total	100	29	14	7	7	4	29	10	
Agriculture	100	28	17	7	15	10	21	2	
Forestry	100	†	†	†	†	†	†	†	
Coal mining	100	18	8	6	8	4	44	12	
Manufacturing and mechanical	100	34	22	7	5	4	20	8	
Transportation and communication	100	31	15	7	10	6	23	8	
Trade	100	38	19	8	7	3	17	8	
Public service	100	48	13	5	5	4	20	5	
Professional service	100	38	10	6	5	4	23	14	
Domestic and personal service	100	44	16	6	5	5	10	14	

* Less than 0.5 percent.
† Too small for calculation.
[1] Median.
[2] This figure excludes 1,981 unemployed workers who had never had a full-time job, 1 whose employment status was unknown, 2 for whom the industry of last full-time job was not specified, and 130 whose unemployment duration was not ascertainable.

Table 18.—Unemployed Workers Who Had Never Held a Full-Time Job, 7 Southern Illinois Coal Towns, by Age Group

Age group	Total	Bush	Johnston City	Carrier Mills	Herrin	West Frankfort	Zeigler	Eldorado
Unemployed workers who never had a full-time job___	[1] 1,980	42	378	127	578	546	109	200
Under 25 years_____	1,457	34	286	82	409	434	82	130
25–54 years_____	438	8	82	36	143	96	23	50
55 years and over_____	85	—	10	9	26	16	4	20
Unemployed workers who never had a full-time job as a percent of the labor force [2]	13	19	18	15	14	10	9	10
Under 25 years_____	38	52	50	33	42	34	32	28
25–54 years_____	5	6	7	7	6	3	3	4
55 years and over_____	3	—	3	8	4	2	2	6
Unemployed workers who never had a full-time job as a percent of the unemployed [2]_____	30	24	30	33	37	28	24	30
Under 25 years_____	65	59	67	59	71	63	62	56
25–54 years_____	14	8	13	18	18	10	11	15
55 years and over_____	8	—	5	16	13	4	4	19

[1] Excludes 1 unemployed worker whose age was not ascertainable.
[2] See appendix table 14 for data on labor force and number of workers unemployed.

Table 19.—Status of Families Without Private Employment in 7 Southern Illinois Coal Towns

Status of families without private employment	Number	Percent
Total_____	5,104	100
Without workers_____	1,102	22
With workers_____	4,002	78
Some workers employed within 1 year_____	868	17
All workers unemployed 1 year or more_____	2,607	51
All workers inexperienced [1]_____	457	9
Status of workers not ascertainable_____	70	1

[1] Workers who never held a full-time private job.

Table 20.—Assessed Valuation of Real Property [1] in Franklin, Saline, and Williamson Counties, Selected Years, 1913–1932

[Amounts in thousands]

Type of real property	Assessed valuation of real property				
	1913	1918	1922	1927	1932
All real property [1]	$14,114	$15,694	$31,520	$55,534	$35,415
Land and mineral rights	9,799	10,070	19,628	31,228	19,876
Coal lands and mineral rights	3,341	3,302	8,820	16,495	10,109
Other lands	6,458	6,768	10,808	14,733	9,767
Lots	4,315	5,624	11,892	24,306	15,539
	Percent distribution				
All real property [1]	100	100	100	100	100
Land and mineral rights	70	64	62	56	56
Coal lands and mineral rights	24	21	28	30	28
Other lands	46	43	34	26	28
Lots	30	36	38	44	44

[1] Railroad real property is excluded.

Source: Original tax records in the county courthouses at Benton, Harrisburg, and Marion, Ill.; the annual reports of the Illinois State Tax Commission, 1920–1934; and the annual reports of the Illinois State Board of Equalization, 1900–1918.

NOTE.—Relation of assessed to full value: 1909–1918, 33⅓ percent; 1919–1926, 50 percent; and 1927 to date, 100 percent.

Table 21.—Number of Deeds for Town Real Property Recorded in Franklin, Saline, and Williamson Counties and the Average Value of Deeds in Williamson County,[1] 1900–1938

Year	Number of deeds recorded	Average value of deeds (Williamson County [1])	Year	Number of deeds recorded	Average value of deeds (Williamson County [1])
1900	261	$534	1920	5,960	$1,356
1901	339	280	1921	7,860	1,122
1902	1,092	314	1922	5,235	1,203
1903	1,815	400	1923	4,506	1,274
1904	2,106	409	1924	3,603	1,295
1905	2,941	531	1925	2,720	1,191
1906	2,893	680	1926	2,082	1,456
1907	2,568	660	1927	2,553	1,422
1908	2,102	638	1928	1,685	1,500
1909	2,455	706	1929	1,617	766
1910	2,015	750	1930	1,713	556
1911	1,808	760	1931	1,774	628
1912	2,255	699	1932	1,417	484
1913	3,885	789	1933	1,482	387
1914	4,127	751	1934	1,308	(²)
1915	3,052	735	1935	1,328	447
1916	3,256	743	1936	859	447
1917	4,348	832	1937	580	543
1918	6,015	968	1938	(²)	508
1919	6,099	1,147			

[1] Value of deeds in Franklin and Saline Counties is not available.
[2] Not available.

Source: Original deed records in the county courthouses at Benton, Harrisburg, and Marion, Ill.

Table 22.—Taxes Collected and Current Taxes Extended in Franklin, Saline, and Williamson Counties, 1908–1937

[Amounts in thousands]

Year	Taxes collected				Taxes extended			
	Total	Franklin	Saline	Williamson	Total	Franklin	Saline	Williamson
1908	$490	$79	¹ $135	$276	$611	$147	$183	$281
1909	585	138	¹ 156	291	654	¹ 153	205	296
1910	594	142	¹ 157	295	649	180	¹ 171	298
1911	668	169	182	317	734	205	208	321
1912	744	172	202	370	868	220	277	371
1913	1,028	260	274	494	1,123	300	317	506
1914	1,029	255	¹ 316	458	1,131	299	369	463
1915	1,070	269	¹ 332	469	1,152	¹ 329	348	475
1916	1,327	386	¹ 385	556	1,384	433	386	565
1917	1,393	401	¹ 391	601	1,434	430	396	608
1918	1,494	¹ 432	432	630	1,508	438	432	638
1919	2,244	¹ 846	505	893	2,202	859	437	906
1920	2,450	¹ 926	569	955	2,452	939	545	968
1921	2,898	¹ 1,205	567	1,126	2,924	1,170	661	1,093
1922	3,242	1,268	¹ 691	1,283	3,012	1,144	616	1,252
1923	3,480	1,379	¹ 718	1,383	3,287	1,439	469	1,379
1924	3,632	1,214	¹ 818	1,600	3,592	¹ 1,322	738	1,532
1925	3,792	1,455	¹ 764	1,573	4,038	1,693	822	1,523
1926	3,577	1,381	¹ 768	1,428	3,744	1,577	746	1,421
1927	3,545	1,311	822	1,412	3,822	1,570	864	1,388
1928	3,487	1,280	806	1,401	3,771	1,479	853	1,439
1929	3,145	1,164	794	1,187	3,800	1,522	861	1,417
1930	2,809	1,037	749	1,023	3,481	1,336	803	1,342
1931	2,295	858	621	816	3,091	1,238	728	1,125
1932	2,041	700	564	777	2,720	1,001	671	1,048
1933	1,759	704	525	530	2,352	968	580	804
1934	1,763	634	573	556	2,259	889	568	802
1935	1,856	680	580	596	2,383	958	579	846
1936	1,994	705	638	651	(²)	(²)	(²)	(²)
1937	2,036	737	672	627	(²)	(²)	(²)	(²)

¹ Estimated.
² Not available.

Source: Original tax records in the county courthouses at Benton, Harrisburg, and Marion, Ill.; and unpublished data from the Illinois Government Finance Study, WPA Project No. 3121, sponsored by the Illinois Tax Commission.

Table 23.—Activity of Building and Loan Associations in Franklin, Saline, and Williamson Counties, 1900–1936

Year	Number of associa- tions	Assets	Loans outstanding	New loans made during year	Interest, pre- mium, and fines charged
1900	4	$169, 824	$123, 800	$58, 700	$20, 879
1901	4	135, 164	154, 500	73, 021	25, 979
1902	4	225, 587	210, 850	100, 450	35, 112
1903	4	258, 619	243, 540	79, 450	31, 733
1904	5	368, 527	352, 000	128, 250	38, 899
1905	6	468, 477	445, 203	153, 205	53, 993
1906	6	503, 745	470, 350	127, 650	51, 408
1907	7	596, 227	569, 000	314, 450	70, 708
1908	8	663, 983	619, 000	151, 800	62, 653
1909	8	703, 832	656, 350	139, 750	66, 055
1910	9	730, 570	663, 700	170, 400	74, 876
1911	13	819, 408	741, 050	216, 900	81, 926
1912	13	889, 739	795, 200	211, 750	90, 254
1913	13	991, 287	897, 100	292, 500	109, 013
1914	13	1, 286, 822	1, 187, 300	480, 550	124, 286
1915	14	1, 642, 541	1, 528, 550	558, 700	137, 528
1916	15	1, 954, 276	1, 781, 800	486, 200	155, 715
1917	16	2, 276, 450	2, 113, 100	604, 873	197, 561
1918	20	2, 741, 878	2, 570, 470	920, 270	245, 188
1919	21	3, 503, 741	3, 288, 900	1, 290, 650	325, 623
1920	23	4, 417, 856	4, 100, 370	1, 616, 850	406, 406
1921	28	5, 984, 232	5, 643, 950	2, 508, 103	555, 729
1922	31	8, 662, 156	8, 174, 850	3, 408, 108	769, 503
1923	32	11, 180, 872	10, 216, 190	3, 409, 840	978, 339
1924	35	14, 079, 573	13, 183, 600	4, 272, 435	1, 323, 922
1925	34	15, 208, 247	13, 620, 130	2, 348, 180	1, 386, 080
1926	34	15, 373, 868	12, 750, 591	1, 624, 750	1, 413, 747
1927	34	14, 764, 484	11, 260, 760	806, 510	1, 225, 212
1928	34	14, 296, 866	9, 894, 750	584, 050	1, 004, 912
1929	34	13, 514, 911	8, 425, 435	433, 278	898, 074
1930	35	12, 546, 294	6, 778, 973	394, 430	784, 931
1931	34	11, 328, 167	5, 211, 562	110, 890	553, 405
1932	27	7, 759, 963	(¹)	(¹)	(¹)
1933	26	6, 777, 285	(¹)	(¹)	(¹)
1934	24	6, 117, 357	(¹)	(¹)	(¹)
1935	14	4, 461, 672	(¹)	(¹)	(¹)
1936	7	1, 390, 072	(¹)	(¹)	(¹)

¹ Not available.

Source: Illinois Auditor of Public Accounts, *Annual Report of Mutual Building, Loan and Homestead Associations*, Springfield, 1901–1937.

Table 24.—Number of Banks and Amount on Deposit in State and National Banks, Franklin, Saline, and Williamson Counties, 1900–1938

Year	Total		Franklin County		Saline County		Williamson County	
	Number of banks	Amount on deposit	Number of banks	Amount on deposit	Number of banks	Amount on deposit	Number of banks	Amount on deposit
1900	5	$523,403	1	$113,432	2	$214,438	2	$195,533
1901	5	694,848	1	144,281	2	289,285	2	261,282
1902	7	1,063,427	2	201,659	2	299,185	3	562,583
1903	(1)	(1)	(1)	(1)	(1)	(1)	(1)	(1)
1904	10	1,720,827	2	333,697	2	328,729	6	1,058,401
1905	16	3,430,882	4	784,360	4	852,656	8	1,793,866
1906	23	3,721,876	6	733,064	8	1,005,303	9	1,983,509
1907	26	3,479,619	7	626,554	8	797,541	11	2,055,524
1908	25	2,898,374	7	553,617	7	670,239	11	1,674,518
1909	24	3,694,870	6	724,852	7	800,558	11	2,169,460
1910	26	4,399,258	7	1,005,420	7	960,374	12	2,433,464
1911	26	5,192,961	7	1,129,651	7	1,217,929	12	2,845,381
1912	28	6,348,861	9	1,486,817	7	1,430,282	12	3,431,762
1913	29	7,185,404	10	1,690,776	7	1,544,364	12	3,950,264
1914	28	6,628,093	10	1,602,870	7	1,504,136	11	3,521,087
1915	28	6,686,742	10	1,655,387	7	1,364,409	11	3,666,946
1916	28	7,135,992	10	1,795,738	7	1,509,140	11	3,831,114
1917	28	10,648,946	10	2,901,236	7	1,956,729	11	5,790,981
1918	31	15,560,408	13	4,770,378	7	3,028,466	11	7,761,564
1919	36	17,152,128	17	5,671,076	7	3,180,994	12	8,300,058
1920	45	23,491,709	17	7,511,887	14	5,390,073	14	10,589,749
1921	45	26,433,193	17	8,528,422	14	5,953,001	14	11,951,770
1922	45	24,665,624	17	7,637,453	13	5,831,475	15	11,196,696
1923	45	28,488,893	17	9,394,344	13	6,756,431	15	12,338,118
1924	45	27,758,907	16	9,109,411	13	6,401,354	16	12,248,142
1925	47	29,079,134	19	10,840,617	14	6,539,679	14	11,698,838
1926	46	32,156,935	19	12,474,673	13	6,891,815	14	12,790,447
1927	41	27,791,280	17	9,883,083	10	6,394,534	14	11,513,663
1928	41	28,651,570	17	10,586,529	10	6,451,247	14	11,613,794
1929	36	25,693,027	13	8,498,835	10	6,385,516	13	10,808,676
1930	20	12,124,418	7	3,373,803	9	5,252,650	4	3,497,965
1931	16	7,101,226	4	774,419	9	4,709,718	3	1,617,089
1932	14	5,814,395	4	1,011,500	8	4,258,030	2	544,865
1933	11	5,754,030	3	899,098	6	4,402,015	2	452,917
1934	11	6,177,623	3	1,389,813	6	4,140,871	2	646,939
1935	11	7,245,231	3	1,634,579	6	4,964,009	2	646,643
1936	11	8,528,430	3	2,013,925	6	5,587,894	2	926,611
1937	14	10,256,615	4	2,079,548	6	6,634,370	4	1,542,697
1938	13	10,027,902	4	2,254,588	5	5,694,257	4	2,079,057

¹ Not available.

Source: Illinois Auditor of Public Accounts, *Statement of Condition of State Banks in Illinois,* annual, Springfield, 1900–1938; and U. S. Comptroller of the Currency, *Individual Statements of Condition of National Banks at the Close of Business, December 31, 1900[–1938],* supplements to the annual reports of the Comptroller of the Currency, Washington, D. C.

Table 25.—Number of Depositors and Amount on Deposit in United States Postal Savings Offices in Franklin, Saline, and Williamson Counties, 1914–1938

Year	Total Depositors	Total Amount	Franklin County Depositors	Franklin County Amount	Saline County Depositors	Saline County Amount	Williamson County Depositors	Williamson County Amount
1914	291	$48,738	166	$31,584	24	$3,451	101	$13,703
1915	500	94,958	273	58,018	52	6,888	175	30,052
1916	738	169,367	489	121,423	71	11,648	178	36,296
1917	820	283,047	515	196,881	63	16,636	242	69,530
1918	(1)	(1)	(1)	(1)	(1)	(1)	(1)	(1)
1919	844	430,962	554	300,682	63	30,598	227	99,682
1920	550	275,242	365	197,129	41	20,357	144	57,756
1921	516	293,875	369	220,529	30	19,997	117	53,349
1922	380	249,553	259	183,981	24	11,091	97	54,481
1923	309	196,093	217	147,608	15	5,976	77	42,509
1924	335	251,510	242	186,743	11	5,880	82	58,887
1925	401	309,216	294	235,659	8	6,410	99	67,147
1926	415	336,976	313	272,249	9	6,089	93	58,638
1927	615	519,491	478	422,353	37	23,685	100	73,453
1928	754	672,551	573	532,283	42	31,255	139	109,013
1929	848	793,381	666	636,943	41	31,140	141	125,298
1930	2,028	1,771,566	1,412	1,265,425	124	92,224	492	413,917
1931	4,936	3,484,198	2,841	2,089,292	515	373,316	1,580	1,021,590
1932	7,150	4,344,848	3,682	2,336,541	882	550,583	2,586	1,457,724
1933	7,760	4,640,474	3,736	2,364,638	1,089	677,233	2,935	1,598,603
1934	7,467	4,392,844	3,604	2,168,762	924	598,511	2,939	1,625,571
1935	7,636	4,274,727	3,688	2,066,670	853	565,751	3,095	1,642,306
1936	7,947	4,308,850	3,881	2,054,456	783	552,446	3,283	1,701,948
1937	7,985	4,191,191	3,943	2,022,660	765	520,576	3,277	1,647,955
1938	7,400	4,116,216	3,564	1,929,715	801	542,895	3,035	1,643,606

1 Not available.

Source: *Letter From the Postmaster General Transmitting the Report of Operations of the Postal Savings System, for the Fiscal Year Ended June 30, 1914[-1938]*, annual report to the House of Representatives, Washington, D. C.

Table 26.—State of Birth of Family Heads Residing in Carrier Mills, Johnston City, Herrin, and Eldorado

State of birth	Family heads Number	Family heads Percent	State of birth	Family heads Number	Family heads Percent
Total	8,951	100	Kentucky	750	8
			Missouri	231	3
Alabama	223	3	Tennessee	215	2
Illinois	5,580	62	Other States	409	5
Indiana	173	2	Foreign countries	1,370	15

Table 27.—Population of School Age in Franklin, Saline, and Williamson Counties, 1918–1938

Year	Population of school age (6–21 years)	Year	Population of school age (6–21 years)
1918	46,842	1929	51,168
1919	47,233	1930	49,813
1920	48,314	1931	45,112
1921	52,276	1932	45,144
1922	54,404	1933	43,855
1923	57,959	1934	45,696
1924	57,347	1935	42,996
1925	55,908	1936	39,632
1926	55,666	1937	41,728
1927	52,934	1938	41,098
1928	53,184		

Source: State of Illinois Superintendent of Public Instruction, *Statistical Report*, annual, Springfield, 1918–1938.

Table 28.—Expenditures for Public Assistance by Type of Aid, Franklin, Saline, and Williamson Counties, 1925–1929

[Amounts in thousands]

Year	Expenditures for public assistance			
	Total	Aid to the blind	Mothers' pension	Pauper relief
1925	$95	$27	$16	$52
1926	87	27	15	45
1927	87	26	15	46
1928	109	39	23	47
1929	125	62	23	40

Source: Original pauper records in the country courthouses at Benton, Harrisburg, and Marion, Ill.

Table 29.—Estimated [1] Annual Coal-Mine Pay Roll and Public-Assistance Expenditures in Franklin, Saline, and Williamson Counties, 1925–1938

[Amounts in thousands]

Year	Estimated [1] coal-mine pay roll	Public-assistance expenditures	Year	Estimated [1] coal-mine pay roll	Public-assistance expenditures
1925	$36,992	$95	1932	$8,384	$447
1926	40,221	87	1933	8,667	1,181
1927	25,034	87	1934	9,482	3,509
1928	29,433	109	1935	9,871	3,842
1929	24,540	125	1936	11,020	5,184
1930	19,366	121	1937	11,535	5,454
1931	15,367	89	1938	8,692	8,174

[1] Estimated on the basis of man-days worked each year multiplied by the United Mine Workers of America wage scale each year.

Source: Original pauper records in the county courthouses at Benton, Harrisburg, and Marion, Ill.; *Monthly Bulletin on Relief Statistics*, Illinois Emergency Relief Commission, Chicago; Division of Statistics, Illinois Work Projects Administration, Chicago; Fifth Illinois District, National Youth Administration, Herrin; Old Age Assistance Division, Illinois Department of Public Welfare, Springfield.

Appendix B

LIST OF TABLES

Index

INDEX

○